Democracy's Rebirth

The View from Chicago

DICK SIMPSON

Foreword by
LORI LIGHTFOOT

Library of Congress Cataloging-in-Publication Data
Names: Simpson, Dick W., author. | Lightfoot, Lori E.,
    writer of foreword.
Title: Democracy's rebirth : the view from Chicago / Dick
    Simpson ; foreword by Lori Lightfoot.
Description: Urbana : University of Illinois Press, [2022] |
    Includes bibliographical references and index.
Identifiers: LCCN 2021046123 (print) | LCCN 2021046124
    (ebook) | ISBN 9780252044304 (cloth) | ISBN
    9780252086380 (paperback) | ISBN 9780252053290
    (ebook)
Subjects: LCSH: Chicago (Ill.)—Politics and
    government—21st century. | Chicago (Ill.)—
    Social conditions—21st century. | Democracy—
    United States—History—21st century. | Political
    participation—Illinois—Chicago—History—21st
    century.
Classification: LCC F548.52 .S56 2022 (print) | LCC
    F548.52 (ebook) | DDC 977.3/1104—dc23/eng/20211026
LC record available at https://lccn.loc.gov/2021046123
LC ebook record available at https://lccn.loc.gov/2021046124

For Margaret, Kate, Jeffrey, Lilian, Polly,
and all who fight for democracy

Contents

Foreword

LORI LIGHTFOOT

Democracy—at its core—represents our acknowledgment of our shared humanity. But rather than being an *end* in itself, it is, in fact, a *means* to something greater. In essence, democracy is an argument that says that our society's greatest success comes by all its members having an equal opportunity to unlock their shared talent and potential.

Democracy's argument also demands that its participants engage with our public institutions, our elected officials, our public dialogue, the facts, and, above all, with one another. Obstructing or denying this democratic engagement in any way not only denies the fullness of our democracy, but also rejects our shared humanity, leaving us all lesser for it.

For more than fifty years, Dick Simpson has been actively engaged our democracy here in Chicago and across the nation as both a participant and an analyst. He served as a Chicago alderman, ran for the U.S. Congress, worked on a dozen transition teams for new chief executives, and was an advisor in my own mayoral campaign. In addition to that, he has taught and mentored thousands of students as a professor at the University of Illinois in Chicago and written more than twenty books on elections, ethics, and local and national government.

Taken from the vantage point of Chicago's own challenges and successes, Professor Simpson's latest work, *Democracy's Rebirth: The View from Chicago*, provides a unique analytical prospective on the current state of American democracy as we transition to a post-Trump era nationally and a post-machine era locally.

Published during one of the most challenging moments in our modern history, this book serves as the summation of his decades of experience, research, and advocacy as we seek to develop the solutions we need to address the systemic and increasingly urgent challenges we face.

His proposals represent nothing short of the rebirth of our democracy on both a local level and the national level—values that I have personally fought for in my mayoral campaign and administration. *Democracy's Rebirth: The View from Chicago* helps illuminate both our past and our way forward toward a government and society that are more fair, equitable, and effective for all its residents, and a successful future that we can all equally engage and benefit from.

Democracy's Rebirth

Black Lives Matter protest in Chicago, November 27, 2015.
(Photo by Marcus Robinson)

1

Challenges to Democracy

In the third decade of the twenty-first century, we face major challenges to our democracy. We are struggling to build a modern, multiracial, multi-ethnic democracy based on political and social equality. This is something never before accomplished. As part of this process, we are finding it especially difficult to create an economy that empowers everyone and distributes economic rewards fairly without extreme gaps between rich and poor.[1] The COVID-19 pandemic and the economic recession that followed have only made the income and wealth gap greater.

In the pages to follow, I outline some specific challenges to our democracy. With so much attention on the chaos presented by President Donald Trump and the tumultuous 2020 election, it is important to stress that these broader challenges predate his election and administration. And they have continued after his administration ended. Donald Trump was a symbol and example of our problems, but they transcend him and his administration.

As the photo opening this chapter illustrates, other challenges such as institutional racism highlighted in Black Lives Matter protests, counterprotests by right-wing groups, the pandemic, January 6, 2021, insurrection, and the economic recession are all manifestations of problems we still face.

These challenges exist not only at the national level but in cities like Chicago. Since 84 percent of the world's population now live in cities, undemocratic regimes, racial discrimination, and economic gaps between rich and poor in our cities and suburbs are not trivial.[2] So I use Chicago as a case study of how these social, political, and economic challenges play out at the local level. Chicago is in many ways the epitome of American politics and society. It is an extreme case, exposing these challenges more starkly. As such,

Chicago allows us to examine our problems in more detail than just general discussions of our national circumstances involving 328 million Americans or global trends involving seven and a half billion people with diverse histories and cultures.

The challenges to democracy that I highlight are local, national, and global. They are both theoretical and very practical. It is not enough to find an acceptable philosophical or theoretical solution to democracy's challenges and crises; actual solutions must be implemented in the real world in cities like Chicago. Any genuine solutions will require public support and action at the local level. In turn, public support will have to be built by a movement for change created from the bottom up if we are to achieve radical national transformation.

This raises the question of how to weave together disparate local and national, theoretical and practical threads into a unified tapestry. Most chapters in this book begin with a description of the specific challenges, such as racial and income inequality as they play out in Chicago. I then describe the problems at the national level in the United States. This leads to an investigation of the political consequences of these conditions and the crisis they have created. Finally, I discuss how these problems might be overcome along with the fundamental changes required in order for democracy to be reborn.

The challenges facing our democracy are interrelated. It is important to assess honestly how we have fallen short of our nation's goals in order to undertake the steps necessary to overcome our most egregious flaws.

Thus, I present separate chapters on income and racial inequality, systemic racism, the insidious role of money in politics, the low level of participation by voters, the extreme polarization that has led to a politics of resentment, political corruption that undermines government, and a myriad of structural problems subverting our democracy. I also focus on crises such as the COVID-19 pandemic and current economic recession, which make repairing our democracy more difficult but that at the same time provide the momentum needed to mobilize the public to undertake necessary reforms.

In the final chapters, I present the steps necessary to create a more participatory and deliberative democracy. A higher level of civic virtue and pubic spiritedness will be needed to make possible democracy's rebirth.[3] So will sustained public support for radical changes in our lives, our communities, and our country. As in the past, we, the people, will determine whether or not democracy is reborn in our time.

Manifesto

I bring to this book not only fifty years of study, but my unique perspective as a former political candidate, elected official, campaign strategist, and government adviser. I know how the sausage is made because I have been a sausage maker. I have seen government and politics from inside. This firsthand experience allows me to understand the practical aspects of these social and political problems and the challenges in implementing solutions in the real world. These include the difficulty of mobilizing public support and passing the necessary new laws, procedures, and regulations with the officials now in power as well as preserving and reforming institutions that currently exist. Because of these difficulties, we must educate a new generation of citizens and leaders since reinvention of our politics and government will take years of effort. Nonetheless, the process of change must begin with where we are.

The observations and conclusions in this book are not simply my own. A rather remarkable consensus has emerged among scholars—especially, among political scientists—about the problems we face. Unfortunately, there is less consensus about what must be done to confront those problems. My effort here is to combine the findings of many theoretical and empirical studies, merge these with my own practical political experience, and frame them into a single coherent vision of what is to be done at this critical juncture in our history.

So this book is both a theoretical discourse and a practical manifesto. It is, of course, possible that the effort to assist in democracy's rebirth will fail. Some form of autocracy, oligarchy, dictatorship, imperialism, or totalitarianism may win in the end. But the fight for justice and democracy is well worth making.

If we are to succeed, democracy requires a citizenry willing to participate and hold their government accountable. To sacrifice for the greater good. Democracy can be reborn only if we can rouse democratic citizens to make the sacrifices required. To inspire those efforts, we must offer a clear and achievable vision. Moreover, new institutions of a more deliberative and participatory democracy must be created for a government of, by, and for the people to flourish. This is our task and calling in our time. And it begins with a vision of the type of democracy we want in the twenty-first century. We must act to preserve the good aspects of what we have and correct the flaws that exist in our communities and country.

Our goal is not utopian. Not heaven on earth. We know if a better form of democracy is to be born, real challenges must be overcome in Chicago and across America. We must create both a more participatory *and* a more deliberative democracy led by strong democratic leaders. For that to occur, our society and economy will have to be reformed and improved because the political system rests on social and economic systems. While the final form of politics is not economically determined, a literate middle class and modern technology are prerequisites of the democracy we aspire to build.

As I stress throughout this book, the most fundamental requirement is that we have a democratic people. Because of that, our educational system will have to retool to educate citizens for democracy.[4] And the proposed changes in the economy, society, and our educational systems will have to occur not only at the national, but at the local level.

During the Trump presidential era, our national failings exposed societal problems that have been present over a long period of time. The reaction to the excesses of the Trump era, the pandemic, and continuing injustices provide energy for fundamental changes. Hopefully, we now understand that we cannot ignore the challenges to democracy in the hope that they will cure themselves. That approach only destines us for failure and misery. This unique moment in our history is foundational. Transformative changes are possible despite immediate challenges of racial tensions, the continuing COVID-19 pandemic, and the worst economic recession since the Great Depression. We dare not squander this opportunity. Just as the Great Depression gave birth to the New Deal and World War II gave birth to a time of affluence, our current crises can give birth to a better society and a better democracy.

Reinventing our democracy and overcoming the unique challenges of our time require us to act. But to be successful, a new social movement must arise. We, the people, must shake off our apathy and rise up. However, to act wisely, we must understand the situation we are in and the resources that we possess. To overcome our challenges, we must renew the "spirit of democracy" and forge new institutions and norms. We must understand, act, and act again until our democracy is reestablished on a sounder footing.

U.S. vice president Charles Dawes and his wife vote in Chicago in 1928.
(DN-0086817, Chicago Sun Times/Chicago Daily News collection,
Chicago History Museum)

2

The Rise and Fall of Democracy

We can envision a world of justice and democracy, even as we fear a possible future of injustice and tyranny. However, in attempting to obtain a better world for ourselves and our descendants, we are faced with the same problems as previous civilizations: the choice between the extremes of oligarchy or chaos, dictatorship or collapse. In our country, we have not fully achieved the representative democracy, equality, and justice promised in our founding creed because of problems in our economy, society, politics, and government. Because of this, the 2016 and 2020 elections have been extremely divisive. We are still beset by fear that justice and democracy will not be achieved in our lifetimes.

Since previous civilizations have fallen, we worry: Is America next? Are we a new Rome? Do we face a bleak future as pictured in dystopias like the *Blade Runner* movies? Or can a new republic arise as in the *Star Wars* movies? We live in turbulent and critical times. What we do matters. We will determine America's future.

Machine Democracy in Chicago

American democracy in the nineteenth and twentieth centuries, especially in big cities like Chicago, New York, and St. Louis, did not fulfill the principles of our own founding either. Instead, these cities manifested a more rough-and-ready, party-dominated "machine politics." This is a very limited form of democracy. Will things be any different in U.S. cities in the twenty-first century? For surely, the rise or fall of the broader American democracy will be determined in the cities where 80 percent of Americans now live.

First, definitions. A political machine, like the one that has dominated Chicago for most of the last 150 years, is a political party characterized by patronage jobs, favoritism, nepotism, precinct workers, and party loyalty. It seeks to control government by winning elections, but it inevitably has, as a byproduct, political corruption. Political machines are strongly hierarchical, usually centered on a political boss who controls the party and local government. Political machines historically have been involved in voter fraud as well. The dominant machine political party tends to control all units of government and suppress reforms.

In Chicago, the Democratic Party machine created a rubber-stamp city council under the thumb of party boss mayors like Richard J. Daley. The party also controlled subservient units of local government, among them Cook County, Chicago school board, and the Chicago Park District. They all gave out patronage jobs, made the laws, and delivered local government services, often as political favors.

Political machines developed mostly in the larger eastern and midwestern industrial cities during the nineteenth century as immigrants were being absorbed and assimilated. The political machine in Chicago grew up with the city after the Great Chicago Fire of 1871. The first dominant political boss was Michael McDonald, a gambler-saloonkeeper who noticed the common bonds between the criminals and politicians and introduced them to each other. McDonald's occupation of saloonkeeper was not that unusual for the time. Saloons are closely associated with the history of machine politics in Chicago and in most other industrial U.S. cities. They provided politicians with the means to contact and organize voters, and in return the political machine protected saloons from raids by the police.

More than spawning corruption, the machine served the rapidly growing immigrant and ethnic communities of Chicago. The Chicago political machine acted as a social welfare service for the poor and immigrant populations. A precinct captain controlled blocks and neighborhoods within the fifty wards of Chicago. Immigrants depended on their precinct captain for services, jobs, and advice, particularly when they first moved to the country. On Election Day, precinct captains expected their services and favors to be repaid through votes.

Originally, there were multiple political machines in Chicago entrenched by patronage and corruption. The city council of Grey Wolves (1890–1931) was run by cliques of machine aldermen in a constant struggle with Progressive Era reformers. Then, in 1931, Mayor Anton Cermak created a single, unified Democratic machine, which was continued after his death by Mayor Ed Kelly and party boss Pat Nash. After a brief interlude under Mayor Martin Kennelly, Richard J. Daley came to power and perfected the Democratic Party machine in Chicago.

The political machines of Chicago have been both Republican and Democratic, suburban and inner city. However, the Richard J. Daley machine's distinctive set of features refined the machine politics that had governed most of the larger cities on the East Coast and in the Midwest. Patronage jobs at city hall begat patronage precinct captains—the ones who contacted voters and persuaded them to trade their votes for favors and city services. Government contracts from city hall convinced businessmen to make campaign contributions necessary to fund campaign literature, walking-around money, and bribes. These contributions of precinct work, money, and votes won elections for the Daley machine during the twenty-two years of his reign. With Richard J. Daley controlling both city and county governments, he was able to distribute the spoils necessary to keep the machine running. But a little election fraud also helped elect the party candidates so the spoils could keep flowing.

Election fraud and stolen elections are a tradition not only in Chicago but in America more broadly, and not just in local elections. For instance, Republicans claimed that John F. Kennedy's election over Richard Nixon in 1960 was stolen in Illinois by Richard J. Daley. We also have had the hanging chads in Florida during the 2000 presidential election, the interference by Russia, China, and Iran in 2016 and 2020 elections, and the false claims of election fraud by Donald Trump after the 2020 election. By 2018, the Heritage Foundation, a conservative think tank, had compiled a data base of over a thousand proven cases of election fraud.[1]

Famed Chicago journalist Mike Royko describes the fraud in Chicago elections in the 1970s this way:

> The Machine never fails to run scared. For this reason, or maybe out of habit, it never misses a chance to steal a certain number of votes and trample all over the voting laws. Most it goes on in the wards where the voters are lower middle class, black, poor White, or on the bottle. To assure party loyalty, the precinct captains merely accompany the voter into the voting machine. They aren't supposed to be sticking their head in, but that's the only way they can be sure the person votes Democratic. They get away with it because the election judges who are citizens hired to supervise each polling place don't protest. The Democratic election judges don't mind, and the Republican election judges are probably Democratic.[2]

Thus, vote fraud was an intrinsic aspect of machine politics. Reporter William Rechtenwald went undercover to describe one example of election fraud in the Chicago elections in 1972:

We started out by very simply getting the voters list and driving up and down the streets. We would go into an area and we would see an address . . . that had fifteen or twenty registered voters . . . and we'd see it was a vacant lot. . . .

[Then] we got into an area . . . called the skid row area on West Madison Street where there are a lot of transient hotels . . . [We took up residence in one before precinct registration day.] When the precinct registration sheets came out some of those names [we had chosen to register under] appeared on the polling list as registered voters. Now I had never registered under the name of James Joyce . . . someone had registered [me] to vote without [my] knowledge . . . that's the total service here in Chicago to the voters.[3]

Stealing elections is just one of the defects of machine politics in comparison to the grand ideals of the American Constitution. With Machine Democracy—Chicago style—it is not that elections weren't held frequently, they were simply rigged.

Likewise, with Machine Democracy there were regular public meetings of legislative bodies like the Chicago City Council, the Cook County Board of Commissioners, and the Illinois State Legislature. But the fix was in. When a political machine is successful, it controls the government. It passes laws and governs in a way that keeps majority support for it at election time. It isn't a totalitarian government like twentieth-century fascist Germany or the communist Soviet Union—but it rules "for the people," not "by the people." And the most important people are the party bosses, their business allies, and loyal supporters. The political machine controls the voters rather than voters controlling their government.

Machine politics in its heyday had the trappings of democracy, like regularly held elections and a theoretical separation of powers between different branches of government. However, it is a very weak form of democracy. It subverts elections, intimidates opponents, and gives government jobs to less qualified applicants, thereby creating waste and corruption. It fails to deliver government services fairly, effectively, and efficiently.

In the nineteenth and twentieth centuries, Machine Democracy was the norm in many U.S. cities. In the twenty-first century, it is said that we have outgrown Machine Democracy. Chicago was declared by the media to have had the last of the big-city machines.[4]

Despite reformers in Chicago history such as Mayors Edward Dunne, William Dever, and Harold Washington. Despite progressive leaders like Jane Addams, Clarence Darrow, and Saul Alinsky. Despite many ethics and good government reforms adopted over the years, the machine continued.

In 2019, however, Lori Lightfoot was elected as a reform mayor along with a significant number of "progressive" aldermen dedicated to a reform platform of further weakening the political machine. Yet, despite reforms adopted in the Lightfoot era, a democracy of citizen participation and representation has yet to be fully achieved either in Chicago or elsewhere in our nation.

To declare, as Mayor Harold Washington did back in 1983, that "the machine is dead, dead, dead," is premature. The basic aspects of machine politics—one-party rule—is still alive and well in Chicago and in many parts of the country. As the election of Donald Trump illuminated in 2016, the possibility of electing an unstable demagogue locally or nationally still remains. Our democracy is not yet secure.

While the simple vote fraud perpetuated by the Chicago political machine during its heyday does not characterize elections in Chicago and across the United States today, more sophisticated attempts now occur, such as cyberattacks to hack election results by the Russians in 2016 and 2020. Thus, Chicago machine politics remains emblematic of our failure to fully live up to our democratic promise.

In many parts of America today, one political party dominates the government. Whereas democracy requires two or more competitive parties in order to offer a choice to the voters, gerrymandering and partisan dominance make that unavailable in many jurisdictions. By controlling the elections, dominant political parties control the government locally and bias our representation nationally.

There is no one silver bullet, no one government policy, that can cure the problems facing our democracy. But guaranteeing free, fair, and vigorously contested elections remains the foundation of any democratic renewal.

The American Republic

The Declaration of Independence affirms: "We hold these truths to be self-evident, that all [people] are created equal; that they are endowed by their Creator with certain unalienable rights; that among these are life, liberty, and the pursuit of happiness. That, to secure these rights, governments are instituted among [people], deriving their just powers from the consent of the governed." Government under this conception is instituted to protect certain natural and inalienable rights. When it fails to do so and reforms cannot be achieved by peaceful means, there is a permanent right to revolution. Thus, we freed ourselves from Great Britain by a revolutionary war and, when the Articles of Confederation failed, we adopted a new constitution to achieve "a more perfect union." We were later refounded by the Civil War as our democracy was expanded to include former slaves. Then in the twentieth century, women, former slaves, and youths by their protests won the vote.

In founding our nation, beyond just the right to vote, it was thought essential that a "republican form of government" or representative democracy be established. The system of representation and checks and balances created in the Constitution has served us well for over two centuries. In the twenty-first century, we will need to adopt some amendments to the Constitution to reflect our changed circumstances over the last 250 years, but the fundamental republican principles remain unchanged.

Yet, some of our founders envisioned an even more just and participatory form of democracy. For one, Thomas Jefferson, even though he was himself a slave holder, envisioned a system of graduated government or republics in which the average citizen would have more power. He believed that the "equal rights of [people] and the happiness of every individual are . . . the only legitimate objects of government . . . the will of the people is the only legitimate foundation of any government and to protect its free expression should be our first objective."[5] Jefferson also recognized that governments often usurp their powers and reached the following conclusion:

> We think experience has proved it safer, for the mass of individuals composing the society, to reserve to themselves personally the exercise of all rightful powers to which they are competent, and to delegate those to which they not competent to deputies named, and removable for unfaithful conduct, by themselves immediately. . . .
>
> . . . Action by the citizens in person in affairs within their reach and competence and in all others by representatives, chosen immediately and removable by themselves constitutes the essence of a republic; that all governments are more or less republican in proportion as this principle enters more or less into their composition.[6]

Jefferson, although he never wrote a systematic treatise on government, understood that citizens must maintain republican control of their government. His scheme began with the ward, six miles square, whose citizens met at the call of warders on the same day throughout the state much like the town-hall meetings that developed in New England. These local participatory units of government would keep the various higher levels of government in touch with the needs and criticisms of the people, serve as a check on petty tyrants, and train local citizens to assume the responsibilities of higher office. In Jefferson's conception, each ward would be a small republic where citizens would transact a great proportion of their political rights and duties. The wards would also serve as a check on the higher levels of representative democracy and allow citizens to instruct their elected representatives on their policy views.

In drafting and ratifying the Constitution a decade after the Declaration of Independence, Madison and the other delegates relied on other republican principles to allow the people to control their representatives. They conceived their goal as preventing tyranny such as the colonists had experienced under English rule.[7] "Tyranny" they defined as absolute rule by one, a few, or many. Later political philosophers have continued to propose methods that might prevent domination—especially domination of the wealthy few over the many poor.[8] Both then and now, the philosophical and practical debate has been about which methods might best protect against tyranny and domination, thus safeguarding our human and political rights.

So, from the American experience and from the philosophy on which our nation was founded, we derive the principles of representative democracy, greater citizen participation, and institutional checks and balances meant to prevent tyranny. Jefferson and later participatory democratic theorists stressed a desire for citizens governing more directly at the local level and holding their representatives accountable. Madison and other founders stressed mechanisms like the expanse of the new republic, separate branches of government, and federalism to prevent tyranny.

We face particular challenges in the twenty-first century in which different social, economic, political, technological, and international conditions exist than at the time of our founding. Thus, the central issue is how these principles of participatory, deliberative, *and* representative democracy, along with institutional checks and balances, might best preserve democracy against both tyranny and anarchy under today's conditions.

Representative Democracy

Achieving the American ideal of a representative democracy, rather than a pure, participatory democracy, is not as simple as it would first appear. There are four different types of representation: formal, symbolic, descriptive, and active.[9] Ideally, we want our local and national government to embody all of these types, but the most critical is active representation.

The first type, *formal representation*, requires free, fair, and frequent elections in which all citizens have an equal vote. The values, interests, and informed preferences of every citizen are to be represented in elections and the government. We fail to meet even this simple standard. For instance, we have twelve million undocumented immigrants who have no vote and little voice. Former felons in many states are not allowed to vote or face high hurdles to do so. And even in the 2020 presidential election, with the future direction of the country to be decided, only 67 percent of those eligible to vote did so. In off-year national elections, often only 40 percent vote, and in local elections the number is much lower.

The United States does hold regular elections for about 540,000 elected officials, which guarantees some aspects of formal representative democracy. But there are also undemocratic aspects to our elections. So, chapter 9 is devoted to structure problems like voter suppression, the undemocratic Electoral College, and gerrymandering, all of which threaten formal representation.

The second type of representation, *descriptive representation,* occurs when a characteristic is present in about the same proportion as in the population. The representative body under this conception is like a mirror that accurately reflects the citizens. Today, minorities such as African Americans, Latinos, and Asian Americans are still underrepresented descriptively in many legislative bodies. So are women. By 2020, only 27 percent of the members of Congress were women, although 52 percent of the U.S. population is female. Likewise, only 23 percent of the Congress were racial or ethnic minorities. By contrast, the Chicago City Council is much more descriptively representative of Chicago. In a city that is roughly one-third White, Black, and Latino, among the fifty aldermen elected in 2019, 38 percent were Black, 24 percent were Latino, and 38 percent were White.[10] Thirty percent were women.

Descriptive representation occurred to some degree in the Chicago City Council even during the reign of Mayor Richard J. Daley, when just six African American aldermen represented the Black community. However, they were Uncle Toms known as the Silent Six. They served as rubber stamps for Mayor Daley as part of his political machine and didn't represent the interests of their African American constituents even on issues of racial segregation. During the 1960s, a White alderman, Fifth Ward Alderman Leon Despres, was said by African American media to be "the lone Negro spokesman in the Chicago City Council" because he spoke and acted for the African American community when the African American aldermen did not.[11] Thus, descriptive representation does not always bring active representation of the interests and views of the electorate.

Then we have *symbolic representation,* which is when officials, usually those holding executive office, stand for the country (or city or state) in the same way that a flag does. George Washington was symbolically representative of America, although Donald Trump was not representative in the same way, except for his strong supporters. Often monarchs like the kings and queens of England more clearly symbolically represent their country than our leaders do in the United States. Ideally, leaders should symbolize or "stand for" their country.

The most critical type of representation is *active representation*. This occurs when officials are not just mirroring constituents, winning elections, or symbolizing the nation, but acting to represent them by passing laws and regulations that protect their interests or reflect their views. We can have formal, descriptive, and symbolic representation but still fail as a representative democracy if representatives do not represent their constituents by their actions. Minorities often feel they are not fully incorporated politically. That their issues and desires are not carried out by government.

Later chapters explore both how we have fallen short locally and as a nation in encouraging a more participatory, deliberative, and representative democracy. I focus particularly on how we have failed in active representation and the reforms needed for a flowering of representative democracy in our time.

Lessons from the Past

Mark Twain reputedly said, "History doesn't repeat itself, but it rhymes."[12] We are not doomed to repeat history exactly, but there are lessons we can learn from past experience.

The usual lesson drawn by students of history is that all civilizations begin small, grow, decline, and fall just as individuals do in their personal lives. Thus the frequent reference to the decline and fall of Rome with the inference that America is in decline and cannot be saved from Rome's fate. It is true that all democracies fall, as all previous civilizations have. Someday that will be our fate. Yet, there is no particular reason to believe that after only 250 years the American democratic experiment must come to an end now. There is no reason that we can't reinvent, refound, and reform our democracy for the twenty-first century. This is, after all, what happened with the Civil War as Lincoln proposed with his Gettysburg Address, which begins "four score and seven years ago" and ends with his call for a "new rebirth of liberty." With the defeat of Donald Trump in 2020, we have the opportunity for America to again experience a new beginning. President Joe Biden has reversed many Trump policies, begun the defeat of the COVID-19 pandemic, and laid the groundwork for recovery from the economic recession that accompanied the pandemic. The question is whether we will seize the opportunity now to build on this beginning or continue the decline in our representative democracy.

In the United States, we have historically sought to revitalize our democracy as voting rights have been won by more groups—poor Whites, African Americans, other minorities, women, and youths. We have expanded the electorate from the days in which only relatively affluent White males could vote and serve in government. At the local level in Chicago, there has been a continuous battle between machine politicians and reformers. In modern times, the city has been made more just and more democratic under progressive, reform mayors like Harold Washington and Lori Lightfoot. But the battle to reform Chicago is ongoing.

The complexities of our twenty-first-century world make it difficult for us to create at the national level "a more perfect union." Today, the ever-widening gap between the rich and the poor, which approaches levels of the Gilded Age before the Great Depression, threatens our democracy. President Lincoln said that we cannot long exist half slave and half free.[13] Today, we cannot long exist with a too-rich 1 percent, a too-poor 99 percent, and a disappearing middle class. Added to these challenges is institutional, structural racism, which has been the most common cause of the demonstrations and protests for more than the past six years. It continues to prevent equality for all. Thus, income and racial inequality inevitably set the stage for oligarchy in the form of the rule by a small wealthy class. Slavery in Lincoln's America has given way to a permanent underclass today.[14] Racial inequality is also apparent in our treatment of the twelve million undocumented immigrants in our land with no path to citizenship. America used to be a great melting pot where it was believed that everyone could make a good life through hard work and education, if not in this generation then in the next. If there is now a permanent upper class of inherited power and wealth and a permanent underclass and undocumented immigrants living in misery generation after generation, then the American Dream is destroyed. And our nation will fall.

In the American experiment with freedom and democratic government, we have prized the principles of representative democracy and created a constitution whose goal was to prevent tyranny and domination. To be sure, our practice has not always lived up to this promise. In Chicago, we have for 150 years been stuck in a form of Machine Democracy in which dominance by a single political party headed by political bosses and characterized by patronage, corruption, and stolen elections, belied and betrayed the American promise. We have the formal trappings of democracy in Chicago and the country, like elections and a separation of powers, but a collusion of businessmen and politicians have dominated government decision-making.

A robust reform movement has continuously attempted to end the reign of machine politics in Chicago. Certainly, reforms have been made. As already noted, in 2019 Chicago voters elected a reform mayor and a more progressive city council. Both Mayor Lightfoot and many aldermen ran on explicit anticorruption, reform platforms. Since their election, they have enacted a series of new ethics ordinance and regulations to contain corruption and have passed laws to get the wealthy to pay their fair share of taxes, protect immigrants from deportation, and improve the conditions of minorities and the poor.

Chicago's long struggle with machine politics remains emblematic of the nation's struggle. The ideal of liberty, freedom, prosperity for all, and democratic rule has eluded us even as it continues to provide inspiration. Nationally, we continue to struggle with even formal representation. In the very close and highly contested election of 2020, President Trump argued that the election and its results were fraudulent. Many of his supporters and prominent Republican Party officials agreed. While the empirical evidence in fifty court cases since have upheld its basic fairness of the 2020 election and certified the results, some Americans remain unconvinced even today. Our nation is still divided.

American politics has outgrown Chicago machine politics in a number of ways. However, the problems of income and racial inequality, money in politics, low citizen participation, domination by elites, structural flaws, and political polarization remain. Much remains to be done to overcome these challenges.

The tumult in our national politics points to the urgency of democracy's rebirth. We are still more an oligarchy than a democracy. Added to this, we chose for a time a leader, who despite his promises, did not "Make America Great Again." Although the nation has survived his presidency, as we survived mediocre presidents in the past, his election and administration are proof that more reforms are needed. In truth, our fundamental problems did not begin with Donald Trump, nor did they end with his defeat in 2020. But the democracy that was undermined during his presidency must now be repaired.

We begin with the bedrock principle that, in order for us to claim to be a democracy, our elections must be free, fair, and frequent. We must modify our election processes to allow mail-in ballots, early voting sites, automatic voter registration, and eventually, electronic voting to increase participation. During the COVID-19 pandemic, more Americans voted by mail-in ballots and at early voting sites than at any time in our history. The number of votes cast in the 2020 election was the largest in U.S. history. With 67 percent of the voting-eligible population participating, it had the greatest percentage of the electorate participating since the election of 1900. So, these changes in the methods by which Americans vote need to last past the pandemic despite renewed efforts at voter suppression for partisan advantage in many states.

We must ensure that we provide the opportunity for those who wish to gain citizenship and to be registered to vote. And we must guarantee that everyone has their vote counted equally. This is what allows each of us to have a voice in determining our representatives and the policies governing us. In the future we must also protect against continuing cyberattacks on our democracy.

In Chicago, as we continue to confront the legacy of machine politics with more convictions of public corruption by government officials. However, the machine is not yet, "dead, dead, dead," as Mayor Harold Washington so hopefully proclaimed nearly thirty years ago.

Thus, we have work to do at both the local and national level to protect our elections, extend citizen participation, and to remake our government. There is no doubt that our democracy has been damaged. Repair and renewal are required.

Do we have the political will to undertake the major reforms needed for democracy's rebirth? Let us seize this opportunity to overcome our challenges. Let us bring a new dawn in American government.

A couple shops at the Maxwell Street open market in 1978.
(Photo © Marc PoKempner, 1978)

3

Income and Racial Inequality

As Chicago and our country navigate the twenty-first century, we face particular challenges to our democracy. These are reflected in our choice of leaders like Donald Trump, but our challenges are greater than any specific leaders.

In Chicago, the mayors voters elect reflect the changing status of its people. All mayors up to Richard J. Daley and his immediate successor, Michael Bilandic, were White men. Although they represented various White ethnic groups, they were politicians from either a business or working-class background. Most were lawyers or successful businessmen who belonged to the dominant Republican or Democratic Party machines of their era.

This pattern first was broken by the election in 1979 of the White woman mayor, Jane Byrne, and then the first African American progressive mayor, Harold Washington, in 1983. However, the regular pattern of White male mayors returned with the election of the "Son of Boss" Mayor Richard M. Daley in 1989. He was succeeded in turn by Rahm Emanuel who was the first Jewish mayor.

In keeping with our tumultuous political times, White male dominance was shattered again by the election of African American woman, lesbian, and former Assistant U.S. Attorney Lori Lightfoot in April 2019. She defeated another African American woman, Cook County Board president Toni Preckwinkle, in a runoff election, winning 74 percent of the vote. That election, which began with twenty-one candidates of nearly every race, sexual orientation, and background, reflected the diversity of modern-day Chicago.

Since massive income and racial inequality exists in America, how could Lori Lightfoot become mayor of Chicago? And does her election have implications for America more broadly? Does the election of Kamala Harris, an African American–Asian American woman, as vice president of the United States have similar implications? Both women have broken through the glass ceiling that has prevented women from gaining the highest political offices, and both are minorities. Both are American success stories. Of course, there is still a long way to go before the election of minorities and women to the highest offices becomes a common occurrence.

Mayor Lightfoot's personal story does indicate some progress, however. She grew up relatively poor in a small Indiana town. Her father lost his hearing in her early childhood. Despite his hearing loss, Lori's father and her mother both worked multiple low-income jobs to support their family. Throughout her early years, the family faced economic instability and obstacles, living paycheck to paycheck. Racial discrimination kept her parents in low-paying, working-class jobs.

Lori attended the University of Michigan with the help of scholarships, loans, work-study programs, and summer jobs. Her hard work paid off in the form of a full scholarship to the University of Chicago Law School. She later served as a clerk on the Michigan Supreme Court and became an Assistant U.S. Attorney in Chicago.

Lightfoot's legal career took off, and she rose to become an equity partner at the global law firm of Mayer Brown LLP, where she earned a salary of nearly a million dollars a year before becoming mayor. Like Kamala Harris, she represents the success of the American dream, overcoming racial, income, and gender barriers along the way.

At the same time she succeeded in the private sector, Lightfoot held appointed city government positions, such as first deputy of the Department of Procurement Services, chief of staff and general counsel of the Chicago Office of Emergency Management and Communications, chief administrator of the Office of Professional Standards, and eventually, president of the Chicago Police Board. Nonetheless, she held no previous elected offices, unlike most previous mayors.[1]

At the state and national levels, the social, ethnic, and gender representation of the highest elected officials is quite different from the social, ethnic, and gender diversity of Chicago officials. While more women and minorities are being elected to Congress, Republican president Donald Trump, who sat in the highest elected office from 2017 until 2020, was White, male, and a self-proclaimed billionaire, while his vice president and most of his cabinet members were also wealthy White men. He has been succeeded by another White male, Joe Biden. But Biden has Kamala Harris as his vice president and has appointed a much more racially and gender diverse cabinet than Trump.

In Illinois, Governor J. B. Pritzker, a White male billionaire, defeated another White male billionaire, incumbent Illinois governor Bruce Rauner, in 2018. So, while the election of Lightfoot, Kamala Harris, and more minority members to the Chicago City Council and U.S. Congress suggests that our governments are becoming more reflective of society as a whole, White male dominance is still common. It raises this question: does one have to be White and rich to run successfully for the highest offices?

Inequality Today

Perhaps the greatest challenge, which engenders many of our other political problems, is our level of income and racial inequality. When the gap between the wealthiest and the rest of us grows too great, democracy itself is threatened. When the middle class disappears, so does the bedrock of democracy. When discrimination between Blacks, Whites, Latinos, and Asian Americans continues from past slavery, segregation, and discrimination, democracy is compromised. When income and wealth are closely correlated with racial identity; political equality, upon which democracy rests, is undermined.

In a democracy, every citizen must be equal before the law. Their votes must count equally in elections and their voice must be heard, either directly or through their representatives. Political equality isn't possible if racial discrimination and economic inequality grant some individuals and organizations greater clout and political power.

When the rich rule, we have an oligarchy. When only Whites rule, we have apartheid. When White males rule, we have a patriarchy in which men dominate women. None of these forms of elite rule is healthy or just.

Both our nation and our local communities must have democracy as a principal goal. Even if this goal has not yet been realized, it must remain our purpose as a nation and a people to achieve it. Over the past two centuries, we have made progress toward that goal as women, minorities, and youths fought for and gained the vote.

Today's racial inequality grows from a past of slavery and immigration restrictions. Income and wealth inequality seem to be inevitable components of our capitalist economic system. Yet, both racial and growing income inequality make achieving more democracy impossible. So major changes must be made if we are to fulfill our democratic destiny.

We experience today advanced monopoly capitalism intensified by transnational corporations in our global economy. This economy, with its global city nodes and internationally networked production and distribution, inevitably exacerbates income and wealth inequality. The labor competition between countries pressures U.S. wages downward as modern technology limits the number of traditional jobs. The mobile investment capital and the cheap sources of labor overseas increase the level of poverty and make an ever-smaller group of the very wealthy. The effect is worsened by developing technologies that allow goods and services to be delivered more cheaply by robotics, software, and artificial intelligence. In short, frequently products can be made by fewer workers, and more often these are low-paid workers overseas.

These forces produce the ever-growing divide between the superrich and the poor. In twenty-first-century America there is a very wealthy 10 percent, with another 20 percent or so pretty well-off, and a super-rich segment of the population of only 540 billionaires. These few billionaires have greater wealth and income than most of the rest of us combined.

There are political consequences of this income and wealth divide. Benjamin Page, Jason Seawright, and Matthew Lacombe assert: "As the gap between the wealthiest and the rest of us has widened, the few who hold one billion dollars or more in net worth have begun to play a more and more active part in politics—with serious consequences for democracy in the United States."[2] The interests of the billionaires often do not correspond to the interests and desires of the majority.

The number of people who are poor, unemployed, or underemployed is vast. Certainly, the number of people living in poverty in the United States and in cities like Chicago is too large to allow for the economy and democracy we aspire to achieve. In the developing world, the situation is even more dire. Billions of people around the world live on a few hundred dollars a year in a subsistence existence. With the economic recession that has followed the COVID-19 pandemic, the number of unemployed and the poor have only increased.

Various statistics demonstrate the level of income and wealth inequality in the United States today. One of the simplest is that 5 percent of the people obtained 22.1 percent of the income in 2015, while the bottom 60 percent earned only 25.6 percent.[3] This unequal distribution takes us back to the gaps of the 1930s and 1940s, when we hadn't fully recovered from the Great Depression. The wealth disparity today is even greater than the income disparity, with 1 percent of the population owning 40 percent of the wealth.[4]

During much of the twentieth century, America's position as the largest economy to emerge unscathed from World War II, the growth of labor unions, and our national tax policies enlarged the middle class. But it has shrunk for decades. During the Great Recession after 2008, millions of middle-class Americans lost their jobs and homes. The result is that the upper class today has achieved a level of prosperity unheard of since the gap between rich and poor in the Gilded Age at the end of the nineteenth century.

As Larry Bartels writes, "Income inequality was essentially constant from the late 1940s through the late 1960s with families at the 80th percentile of income distribution earning about three times as much as families at the 20th percentile. Inequality increased fairly steadily through the 1970s and 1980s before leveling off once again in the 1990s."[5]

Income and wealth gaps grew again after the recession of 2001 and, even more after the Great Recession of 2008. With the economic recession during the pandemic, the gap has grown again between the very rich who enjoy the highest stock levels since the stock markets began in America, while the unemployment level soared past even the 2008 recession levels.

Today's economic inequality is exacerbated by a political power gap in which the lobbying power of wealthy individuals and large corporations is used to pass laws to lower their taxes and lessen government regulations. Campaign finance laws and court decisions let the wealthy essentially purchase politicians through campaign contributions and offers of lucrative jobs when those politicians rejoin the private sector.

Vast sums of money have poured into political campaigns since the disastrous *Citizens United* and related court decisions opened the flood gates to big (and often, dark) money in politics.[6] In one of the most expensive gubernatorial election to date in U.S. history, two Illinois billionaires in 2018 spent more than $284 million (most of it their own money) to win the post.[7]

Contested congressional elections now cost at least $4 million each, with the most expensive House race costing more than $37 million and the most expensive Senate race costing $224 million in 2020.[8] So incumbent members of Congress have to raise $1,000 an hour during their two-year terms in office to be reelected. The legal limit for individual campaign contributions to federal campaigns is $2,900 per election and $5,800 per election cycle per candidate. But this means that candidates spend more time contacting contributors, while political action committees (PACs) and large dark-money contributions become more valuable. The costs of media advertising, direct mail, phone canvassing, and Internet are a major cause of the ever-increasing need to raise money.

This level of money needed to win political races means candidates cannot raise the necessary funds by depending on small donations from their own constituents. While some money can be raised more broadly with contribute buttons on campaign websites, usually these smaller donations are not enough to prevail.

Even local city council and state legislative races cost a lot. In districts with between fifty thousand and a hundred thousand residents, candidates usually have to raise at least a quarter of a million dollars.[9] Because of the high costs of media, Internet, and staff of most election campaigns, unequal access to wealth means that the rich have a disproportionate effect on electing the candidates who will, in turn, serve their interests. In U.S. elections, money matters.

Not only does big money in elections undermine democracy, but income and wealth inequality provide a great advantage in shaping laws and regulations inside government. When laws and regulations are being drafted, the rich often influence compliant officials they have elected. They influence appointed officials as well by lobbying in the executive bureaucracy. The wealthy also hire high-powered lawyers who represent them and their class interests in all branches of governments, including in the courts, where corporate lawyers frequently become judges themselves.

It is true that public interest groups like older, venerable groups like Common Cause and specialist organizations like the environmentally concerned Sierra Club represent broad citizen and public interests. It is also true that they can sometimes mobilize grassroots lobbying and direct action to force the adoption of laws and regulations opposed by the wealthy. Yet, individuals, working-class organizations like labor unions, and public-interest groups are often overmatched by corporate lobbyists working in the backrooms out of public view. Lobbyists for the wealthy have the advantage because they can bundle large campaign contributions and provide the technical expertise to draft legislation and regulations that the average citizen cannot possibly match. They frequently provide the information and technical expertise to legislators and bureaucrats necessary to decode thousands of pages of legislation and regulations.

During the Trump administration, the advantages of the wealthy grew. Donald Trump appointed lobbyists and corporate officials to positions of power in the Cabinet and administrative agencies. From these positions they were able to deregulate environmental protections, increase military spending, start erecting a huge wall across the southern border, and generally enact policies favored by their previous and future employers.

In short, the principle of political equality of one person, one vote is now overridden by corporate and individual wealth in modern U.S. politics. While this may have been more the case in the Trump administration, it was true long before Trump took office. "Money talks" is an accurate description of our political system today. Simply electing Joe Biden as president, new members of Congress, and local officials is not enough to end the power of the wealthy.

While there have been gains in lessening racial and gender inequality, Whites, Blacks, Latinos, Asian Americans, women, and LGBTQ folks still fall at distinctly different places in the economic hierarchy. While there are certainly examples today of minorities and women who have made it economically and politically into the upper class, they remain the exception. Income inequality still reflects racial and gender inequality in today's America.

For an example of the effects of race on politics, note that 80 percent of majority Black congressional districts elect Black members of Congress, while only 5 percent of Black representatives are elected in majority White districts. Even women, who have made the gains in the private sector, still on average earn less than their male counterparts in the private sector and hold only 5 percent of the CEO positions of giant corporations. Women and minorities are also underrepresented on corporate boards. And these conditions have worsened since the pandemic began.[10]

Before the 2018 elections, women made up only 20 percent of the members of both houses of the U.S. Congress. Additional women were elected in 2018 and 2020, but still made up only 27 percent after 2020, a far cry from the 52 percent of the population they constitute.[11]

Thus, even if minority groups and women like Chicago's Mayor Lori Lightfoot or Vice President Kamala Harris have improved their status, wealth, and power, race and gender still provide a basis for discrimination. This creates an additional barrier to political equality.

Economic and Racial Inequality in Chicago

Chicago and its metropolitan region graphically illustrate the effects of economic and political inequality. Since minorities are the majority and Whites the minority in Chicago, it is a precursor of the future population distribution in America. According to the U.S. Census, by 2045 minorities will become the majority nationally.[12] This has already occurred in microcosm in Chicago.

In the 1960s, scholars declared Chicago the most segregated city in North America.[13] Since then, other cities like Milwaukee and Dallas have occasionally had a higher segregation index. Nonetheless, the Chicago metropolitan region remains one of the most segregated. Chicago's Black/White residential segregation index has improved from 94 percent in the 1960s to 72 percent today.[14] However, that still means that three-quarters of Chicagoans would have to move to live in a community with the same population percentage of Blacks and Whites as in the Chicago Metropolitan statistical area. Latinos and

Asian Americans have a lower segregation index than Blacks. But Chicago remains residentially segregated for all racial groups. Even when minorities move to the suburbs, they frequently are forced to settle in residentially segregated suburbs such as the African American suburbs of Harvey and Markham, while Whites flee to all-White suburbs like Kenilworth.

Residential segregation inevitably leads to segregated schools and job discrimination because schools in minority communities are generally inferior and companies don't locate in ghettoes. Minority communities experience more unemployment, lower educational attainment, and higher crime rates. Racial segregation matters in all aspects of life.

The city of Chicago today is approximately 30 percent Black, 33 percent White, 29 percent Latino, and 7 percent Asian American or other.[15] For practical political purposes it is one-third Black, one-third White, and one-third Latino. Because no one racial group controls the outcome of city elections, a multiracial coalition must be assembled to win and govern. Ever since Harold Washington was elected in the 1980s, it has been true that, to be elected mayor, a candidate must win support of at least two of the major racial groups. In Lightfoot's case, she assembled a "rainbow coalition" with majority support from all three racial groups in the runoff. But despite gains in political power, White males are still dominant in Chicago, as they are more generally in America. While Chicago has become a multiracial, multicultural city, it has done so without achieving even approximate equality in wealth or power.

Race is related to economic success in Chicago as well as to political power. The "color gap" in the economy has been widening ever since it was first measured by Pierre De Vise in the 1960s.[16] Over the last several decades, Chicago has become a global city, more dependent on the service economy than on the manufacturing that characterized it in the nineteenth and much of the twentieth century. Back when it was the "hog butcher for the world, tool maker, stacker of wheat," as Chicago poet Carl Sandburg wrote.[17] Rather than narrowing the income and wealth gap, the new global economy has only widened it. The owners and executives of global corporations end up with ever greater wealth, while their janitors, clerks, and secretaries make near-poverty wages and the unemployed in the city don't even make that.

The racial connection in the gap between rich and poor is shown graphically in the maps of the richest and poorest communities. The richest suburban communities are all White and as shown in the map in figure 3.1 from De Vise's studies in 1966. The latest census data show that they are little changed in 2020. Some wealthier Chicago neighborhoods like the Gold Coast and Lincoln Park have rich people living in them, but the suburbs still tend to house most of the wealthy and those rich suburbs remain mostly all-White.

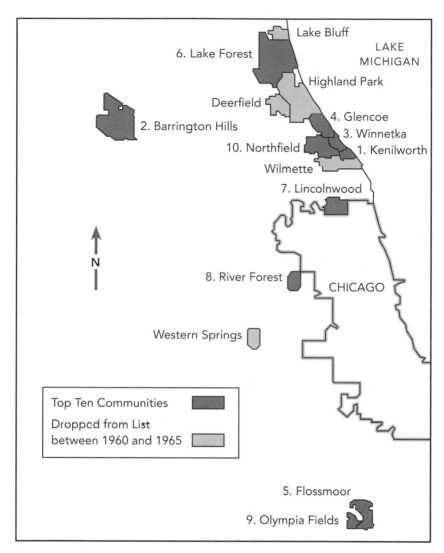

Figure 3.1: The ten richest communities in Metropolitan Chicago in 1966. (After De Vise, *Chicago's Widening Color Gap*, 44, based on information in the *Chicago Daily News*, May 10, 1967, 72)

By contrast, the ten poorest neighborhoods are nearly all Black, inner-city neighborhoods, generally clustered around public housing. Since 1966, the biggest change is that razing public housing has left poverty still concentrated in the same neighborhoods. But where previously the poorest neighborhoods were only one neighborhood wide, poverty has now swollen to two

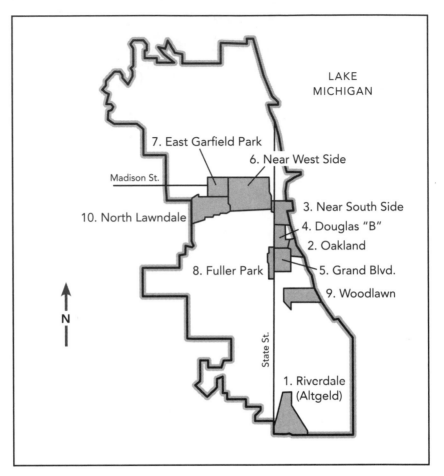

Figure 3.2: The ten poorest communities in Metropolitan Chicago in 1966. (After De Vise, *Chicago's Widening Color Gap*, 59, based on information in the *Chicago Daily News*, May 9, 1967, 24)

or three neighborhoods in width as the concentration of high-rise public housing has been eliminated. The pattern of poverty is mostly unchanged, with the poorest communities still on the South and West Sides of Chicago in all-Black neighborhoods. That is still the situation today although some southern suburbs have become all Black and among the poorest in the region.

The overall gap in racial income and wealth in Chicago remains stark. The median White household income in 2018 was $70,960, Asian American households earned $56,373, Latinos $41,188, and Blacks only $30,303.[18] Thus, Whites on average had more than double the income of Black households.

The data from the 2017 American Community Survey show that the picture is even bleaker and more racially biased for young adults. About 45 percent of Black men age twenty to twenty-four were unemployed and not in school, as were 20 percent of young Latino men, but only 5.7 percent of young White men.[19] This education and job gap is partly responsible for the continuing gap in wealth and income.

The pandemic that began in 2020 has only worsened this gap. We know that deaths have been higher in minority communities due to the COVID-19 virus, and in November 2020, Illinois was the state with the highest cases in the country that month. The economic recession also hit the minority community harder than the White community because more Whites could continue to work from home or were able to hold onto their jobs.

Deaths for Blacks and Latinos from the virus were much higher than for Whites. Whites accounted for 22 percent of the deaths, Blacks 39 percent, and Latinos 33 percent as of June 2021.[20] Even health and mortality rates are racialized. About the high rate of COVID-19 infections in minority communities, Sage Kim writes that "one of the reasons for such racial disparities is due to the fact that African American communities are disproportionately affected by multiple chronic diseases before the COVID-19 pandemic." Further, "Fundamental social inequalities, including economic disadvantage, racial discrimination and spatial exclusion have dismantled community capacity, and residents in highly segregated, disfranchised neighborhoods are exposed to prolonged social stress. These social factors result in health disparities we see in cities like Chicago."[21]

Mayor Lightfoot notes that "80 percent of health outcomes are due to social factors, including housing, safety education, economic opportunity—every single one of which through our history as a nation been impacted by systemic racism . . . we can no longer allow racism to rob our residents of the opportunity to live and lead full, healthy and happy lives."[22]

Beyond the racial aspects of Chicago's economic patterns, even before the pandemic there was a very disturbing pattern of the shrinking middle class. Using data from education scholar Sean Reardon and sociologist Kendra Bischoff, policy analyst Daniel Hertz calculated where the median family income of each census tract fell relative to the entire metropolitan area. In the 1970s, 45 percent of the census tracts were middle class. By 2010, that number was reduced to 16 percent and continues to fall.[23]

In brief, the middle class has greatly shrunk over the last fifty years, and that pattern has worsened in the current recession as more formerly middle-class families have lost their homes and jobs.

The middle class has been shrinking for decades. The middle class was a greater percentage of Chicago's 3.6 million people back in 1970 than it is today. It shrank while both the poverty and wealthy areas of the city have expanded. Our economy, both nationally and locally, is fostering a small wealthy class at the top and a larger, poorer class at the bottom, especially since the Great Recession in 2008 and the pandemic recession that began in 2020. The result is a rapidly shrinking middle class and a color or racial gap. There are more poor minorities proportionally than there are poor Whites, just as there are more rich White people than there are rich minorities.

Political Consequences

It is reasonable to ask: Does continuing racial and sexual inequality coupled with income and wealth inequality threaten democracy? Abraham Lincoln put it succinctly when he declared that a nation half slave and half free could not survive.[24] While our inequality today is not the same as slavery presented in his era, it still poses a problem. When we were founded as a nation, Blacks, women, and Native Americans were not citizens. White males ruled and owned nearly all of the wealth. Over the last two centuries, we have enlarged the electorate and all these groups through struggle and protest have managed to earn full citizenship rights. Yet, Whites have remained at the top of both the economic and political system for the last two hundred and fifty years.

While White men still have disproportionate wealth and political power, in numbers they are a minority and can be outvoted. This is part of the reason for continuing efforts in some states to disenfranchise minorities and suppress their votes. As of the spring of 2021, for instance, lawmakers in forty-seven states had introduced over 350 voter-suppression laws, led by three states with the most bills: Texas, Georgia, and Arizona.[25]

National Civil rights laws since the Voting Rights Act of 1965 have sought to overcome obstacles to voting at the state and local level, but it is a continuing struggle. As of June 2021, Congress had failed to pass new laws to protect voting. Even though new techniques—electronic and automatic voter registration, early voting, and even electronic voting experiments in some states—have made registering and voting easier in an effort to boost civic participation during the pandemic. Despite these efforts, voting rates in the United States remain the lowest of other democratic nations and lower still for minorities and youths.[26] White males still dominate, although this is changing.

It is well established by social science that income, education, and age disparities play major roles in rates of voting and all other forms of political participation.[27] Generally speaking the higher a person's social economic status (SES), the more frequently they vote and participate politically in other ways, such as giving money to campaigns, protesting, and writing public officials. Educational inequality ends up reinforcing economic and income inequality, although for individuals it may be the best way out of the "permanent underclass" poverty.

As Thomas Jefferson wrote, democracy depends on having a large middle class, which in his time were yeomen farmers who owned their own land. "Jefferson envisioned a country populated by small family farms, clustered in rural communities. The yeoman farmer was the backbone of this country, Jefferson believed, who would not be indebted to anyone or anything else."[28] According to Jefferson, these property owners would seek to preserve prosperity for themselves and the nation, and as landowners, they would hold more moderate political views. This moderate middle group would provide stability for the new country.

Today, followers of Jefferson's philosophy argue that democracy still depends on a large middle class with a secure social position, modest prosperity, and economic security. This is exactly the income group that the United States and Chicago are rapidly losing.

The very rich, as a group, have a tendency to support oligarchy and autocracy, while the very poor, having nothing to lose, more often provide support for radical or revolutionary actions and mob rule. The middle-class voters naturally tend to provide common sense support for more moderate policies. So, the shrinking middle class in our time is a threat to democracy.

Times of Crisis

Tyranny and demagoguery are most likely to occur in bad economic times as seen in the famous examples of Hitler, Stalin, Mussolini, and Franco in the twentieth century. On the heels of the Great Depression, there was the rise of fascism and communism and growth of radical movements.

Today, on the heels of a slow, uneven recovery from the Great Recession, which has left many Americans behind and forced millions out of the middle class as they lost their homes and jobs, Donald Trump was elected by voter reaction to their worsening condition. His actions during his four years as president further undermined democracy. His tax breaks for the wealthy and corporations, along with his tariff war with China, widened the economic gap. Thus, a politics of resentment bubbled up among those who had been left behind or whose place in the economy was threatened, and they mobilized.[29]

While his more liberal politics differed from Trump's, Chicago's former mayor Rahm Emanuel was labeled by his opponents as Mayor 1%.[30] During his eight years in office from 2011 to 2019, Chicago's economy was booming, with building cranes and new skyscrapers continually popping up in the downtown Loop and adjacent neighborhoods in order to provide new office space and upscale residencies. These were the physical signs of economic growth as global corporations relocated their headquarters here and Internet startup companies were created in larger numbers. However, in other parts of the city, there continued to be a high crime and murder rate. Chicago became known as the murder capital of the nation. It also had failing public schools; the mayor and his school board closed fifty such failing schools in minority neighborhoods in a single year. Unemployment continued as high as 30 percent in ghetto neighborhoods where economic recovery did not penetrate.

Despite this, Chicago remained resolutely anti-Trump and a sanctuary city that refused to help the national government implement its draconian immigration policies. Chicago voted more than 80 percent in favor of Hillary Clinton in the 2016 presidential election and by a similar margin for Joe Biden in 2020.[31]

Despite being strongly Democratic and anti-Trump in its politics during both the Emanuel and Lightfoot eras, Chicago remains a tale of two cities economically and socially. Many wealthy Chicagoans live on the very narrow strip of the Gold Coast, or outside the city limits in wealthy suburban enclaves like Kenilworth and Winnetka. Meanwhile, the poor live trapped in minority ghettoes on the South and West Sides of Chicago and in the southern suburbs.

Metropolitan Chicago is still sorting itself out as Democratic candidates are beginning to win elections in what was previous all-Republican suburban districts. In short, Illinois is becoming a bluer state controlled by Democrats.

In the turbulent Trump era, people took to the streets in Chicago to protest. The anti-Trump protest at the University of Illinois at Chicago Pavilion in 2016 forced the only cancellation of a Trump political rally during that year's presidential campaign. Black Lives Matter protests since the tragic events in Ferguson, Missouri, the Chicago police shooting of Laquan McDonald, and the murder of George Floyd in Minneapolis led to protest marches that closed streets and snarled Chicago traffic. The national Women's March after President Trump's inauguration in January 2017 drew 250,000 people. It was one of the largest protest marches in Chicago history. Added to these, immigration protests in Chicago have drawn tens of thousands of people for more than a decade.

In short, racial and income/wealth inequality and discrimination have led to political turmoil and instability in Chicago and the nation. That turmoil only increased after Trump's election. The problems of crime, police abuse, and schools have worsened as economic recovery was slow to arrive in some Chicago neighborhoods after the Great Recession of 2008.

This turmoil set the stage for the 2018 congressional elections in which the Democrats made substantial gains. They fell short of taking over both houses of Congress. However, they gained control of the House of Representatives by winning forty additional seats. Then, in 2020 Democrats not only retained control of the House but gained control of the Senate, with Vice President Kamala Harris able to cast the tie-breaking vote in a body divided 50–50 between the Democrats (and two Independents who caucus with them) and Republicans.

Meanwhile, in Chicago, the 2019 mayoral and aldermanic elections were fought as a continuation of old policies versus fundamental reform. A number of candidates framed it as experienced political and governmental officials versus an inexperienced newcomer. Lori Lightfoot ran on Mayor Harold Washington's earlier progressive platform of a "Chicago That Works for All of Us." She proposed reforms of Chicago policing, schools, and neighborhood economic development with no major new taxes. Many winning aldermanic candidates offered similar progressive programs that appealed to Chicago voters.

The results of the 2019 Chicago elections paralleled the 2018 and 2020 national elections. Lightfoot won all fifty Chicago wards, garnering 74 percent of the vote. By doing so, she gained a mandate for change along with eighteen newly elected aldermen who would help provide the majority she needed to govern. In the first two years of her administration, she was able, with the support of the new city council, to enact ethics reforms and to begin to tackle the intractable problems of crime, violence, schools, and budget shortfalls. She then had to tackle the pandemic and economic recession that slowed the enactment of the progressive reforms she had advocated in the campaign.

At the national level, the 2020 election became a referendum on the Trump policies and his administration's handling of the pandemic. With Joe Biden's election and Democratic control of congress, there is now an opportunity to remake America into a fairer and more equitable society.

Overcoming Inequality

Racial, income, and wealth inequality continue to pose a threat to our democracy. This will not be resolved by the outcome of a single election. Based on our history and the history of other democratic countries, lesser forms of democracy can be maintained even in the face of severe racial discrimination and wide economic inequalities. These lesser forms, like conservative democracy, polyarchy, or Machine Democracy, contain some democratic features. However, racial and income inequality is a threat to continuing, much less improving, American democracy.

Ever since the civil rights of the 1960s, followed by women's rights, LG-BTQ rights, and Native American rights movements, we have made progress toward ending various forms of discrimination. However, as Chicago demonstrates, there is still a direct link between race and economic success.

Under President Donald Trump, racial issues were raised in his campaign and in White House attacks on Latino and Muslim immigrants, whom he labeled terrorists, criminals, and rapists who take American jobs from "true Americans." His travel ban against Muslims was even eventually upheld by the U.S. Supreme Court. Over the four years he was president, thousands of refugees seeking asylum were turned away at the borders and a large border wall was under construction. His administration threatened eight hundred thousand DACA (Deferred Action for Childhood Arrivals) students with deportation. The twelve million undocumented individuals and families living in the United States faced similar deportation threats. This is one face of racism today.

At the same time, we are seeing a fundamental shift in American society. Yoni Appelbaum puts it this way:

> The United States is undergoing a transition perhaps no rich and stable democracy has ever experienced: Its historically dominant group is on its way to becoming a political minority—and its minority groups are asserting their co-equal rights and interests. . . .
>
> . . . Sometime in the next quarter century or so, depending on immigration rates and the vagaries of ethnic and racial identification, nonwhites will become a majority in the U.S.[32]

As this occurs, Whites, especially White conservative Trump supporters in the Republican Party, have to become convinced that there is a still a viable political path to maintain their rights as a new minority.[33]

However, an even more insidious problem than the ongoing demographic shift is the growing economic inequality in the United States. All citizens must have economic security if they are to have the leisure, skills, and time to carry out their political duties as citizens. A rough equality is a necessary precondition for democracy.[34] The gaps between classes must not be too great or hereditary. Ideally, the middle class should be the largest class in order to provide a bulwark of support for democracy. Unfortunately, that is no longer the case in either Chicago or the nation.

Instead, the middle class is shrinking while the income and wealth gap is widening. Those in and near poverty are growing and that has only worsened during the pandemic and the economic recession that followed it. Globalization is making that gap wider, not narrowing it. At the same time, the rich have the dominant voice in government and affect government policies at all levels. We are rapidly becoming a government of, by, and for the rich rather than a government of, by, and for all the people.

Under these circumstances, what does democracy's rebirth require? It requires progress in lessening racial discrimination and the unhealthy link between race, class, and wealth. It requires an immigration policy that, while restricting immigration to manageable levels, recognizes the value of immigrants and their innate human rights. It requires that we end anti-immigrant rhetoric, policies, and racism.

We must narrow the wealth and income gap, which if left unchecked will destroy democracy. This is complicated because democracy flourishes best when coupled with capitalism that is able to harness ambition, initiative, and inventiveness by the lure of profit and property accumulation. Although under capitalism there cannot be complete economic equality, there can be equality of opportunity and a smaller gap between rich and poor.

The cure for the dichotomy between the imperatives of capitalism and democracy lies in government regulation of the economy, a fairer system of taxation, and more generous government programs in education, health, and welfare. What is needed is the Goldilocks effect—neither too much nor too little government. We need government regulations and programs that allow capitalism to succeed without destroying either competition or democracy. We need policies that tax wealthy individuals and corporations more fairly and that provide a basic income to the poor to raise them and their children out of poverty.

Successful capitalists must be able to accumulate wealth and corporations must be able to succeed, but within tax and regulatory limits. As political scientist Stephen Caliendo puts it, "in a capitalist system, some individuals will acquire, accumulate, or otherwise possess more wealth than others. Accordingly, reducing inequality does not entail allotting the same amount of possessions, money, and debt to each individual. Rather it refers to the dramatic (and increasing) gap between the wealthiest and poorest Americans, and the disproportionate levels of poverty . . . in communities of color."[35]

Today, our governmental policies let some individually accumulate too much wealth and others too little. For instance, contrary to President Trump's claims and the goals of his tax policies, wealthy Americans and corporations are not taxed too much, but too little. In the Eisenhower administration after World War II, the wealthiest Americans paid 66.4 percent in income taxes.[36] Today the official highest tax rate is 33.4 percent. With the Trump tax laws and many exemptions, the actual tax rate today is much lower. Most wealthy people pay a much lower percentage of their income than the official rate. As wealthy investor Warren Buffett says, it is unfair that he pays a lower tax than his secretary.

We do not want government laws and policies that cause everyone to have the same income and wealth, but we also don't want the gap between rich and poor to become too extreme. Nor do we want to eliminate the middle class. So, we need to raise taxes on the wealthy; provide benefits and assistance to help raise the poor out of poverty; and enlarge the disappearing middle class. Despite the fact that such a change in policies would benefit the majority of Americans, this is not an easy change to make. As Mayor Richard J. Daley used to chide me when I was a Chicago alderman, "you ain't got the votes, kid." So even if the economic and social agenda needed to reinvent and sustain democracy is accepted, the political will and strength is not yet there to enact it. In the 2020 campaign, Bernie Sanders and Elizabeth Warren were among the candidates promoting such policy changes, and a growing proportion of the public now support them. But any substantial change will come slowly. These issues will continue to be central to the divisions in the elections throughout the coming decade.

Moreover, the problem is not just inequality between individuals, but the inequality between individuals and global corporations. Massive, transnational corporations clearly need to be regulated, but this is difficult because no single national government can regulate them effectively. If national laws get too restrictive, corporations can relocate their headquarters or production facilities to other countries. They can arrange their bookkeeping so that their profits are officially acquired in countries with low taxes and few regulations.

Effective regulation of transnational corporations will require a new international order, as happened with the global institutions that arose after World War II. Those served us reasonably well in the twentieth century. Unfortunately, these economic institutions and regulations are no longer adequate. For us to create a new international order adequate for the twenty-first century, the United States and the European Union must take the lead in creating institutions and regulations to curb transnational corporations. This will be one of the greatest challenges of this century.

Overcoming inequality is not as simple as adding new taxes or government regulations. In a time of automation and artificial intelligence, the nature of work itself is changing. As are the roles of humans in production, jobs, and leisure. We will require new job training, education, and skill development as a minimal first step in confronting these changes.

The standard work week that is today forty hours will need to decrease while minimum wage and income will need to increase to a livable wage. In the future, humans will be directing the work of machines using computer software and artificial intelligence. On the other hand, professionals are ever more tied to electronic communication so that they are in many ways more tied to their jobs for longer hours. The nature of work will need to change in ways that are more humane for everyone.

In this new economy, education will not end with a high school or college degree; rather, workers will be continuously retraining and upgrading their skills. Online education will move from courses and webinars to virtual reality training and personal avatars. It will indeed be "a brave new world." But, while educating new workers and retraining former workers will be important, fundamentally we will need to find ways to subsidize income. We need to better share the gains that come from both international trade and automation. Everyone can gain from the new economy, but only if these gains are shared more equitably.

Our societal goal has always been to provide as many people as possible with meaningful work. With new technology that should become possible. If more people play responsible roles in the economy, and thereby, develop their creativity and thinking, we will potentially raise better citizens able to play a more direct role in electing representatives and in holding them accountable. Citizens will become capable of participating more directly in making those policies that most affect their lives and communities.

There is, of course, the darker possibility that this same technology could be used to create a totalitarian dystopia as often portrayed in the science fiction books and movies. The challenge we face now is to direct our new economy so that a positive economic and political future is achieved. To do so will require some government restrictions, regulations, direction of the economy, and a way to better share the wealth. The first step is to eliminate, or at least narrow, existing racial and economic disparities. The second is to create a more humane workplace. The third is to ensure that communities, neighborhoods, and individuals are not left behind in this new economy created after the pandemic and economic recession lift.

Fortunately, under capitalism it is possible to achieve these goals. Governments simply need to create laws and rules that make profits greater for individuals and corporations making positive contributions to eliminating inequality and creating a workforce that is educated, employed in useful work, and better trained for their role as citizens. However, this redesign of the economy first requires a redesign our politics.

Government has a positive role to play. For example, in Chicago, the Lightfoot administration has focused on lessening poverty especially in ten neighborhoods on the South and West Side wards in predominantly African American neighborhoods. The city has created a public-private commitment to spend more than $750 million in these ten target communities to promote economic development. Despite the pandemic and economic recession, progress has been made in the first year of the commitment.[37] In February 2020, before the pandemic fully took hold, a poverty summit was held with more than seven hundred leaders from community groups, civic organizations, academia, and the effective neighborhoods to kick off the effort. By October 2020, $70 million in city funds and $300 million in private funds had been allocated. Since then several hundred million dollars have been committed to economic development in these poverty neighborhoods. "This is just the beginning of something great and special happening in our city," Mayor Lightfoot said. "We won't be stopped by a pandemic, we won't be stopped by economic and fiscal challenges because we are more determined and united than ever to lean into our values and make sure that we continue forging a path for more inclusive development in every neighborhood in our city that has been deprived of development for way too long."[38]

This chapter opens with a photograph of an African American couple shopping at the Maxwell Street Market in 1978. On Sundays, that market was where the working class and the poor shopped for bargains. Many Jewish business owners got their start there, and nearly every great Chicago jazz and blues performer got their start playing on the street. The market was demolished in the twenty-first century by urban development and expansion of the University of Illinois at Chicago. It was moved several blocks away and has essentially disappeared, just like Chicago's middle class is disappearing. It is another symbol of what has been lost.

Despite the pandemic and recession, city government and partners in the private sector (including businesses, civic organizations, and universities) in Chicago are attempting to create a more balanced economic development in which poor neighborhoods are not left behind in the recovery. Limiting poverty, lessening economic inequality, and increasing the size of the middle class cannot be achieved at the local level alone. But new policies of fairness in cities around the country must be part of democracy's rebirth.

The author raises funds for his 1971 aldermanic campaign in Chicago. (From author's collection, photographer unknown)

4

Money in Politics

Income inequality has meant that elections have become much more expensive. The rich simply have more money to give. At the same time, elections have become more expensive because most campaigns have had to adopt expensive techniques previously reserved for national campaigns. Take, for example, Chicago elections held on February 26 and April 2, 2019. More than $40 million was spent to elect Chicago's mayor and city council. Chicago elections in 2015 and 2019 were the most expensive in Chicago history. Beyond broader social problems like the loss of the middle class and the dangers of racial and income inequality, the flood of money has skewed nearly all elections and undermined the equality of the voters, which is essential to democracy.

From 1955 to 1976, when Richard J. Daley was mayor of Chicago, he spent less than $1 million on each of his campaigns. By contrast, when his son, Richard M. Daley became mayor from 1989 to 2011, he spent from $4 million to $7 million. This changed radically when Rahm Emanuel spent $12 million in his 2011 election and $32 million in 2015 to be elected mayor. Over time, Chicago city elections have become mini-presidential campaigns, both in campaign techniques and their cost.

In 2018, when it appeared that Rahm Emanuel would run again for re-election, he began raising the necessary millions to do so. After Labor Day when he announced he would be retiring, the number of candidates seeking to replace him ballooned from seven to twenty-one. At the same time, there were 212 aldermanic candidates vying for the fifty city council seats. The 2019 elections with their multiple candidates would again turn out to be the most expensive in the city's history. Each of the mayoral frontrunners would need to raise at least $5 million. Of the two candidates who made it into the runoff, County Board president Toni Preckwinkle raised $6.9 million, while the winner, lawyer Lori Lightfoot, raised $5 million. In the primary, several other mayoral candidates also raised a lot of money, including Bill Daley, son of Richard J. and brother of Richard M. Daley, who raised $7.2 million; and lawyer Gery Chico, who raised $2.9 million.[1]

Chicago aldermanic campaign fund-raising was equally robust with dozens of candidates raising more than $200,000 and four campaigns passing the $1 million mark. Fourteenth Ward alderman Ed Burke led with a war chest of $12 million built up over the years by contributions from businesses in the global economy. These included the Trump International Hotel and Tower and American Airlines, which as an attorney he aided in getting property tax reductions in addition to using his clout as the floor leader of the Chicago City Council to pass legislation favorable to them. In the end, Burke spent $715,000 to be reelected, far more than his challenger. Despite being indicted on corruption charges at the time, Burke managed to win reelection due to his formidable war chest and political power.[2] Altogether, aldermanic candidates in 2019 spent $22.7 million.[3]

Even though he was retiring, Mayor Rahm Emanuel continued to play a role in the 2019 election by giving checks of $20,000 each from his campaign funds to support the reelection campaigns of the aldermen who had voted with him most frequently in the city council. Despite Emanuel's support, a number of these aldermen lost their reelection bids, including Fortieth Ward alderman Pat O'Connor, Mayor Emanuel's political floor leader. In general, Chicagoans voted for reformers in 2019 election in reaction to continuing corruption scandals, but all the winning campaigns raised and spent a lot of money.

Thus, money counts heavily in local as well as national elections. At the city level, large campaign contributions from wealthy individuals, corporations, and labor union PACs count for more than small contributions by constituents. To paraphrase former U.S. Senator Everett Dirksen, "a million here and a million there, and soon you are talking about real money."[4] Campaigns for mayor and aldermen in cities like Chicago cannot be run successfully without big bucks any more than modern-day races for members of Congress and president can.

Successful candidates have to purchase staff, headquarters, software and computer programs, and most importantly, mass media, cable TV, and social media. This is in addition to the usual campaign brochures, buttons, direct mail, and the like. Getting the word out to tens of thousands or a couple million voters does not come cheap. For citywide campaigns, TV ads are needed, and a week's worth of saturation ads on a few key stations cost more than

$250,000. Despite a robust and successful social media campaign, volunteers, and paid workers going door to door, Lightfoot won only after the *Chicago Sun-Times* endorsement allowed her to raise sufficient funds to mount a TV ad campaign with professional, well-made ads utilizing the findings of public opinion polls to guide their development.

Regulating Money in Politics

The use of money in political campaigns that flows directly from economic imbalance has been a continuing problem in American democracy. Although attempts to regulate money in politics goes back to the early twentieth century when corporations and labor unions were prevented from contributing directly to federal elections, these efforts have not always been successful. In the 1970s, after the Watergate scandal, Nixon's impeachment, and his resignation, there was a systematic effort to restrict campaign contributions and to establish partial public funding for presidential campaigns. The public recognized that campaign contributions sway elected officials. Large contributions give the wealthy, corporations, and labor unions unfair access, if not direct control over, government officials who win their elections with the help of "big money." Wealthy individuals, interest groups, and political parties control which candidates get on the ballot and have the resources to run viable campaigns. Because of this imbalance in who funds campaigns, we are in danger of becoming an oligarchy rather than a democracy.

Attempts to restrict the influence of money in politics have taken several forms. The least controversial is based on the premise that "sunlight is the best disinfectant." Following that idea, campaign reform legislation focuses on making publicly available the names of contributors and the amount they give to candidates. The belief is that, if the actions of the elected officials too blatantly reflect the interests of their contributors, then voters would elect other candidates at the next election.

Despite campaign reporting laws, however, not all organizations today report who actually contributes. In the 2012 elections, for instance, more than $300 million was spent by groups that did not report their donors, creating "dark money" in election campaigns. More than $184 million in dark money was contributed in 2016 and nearly as much in non-presidential elections in 2018. The 2020 elections saw the amount of dark-money contributions continue to be more than $119 million.[5]

Another approach to regulating money in politics has been to pass anticorruption laws and to prosecute vigorously outright bribing of public officials. It is hard to estimate how effective this criminalizing approach is, however. Since 1976, more than 2,100 public officials in Illinois and more than 1,700 in metropolitan Chicago have been convicted in federal court of corruption.[6] In 2020 and 2021, there were three major corruption cases involving more than a dozen aldermen, state legislators, and lobbyists at various stages of trial in federal court. Yet, corruption—from simple bribery to illicit use of political campaign funds—and more elaborate corruption schemes continue unabated even as thirty or more public officials in Illinois are convicted each year. Four of the last ten Illinois governors have gone to prison, with two imprisoned at the same time. Five congressmen, nineteen judges, and thirty-five Chicago aldermen have also gone to prison since the 1970s.[7] While anticorruption laws and convictions have obviously had some effect, they are not by themselves a cure. The problem is not a "rotten apple in the barrel" or just a few bad individuals, but a rotten apple barrel. The system is broken because the misuse of money in politics has become imbedded in the political culture itself.

The third approach to curbing the misuse of campaign contributions has been to restrict the amount that can be contributed, and sometimes, to provide public funding of elections as we partially do in presidential campaigns. This has been done in cities like New York and states like Maine. For instance, individuals are restricted to giving only $2,900 per congressional candidate for each election cycle, so they can't give millions of dollars to elect a candidate who may favor their interests. However, setting limits on campaign donations by itself is insufficient.

Public funding is essential to make sure that all viable candidates (those with public support as shown by petition signatures or standing in public opinion polls) have sufficient funds to get their message to the voters. Candidates don't have to have funding equal to that of their wealthy opponents or those funded by wealthy interest groups. Additional money tends to have less effect after a minimal threshold is met. But candidates do need enough funding to be competitive. Of course, public funding can be made contingent on full campaign disclosure and accepting limits on the size of private campaign contributions.

Unfortunately, *Citizens United* has undermined setting limits on campaign contributions. As early as the *Buckley v. Valeo* Supreme Court decision of 1976, the official definition of corruption has been "confined to quid pro quo bribery." In *Citizens United* in 2010, the Supreme Court struck down all limits on corporate political expenditures and concluded that "as a matter of federal constitutional law *corruption* now means only quid pro quo corruption" (emphasis added).[8] The courts have further ruled that laws limiting campaign contributions can't infringe on either individuals' or corporations' right of free speech. This includes their right to use their money for political advocacy in support of candidates, purchasing their own independent media ads, and lobbying governing officials.

As Stephen Wayne writes, "The financing floodgates had been opened by the Court's ruling in *Citizens United v. Federal Election Commission* (558 U.S. 08-205). In that decision, the court held that corporations and by implication labor unions, could raise and spend unlimited amounts of money on election activities so long as they did not do so in coordination with the candidate's campaign. . . . During the 2015–2016 election cycle, approximately $4 billion was spent independently by nonparty groups and individuals."[9] By 2020 a similar amount was spent.[10] These vast sums of money that now pour into campaigns from wealthy individuals and groups undermine the principle that every citizen by their vote and voice should have an equal influence on the outcome of elections. Money clearly amplifies the voice and clout of corporations, PACs, and wealthy individuals.

Subsequent court decisions have made possible unlimited contributions by candidates themselves and lifted limits on how much wealthy individuals can give. For instance, in the 2016 election, twenty wealthy individuals gave or spent over $10 million each in attempting to influence the outcome.[11] There is no doubt that they had more influence on who got elected and what policies these representatives supported afterward than citizens who gave nothing or only a few dollars. Now, by law, there is even the opportunity to give unlimited money through various organizations without them disclosing the names of their donors. This dark-money option means that we voters don't even know who is buying the election and politicians with secret contributions.

In practice, these new rules by the federal courts have opened the floodgates to nearly unlimited and unregulated campaign contributions. With President Trump appointing more conservative judges since 2016, it seems unlikely that judicial opinions will regulate campaign funding in the near future.

The clearest alternative to the current state of affairs is public funding of campaigns and the full reporting of all donors by campaigns that accept public funding. But while there is general public support for reigning in the Wild West of money in politics, there is less support for using tax dollars to fund campaigns. Public opinion must first be changed if the court decisions are to be changed by legislation.

Cost of Elections

The clearest trend of money in politics is that every election is more expensive than the last one. For instance, the 2016 presidential election year saw more money raised and spent than 2012. According to the Open Secrets website maintained by the Center for Responsive Politics, $6.5 billion was spent on federal elections in 2016, with more than $100 million spent on the single U.S. Senate race in Pennsylvania.[12]

Even though 2018 was a non-presidential election year, federal election spending was still a whopping $5.7 billion. That year, both the Florida and Texas U.S. Senate races topped $110 million.[13] Spending on state and local races also increased exponentially. In the 2018 race for governor of Illinois, more than $255 million was raised by billionaire Democratic and Republican candidates.[14] U.S. Senate and gubernatorial races cost potential candidates up to $100 million each. Contested House of Representative races cost on average over $4 million and even local elections averaged $250,000. When elections cost this much, it is hard for qualified candidates who are not wealthy or backed by rich individuals, labor unions, or business corporations to compete. As a result, we frequently don't elect the most qualified candidates anymore, but only the candidates backed by wealthy interests. Big money selects the candidates that the voters choose from. As New York Machine "Boss" Tweed famously put it over a century ago, "I don't care who does the electing, if I get to do the nominating."[15]

By 2020 campaign spending had increased again. The most expensive House of Representatives race cost more than $37 million and the most expensive U.S. Senate race cost $260 million.[16]

For more than a decade, in order to run successfully for president, one must first win what is called the money primary. A candidate, no matter how qualified or level of public support, must raise millions of dollars to compete successfully because running for president is ghastly expensive. Those who can't raise enough money to hire the staff, do the polling, and run both a traditional and a social media campaign can't win. This occurs many months before the first official primary or caucus in which the voters get a voice. Then, candidates who don't win the early primaries and caucuses are forced to drop out because their campaign contributions dry up. Wealthy donors and organizations want to back winners in order to gain access.

The result of court decisions and ever-increasing campaign expenses is that we get the "best government that money can buy." Big money and dark money in campaigns has skyrocketed. In the 2016 election, super PACs spent $1.4 billion, over $181 million of which was dark money, with the donors hidden from the public.[17] That massive influx of PAC money increases every election cycle. These huge sums of PAC money result in more negative attack ads rather than thoughtful debates of public policy. The "independent expenditures" by these committees mostly fund negative television ads and social media attacks that further alienate voters, lower election participation, and undermine faith in democracy.

U.S. senator and presidential candidate Bernie Sanders, in his 2019 New Year's e-mail put the situation this way:

> The bad news is that in the United States and other parts of the world, the foundations of democracy are under severe attack as demagogues, supported by billionaire oligarchs, work to establish authoritarian type regimes. That is true in Russia. That is true in Saudi Arabia. That is true in the United States. While the very rich get much richer these demagogues seek to move us toward tribalism and set one group against another, deflecting attention from the real crises we face. . . . Politics in a democracy should not be complicated. Government must work for all of the people, not just the wealthy and the powerful. As a new House and Senate convene next week, it is imperative that the American people stand up and demand real solutions to the major economic, social, racial and environmental crises that we face.[18]

When elections are badly skewed by big money and dark money, it is hard to have faith that when the Congress or state and local officials take office that there will be fundamental policy changes.

Overall, money speaks and officials listen. The wealthy have powerful influence because their campaign contributions determine the outcome of most elections. Because of this, curbing the massive influence of money in politics is central to democracy's rebirth.

The 2018 midterm elections were essentially a referendum on the Trump administration and its policies. With all the money spent by candidates of both political parties, the clearest outcome was that, while the Democrats were not able to take back the U.S. Senate, they won a majority of seats in the House of Representatives.[19] Similar results were seen down ballot, where Democrats won more state legislative seats and governorships, coming closer to parity with Republican control of the states. These elections were, however, the most expensive off-year, non-presidential elections in U.S. history. The Democrats were able to win these seats only because of Trump's unpopularity. But in 2018, Democrats also owed their electoral success to the fact that they were able to raise more money for these races than ever before. Altogether, more than $5.7 billion was raised. Congressional Democratic candidates Jon Ossoff (GA), David Throne (MD), and Scott Wallace (PA) led the pack by raising between $14 and $30 million each for their campaigns. And Texas U.S. Senate candidate Democrat Beto O'Rourke raised an astounding $38 million in a single quarter even though he lost the election.[20]

The Democrats raised much more from "small donors" than Republicans in 2018, but Republicans did better with outside PAC money and contributions from big contributors. Big money and dark money continued to affect election outcomes for candidates from both parties. It was simply that in the 2018 election Democrats were able to spend as much or more in contested districts than Republicans, who traditionally have the money advantage with support from wealthy individuals and big-business contributors.

The 2020 elections continued this trend of ever more expensive elections. The Democrats won the presidency, kept control of the House of Representative (despite losing some seats), and gained a razor-thin control of the U.S. Senate in a 50–50 split, with Vice President Harris able to cast the tie-breaking vote on critical issues.

Translating Campaign Giving into Government Influence

There is little doubt that all this money in politics has a corrosive effect that undermines democracy. As Benjamin Page and Martin Gilens put it, "We believe that *both* major parties tend to be corrupted—and pushed away from satisfying the needs and wishes of ordinary Americans—by their reliance on wealthy contributors. We see this reliance as one of the major reasons for today's feeble state of democratic responsiveness. . . . U.S. officials are clearly *dependent* on private money. . . . [Moving from a principle of one person, one vote] toward a principle of *one dollar*, one vote."[21]

Money translates into control of the government and governmental policies in a number of ways. The first and most obvious is that the inability to raise the large sums of money necessary to run for elected office limits the potential pool of candidates. Incumbents are aided by the fact that a majority of members of Congress have a net worth of more than a million dollars. This is obviously not true of the majority of Americans they are supposed to represent.[22] So many of them can support their campaigns with their own money. These days, candidates either have to be personally wealthy or have wealthy individuals, businesses, or unions to pay for the ever more expensive campaigns costing from hundreds of thousands to millions of dollars. The high cost of campaigns filters out candidates who are not wealthy themselves or who hold policy views unacceptable to wealthy individuals or organizations.

One of the clearest examples of how this skews representation is that "people with *working-class jobs* still make up a majority of the labor force. But people who work primarily in these kinds of jobs make up less than 10 percent of the average city council and less that 3 percent of the average state legislature. The average member of Congress spent less than 2 percent of his or her adult life doing the kinds of jobs most Americans go to every day. None of America's governors were blue-collar workers when they got into politics" (original emphasis).[23] So there is a clear class bias as to who can be elected to office, from city council to president. This inevitably means that the class bias in office holders eliminates life experiences and perspectives of the working class and often even middle-class perspectives.

Beyond the class biases of elected officials themselves, campaign giving is a way for the wealthy to buy access to influence those officials. When an elective official decides which phone call to return or with which group to meet, large campaign contributors go to the top of the list. It does not mean that public officials always grant every wish of every large donor, but donor requests are listened to and their wishes are factored into decision-making. When the wishes of a strong majority of their constituents are known, an elected official who wants to stay in office will vote accordingly. But when there is not overwhelming public opinion on an issue, why not favor the campaign contributors who help you stay in office? If nothing else, money buys access for wealthy individuals, corporations, and unions to present their requests to office holders, who are only too anxious to please them in gratitude for their past contributions and in hope of continued largess.

In addition, wealthy individuals, corporations, and unions hire lobbyists who press their case for laws and regulations that favor their clients. For many government units such as Congress, there are more lobbyists than public officials. And they can focus on just the issues that concern their clients, not the several thousand proposals a member of Congress or a bureaucrat must consider. These lobbyists present detailed information and, sometimes, actual drafts of the legislation or regulations they wish to see enacted. Business lobbyists and conservative groups like the American Legislative Exchange Council (ALEC) push a pro-business agenda at the state government level as well.

If there is no organized opposition, elected and appointed officials are likely to heed the advice of these lobbyists, as they don't have the time to conduct research on their own, and even with staff help there is a limit to what they can know about complicated problems and issues. Finally, there are many more lobbyists for wealthy interests and business groups than there are for labor unions and the poor.[24]

It might not matter that the wealthy were influential if they represented the same views as other constituents Therefore, one of the key questions about donor and lobbying influence has been whether the policies favored by the wealthy interests differ significantly from popular opinion and the desires of other citizens. Special regulations or tax breaks that favor individuals or corporations are obvious examples of where access pays off in favorable policies for the wealthy as opposed to average citizens, who end up paying higher taxes and having fewer protections. But what about more general issues that affect people across the society, rather than just special breaks for the connected few? Benjamin Page, Larry Bartels, and Jason Seawright assembled a unique database that allowed them to determine that the policies on some important issues favored by the wealthy differ greatly from the rest of society.[25]

Moreover, the wealthy get their way—not all the time, but a significant amount of the time—on these important issues. In interviews with multimillionaires, the authors were able to determine that their policy preferences were indeed different from the public. For example, based on public opinion polls, two-thirds of Americans said that the federal government ought to see to it that everyone who wants work can find a job, while only one-fifth of the wealthy held this opinion. The same sort of differences of opinion occurred over providing jobs for the unemployed, national health insurance, Social Security, and funding for education. As Page and Gilens conclude in *Democracy for America*: "What wealthy Americans want—and what they get—from government is often quite different from the relatively progressive economic policies that most Americans want."[26]

Nicholas Carnes reached a similar conclusion, writing about the class bias of members of Congress along with other elected officials. He discovered that "members of Congress who are wealthier have been found to be more likely to oppose the estate tax. Mayors from business backgrounds have been found to shift city resources away from social safety net programs and toward business-friendly infrastructure projects. Legislators with more education and income are less likely to support policies that would reduce economic income inequality. Lawmakers with more money in the stock market are more likely to raise the debt ceiling (and thereby protect the stock market)."[27]

In my studies of Chicago politics and government, I have shown that funding by wealthy individuals and corporations involved in the global economy as Chicago has become a "global city" has produced policies that favor big contributors and provide the amenities that they desire over better public schools, public safety in ghetto communities, higher wages for workers, and greater benefits for the poor.[28] While big civic projects—Navy Pier, the Mc-Cormick Convention Center, and Millennium Park—that the wealthy favored have moved forward, attempts to solve broader social problems have stalled. Smaller, and relatively low-cost, beautification projects like wrought-iron fences around schools and parks as well as flowers in the parkway have been accomplished, while public housing has been demolished, fifty public schools were closed in a single year, and the city's mental health facilities were eliminated. As many as eighty thousand Chicagoans are homeless at least some time in the year. At the same time, thirty public officials in Illinois are convicted each year of outright corruption, including taking bribes for specific government actions such as corrupt contracts, zoning changes, licenses, or building permits. This "corruption tax" costs taxpayers at least $500 million a year.[29]

It is not just individual campaign contributions that allow the wealthy and corporations (and sometimes powerful labor unions) to get their way in government. The leading theory of urban politics is that public-private partnership regimes, sometimes called growth machines, govern U.S. cities and suburbs.[30] That is to say, top political and governmental leaders join with leaders in the private sector, principally major corporations, to create a stable governing regime to keep politicians in power and to deliver policies that favor economic development by those in the private sector. Neighborhood organizations and civic groups, although they may play some role in shaping policies, are only rarely and briefly dominant in this power-sharing arrangement. Campaign contributions and election financing are only a part of the system that governs cities like Chicago. Yet, the ability of the well-to-do to fund campaigns for mayor, alderman, and other local officials is a part of what keeps pro-business regimes in power in American cities and towns.

To the extent that a power elite of politicians and the wealthy govern both nationally and locally depends on their being able to raise enormous amounts of campaign funds. Democracy, political equality, and an equal voice in determining the government decisions that most affect our lives are undermined by this imbalance of political contributions.

Public Opinion

The Kettering Foundation back in 2006 funded a National Issue Forums series with a cross-section of the population. This is what those forums revealed:

> The deliberations painted a picture of distress, disenchantment, and alienation among U.S. citizens . . . [who] express low levels of confidence in the leaders of both political parties, anger at the disproportionate power of the special interests that dominate campaign giving, impatience with the polarization of political life, and a feeling that they were powerless to change things. Overwhelmingly the participants said that elected officials "are more responsive to special interests and lobbyists" than to the public and to the public interest. . . . Money talks . . . [and] the average citizen has no voice and is unrepresented.[31]

If this is what the public believes, is it any wonder that so few people usually vote and that they hold public officials in such low esteem? Beyond funding election campaigns and lobbyists, money in politics is used more broadly to shape public opinion. Money, as conservatives have demonstrated over the last several decades, can be used to create think tanks with particular ideological bents and to sponsor radio talk shows, TV networks, newspapers, blogs, and electronic news sources that shape the news that members of the public receive. Money can also be used to shape public opinion and "astro-turfing" campaigns to create the illusion of widespread grassroots support for a candidate or policy, when such support doesn't exist.

More long term, money can endow professorships at universities to provide intellectual ammunition for particular political points of view. Money can fund lawsuits to change the legal interpretation of what is permitted (e.g., changing to unlimited campaign contributions, new restrictions on abortion, or the right to bear arms without legal restrictions). Nor does money have to support only conservative points of view. It can also support liberal views. For instance, wealthy donors have used their influence to get the Democratic Party to take more liberal positions than the majority of Americans on some social issues.

As a side effect, these uses of money to control think tanks and the media have increased political polarization which makes consensus governing more difficult. This, in turn, has created gridlock and governmental failures.

In addition, giant media corporations make a profit entertaining the public rather than educating it for the tasks of citizenship. Media as entertainment can make happy, passive consumers, but this does not provide the information and enlightenment necessary to produce democratic citizens. Thus, we face twin perils.

On the one hand, we can have government and private corporations that create a system like in George Orwell's 1949 novel *1984*, where Big Brother is always watching. With new computer tools and Internet connectivity, media and government can be particularly invasive. Foreign and domestic hackers also now threaten our privacy and the integrity of our elections.

On the other hand, when big media is profitably used to provide entertainment instead of political news, the result is more like Aldous Huxley's 1932 novel *Brave New World*, in which we are lulled not only by drugs but by the distractions of entertainment. Since media corporations are private companies, their first goal is to make money for their owners and shareholders. Any duty to provide information needed to make our democracy function or to protect our privacy is a secondary concern. Profits have become the driving force behind both mass and social media today.

Democracy requires democratic citizens and democratic leaders. To make good governmental decisions, citizens and leaders have to know the facts and hear competitive arguments about the best policy to follow. Traditionally, over the last several hundred years, we have depended on newspapers, magazines, and books to provide us the information we cannot hear directly in person. Today, we depend on our electronic devices and the Internet to transmit the information necessary to vote, voice our opinions, and hold our officials accountable. We learned to use them more extensively during the pandemic that started in 2020, but we still haven't been able to make them work for democratic governance. That is going to take major changes in how we get and process political news.

Newspapers still exist, but as a source of news they are being replaced by television and electronic media that, when they provide information at all, usually provide just a brief story rather than an in-depth analysis. To be sure, our elected officials read and hear more news and debate about public policy in legislative bodies. However, they are influenced by and dependent on lobbyists. They are also hindered by political party and ideological polarization. In the meantime, they must cope with ever more complicated issues (when laws can run to thousands of pages that require technical expertise to parse), structural problems in the political system like gerrymandering, the need to raise enormous amounts of money to run for office, and the problem of time to attend to the tasks of government that rarely includes time for serious reflection.

Money isn't spent just on elections and lobbying. More fundamentally, money affects what we as citizens know. The lack of money makes some citizens so concerned with getting bread on the table, a roof over their heads, financial security, health care, and paying taxes, that they have no time to attend to citizen duties. What little time they have left goes to recreation and renewal, escape from the daily grind, and the pleasures of private life. Citizenship and government policy making don't make the list of priorities unless some demagogue whips them into a frenzied mob. A case in point is the mob that stormed the U.S. Capitol on January 6, 2021 to prevent the certification of the election of Joe Biden as president.

Despite some funds from foundations, enlightened wealthy individuals, and the government, little money is available for institutions of education and programs to create and sustain democratic citizens. As a result, we have a diminished public space where citizens can be informed, debate, and decide public policy.

Democracy cannot exist without the *demos*, the people. As Lincoln taught us, we must have government of, *by*, and for the people. To achieve that goal, we, the people, must be imbued with what our forebears variously called the "spirit of democracy," "spirit of Liberty" and "spirit of 1776." We must not allow public opinion to be manipulated by big money interests. Instead, we citizens must have the information, knowledge, and desire to create a public supportive of good leaders and good policies.

Money undermines political and governmental processes in Chicago in ways similar to the ways money distorts national politics. The public, despite occasional outcries, is forced to tolerate corruption and crooked contracts "with thievery written between the lines."[32] Government policies tilt away from the public interest to favor private interests represented by the machine growth regime.

In Chicago as in the nation more broadly, wealthy individuals and businesses bribe politicians, either legally through campaign contributions or illegally by money passed under the table. Therefore, public trust in fair and honest government is undermined. Many citizens come to believe that "you can't fight city hall." In Chicago, we have accepted an attenuated Machine Democracy rather than demanding genuine democracy.

During Mayor Lightfoot's first years in office, Chicago adopted a series of reforms to undermine machine politics. The mayor and the city council adopted stricter ethics laws, strengthened the inspector general, and eliminated aldermanic privilege and prerogatives over administrative decisions such as building permits. They televised city council meetings, broadened public hearings on the city budget, and instituted antipoverty programs. The move from Machine Democracy to real democracy is not completed, but it has begun.

Public Financing and Lobbying Restrictions

At both the national and local levels, reformers have continually sought to restrict money in elections and illegal lobbying. This is made more difficult because of the need to protect freedom of speech at the same time. The courts, especially since the *Citizens United* decision in 2010, have ruled that the use of money other than in direct quid quo pro bribes is just another form of speech to be protected. Court decisions since 2010 have even made it possible for organizations to keep secret who really provides the money, so that when dark money contributes to campaigns and lobbying, citizens don't even know whose money and influence it is.

Nonetheless, strides have been made to provide more information about money in politics, and some restraints have been put in place. Individuals and organizations who contribute directly to federal, and most state and local, election campaigns have their contributions revealed in a timely manner before the election so that voters can take that information into account.

Lobbyists must register and reveal their clients and expenditures. Inspectors general at both the local and national level have been given greater powers to investigate corruption and waste. Ethics laws have been strengthened. Public officials and those running for office must usually reveal the sources of their wealth and income to some limited extent, although they are seldom required by law to make public their entire income tax returns. The most visible case of refusing to provide information on income and possible conflicts of interest was President Trump's refusal to make his tax returns public before his election and throughout his four-year term in office.

Beyond campaign contributions and lobbying, outright corruption continues. This is despite literally thousands of convictions of public officials and those who bribe them. However, the larger problem is not outright bribery and corruption, but the legal corrupting influence of money in politics. It is clear that neither disclosure laws nor anticorruption laws are sufficient to prevent this corrupting influence.

There are some restrictions on the amount of money an individual, business, or organization can contribute to election campaigns. New court rules, however, make simple restrictions difficult to impose. And when they are imposed, the vast advantages of incumbency mean that more than 90 percent of the incumbents are reelected. So, simply setting contribution limits is insufficient, just as merely requiring lobbyist registration is an insufficient bar to money tilting the balance in government policy making.

To overcome the negative effects of money in politics, we have to change public opinion from "you can't fight city hall" to people demanding that legitimate candidates have sufficient funds to campaign effectively and that representatives actually represent a majority of their constituents, rather than outside lobbyists or a few wealthy interests.

The most effective solution to the undue influence of money in politics, while still allowing the wealthy and interest groups a voice in elections and policy making, is public funding of campaigns. Today, fourteen states and some cities provide some form of public funding, along with the partial public funding of the U.S. presidential campaign.[33] As the National Conference of State Legislatures indicates, however, "States [and other governments] cannot require candidates to use public financing programs, and the financial advantages of private fundraising frequently prompt candidates to opt out of public financing programs, which often include expenditure limits for participants. Candidates who opt not to use public funds can solicit contributions from individuals, PACs, unions, parties, and corporations, without having to abide by state [or other government] expenditure limits."[34] Even with these limitations, public funding levels the playing field so that legitimate candidates have sufficient funds to get their message to the voters.

There are various ways to provide public funding. The most common is for government to match small private donations to candidates by a formula such as six to one: six dollars from the government is provided for each small, individual dollar donation up to a set amount, such as $250.

Another method has been to provide democratic vouchers. Under this method, vouchers for a set amount, such as $50, are provided to each registered voter to give to the candidate or candidates of their choice. And of course, for presidential elections there is a tax check-off system that allows taxpayers to designate a small portion of their taxes to publicly fund presidential campaigns that abide by contribution and reporting rules. We have decades of experience with public funding and could easily adopt one of these systems if there were a will to do so.[35]

Beyond the impact of money in election campaigns, business lobbying occurs in backrooms, legislative offices, and administrative offices behind closed doors. One modest step that could be taken is to require that all written lobbyist communications be published in a public government database and website. It is not possible to make public what is said in private, however.

Three-quarters of all lobbyist expenditures in the United States represent businesses.[36] In some ways, regulating money and its lobbying effects is more difficult than controlling campaign contributions. Elections at least occur in public and contributions to candidates for public office can be required to be publicly disclosed. Lobbying, by its very nature, occurs in private settings with little public oversight or public disclosure. Added to these concerns, once public officials leave office they often become lobbyists themselves, utilizing their insider knowledge and contacts. That is a surefire way for former public officials to use their expertise and influence profitably.

The fundamental problem is that lobbying, like campaign finance, primarily represents those with the most money. Two-thirds of the organized interest groups in Washington, D.C., focus on economic interests, and at least 53 percent represent business interests. *Fewer than 1 percent represent nonprofessional or nonmanagement occupations.* Ninety million people in these nonprofessional occupations are not represented by any occupational association.[37]

In addition to wealthy individuals and organizations buying unequal access to officials by campaign contributions, lobbyists control information that legislators and bureaucrats need to make laws and regulations. A limited solution to this imbalance in information would be to extend the congressional research units with Congress, including a polling office to provide better data on public opinion and to curate the opinion research provided by outside polling organizations like Gallup public opinion polls, news media, and Pew Research. Creating a more deliberative process to inform both members of Congress and their constituents, such as those suggested in chapter 10 of this book, would also allow elected officials to be better able to represent us.

The public has always been suspicious of lobbying, and these suspicions have been deepened by scandals like the Jack Abramoff lobbying scandal in Washington, D.C.[38] Beyond the scandals in the nation's capital, however, there are plenty of lobbying scandals in state capitals and city halls. Like campaign contributions, lobbying elected and appointed government officials is not illegal. Under the First Amendment of the U.S. Constitution, we have a right to petition the government. And private citizens, businesses, and organizations often have important information on how laws and regulations will affect them to share with officials. This information can make laws and regulations better. But bribes, whether in the form of campaign contributions, promises of future employment, or money given under the table, distort government.

Limiting the Effect of Money in Politics

Nicholas Carnes argues that the "cash ceiling" in politics must be changed. He points out that "workers are less likely to hold office not because they're unqualified or because voters prefer more affluent candidates, but because workers are simply less likely to run for public office in the first place . . . because the American political process has a built-in *cash ceiling*, a series of structural barriers and corresponding individual-level attitudes and behaviors that keep qualified working-class citizens out of our political institutions."[39] This is true for candidates from the middle and upper-middle classes as well. And the voices of the poor are even more rarely heard in government.

There is no magic silver bullet that will bring about democracy's rebirth. What is required is multiple reforms like public financing of elections, disclosure of campaign contributions, stricter lobbying regulations, better information and research from neutral sources, lessening public corruption, and ending a corrupt political culture. At the local level, it requires not only transparency and ethics reforms but new ways for officials to heed citizens' voices and for citizens to participate in government decision-making more directly.

Accomplishing all of these reforms will require a renewal of the "spirit of democracy" among the public. When we have the will to limit the impact of money in politics and to repair the deficiencies in our politics, we will find the way.

University of Illinois at Chicago student Allyson Nolde participates in a National Student Issues Convention, October 2016. (Photo courtesy of UIC Bookstore)

5

Nonparticipation

In previous chapters we explored the problems of income and racial inequality and the role of money in elections and lobbying. Limiting inequality and the effects of money on politics are preconditions for democracy. The lack of political equality and the ways in which money skews elections and policy making cause many observers to question whether we have real democracy in the United States today. These problems are even worse in many other countries, especially new and developing nations.

Beyond problems of inequality and the influence of money in our politics and government, democracy requires participation by informed voters. Government of, by, and for the people perishes without participation.

It may seem strange to focus on nonparticipation when more than 159 million people voted in the 2020 election, more than in any previous U.S. election. Moreover, 67 percent of the eligible electorate voted, which is the greatest percentage since 1900, when 74 percent voted.[1] The real problem would seem to be the polarized nature of participation as well as turnout.

The recent presidential election is the exception in participation by voters, however. Over the last several decades, participation has been lower. Participation is also lower in non-presidential years and lower still among young and minority voters. It is also much lower in local elections, often struggling to reach even 30 percent.[2] Democracies cannot survive without citizen participation. The government must ultimately be controlled by the people, rather than people being manipulated by government.

Given the nation's size and the conditions in the twenty-first century, how are we to have government by the people? Since we have fallen short of an ideal democracy, what should we do to bring us closer?

Political scientists, journalists, and citizens have observed correctly that we do not have the information and civic knowledge to guide directly law and policy making. One reason for that is many schools have eliminated civic education or what John Dewey called "educating for democracy."[3] Moreover, the information afforded citizens by our media is inadequate, except for a dedicated minority to discern the best policies. Often, media doesn't even provide the information needed to judge the character and policy positions of candidates running for office, which is the minimum necessary in a representative democracy.

Of course, at the federal level, we don't have a participatory democracy like ancient Greece, Rome, or American town-hall meetings. As U.S. citizens, we don't govern directly. Instead, we elect representatives who make the laws and appoint other governmental officials. Yet, we regularly fall short of standards of informed citizenry required for a representative democracy. Even when we use shortcuts to decide our voting such as party identity, interest-group membership, and voting cues like the race and gender of the candidates, we participate too little and with insufficient information.

Party and group identities are the most important influence on our voting choices.[4] But to hold our representatives accountable, we citizens must have political knowledge beyond the fact that we and our representatives are Democrats or Republicans, Trump loyalists or progressives. We need to know something more about the candidates, offices they are seeking, and their stands on policies to make informed voting choices.

Yet, political scientists and pollsters have consistently found that we citizens lack basic political information, like the names of the members of Congress who represent us or our rights under the Bill of Rights.[5]

Some argue that voters don't have to know all that much about the candidates or policies because it is enough simply to vote retrospectively in order to hold government accountable. That is, we can follow the American tradition of throwing the rascals out if they fail to govern well. These political observers say that voters may not know the intricacies of government, but they know where the shoe pinches. Whether they are better or worse off since the current government took power. If a government leads us into a calamitous war or an economic crisis; misspends funds or significantly increases taxes; we can punish them at the ballot box by electing a new government to set things right. Unfortunately, empirical research has shown that we don't even do that well.[6] Voters often mistakenly blame officials for things like earthquakes over which they have no control or reward governments for improvement in the economy that government policies didn't cause. In short, even retrospective voting is flawed.

There are a variety of reforms that could provide more accurate information to citizens and alternative methods, like citizen juries or assemblies to improve education of citizens and better convey their informed views to their representatives. But these will require major institutional changes.

Another solution to the problem of government's failure to represent the wishes of the public has been to institute voter initiative and referendum. Twenty-six of the fifty states have done so, although some like Illinois have severely restricted the laws that can be adopted by this method.[7] However, even in states where initiatives are frequently used, the outcome is often determined by money and powerful interest groups. And voting directly on policies and laws requires even more information and effort than is required for voting for candidates.

Control by Political Parties in Chicago

Citizen participation has been even more constrained in Chicago than in other places. Inequality and the role of money in politics are clearly present but these aren't the only problems in Chicago. The dominant political force for the last 150 years has been machine politics. Historically, the machine has attempted to limit participation as much as possible to their supporters. We have held elections, but most of the time a single political party has dominated—the Republican Party after the Civil War until 1933, and since then the Democratic Party. One-party government, whether in Africa, China, Russian, or Chicago, is a poor form of democracy even if formal elections are held and legislative bodies follow technically democratic rules of procedure in adopting laws.

On the positive side, voter turnout is often higher in Chicago than in the United States generally. In the 2018 off-year election, the turnout was 56 percent compared to 47 percent nationally. Unfortunately, that meant that, even in Chicago, 44 percent of the eligible voters didn't vote. Likewise, in the critical February and April elections for mayor in 2015, which were highly contested, only 33 percent voted in the primary and 39 percent in the general election. Almost the same percentages voted in the most recent city elections in 2019.[8] Sadly, in these critical local elections, the future of the city was decided by the approximately 20 percent of the electorate who voted for the winning candidates. In 2020, Chicago led the state with 73 percent of the electorate voting, compared to 67 percent nationally.

The chief problem of democracy in Chicago, however, is not a low *level of voting participation* but *control of that vote* by the Chicago machine. Although party labels have differed, machine political control has been a problem in

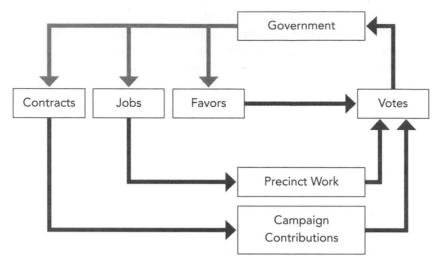

Figure 5.1: Richard J. Daley machine. (Source: Created by the author based on course lectures by Milton Rakove)

Chicago since 1871. From 1871 to the present, there has been an effort by reformers to destroy the different political machines that have ruled in order to create a better representative democracy. They sought a government that would be open, honest, effective, efficient, and capable of delivering government services fairly at the lowest cost to the taxpayers. These reformers have sometimes won and enacted reforms. But ultimately, machine control prevailed most of the time.

Modern Chicago politics dates from 1955, when the classic political machine was perfected under Chicago mayor Richard J. Daley, who was both boss of the Democratic Party and mayor for twenty-two years. Under Daley, the political machine took the form shown in figure 5.1.

The older political machines of the nineteenth and twentieth centuries were strengthened after Richard J. Daley's election in 1955. The Daley machine had distinctive features that refined the machine politics that had earlier governed many East Coast and midwestern cities. It was an economic exchange within the framework of the political party. The resulting regime was an economic growth machine that married the dominant political party, the Democrats, to big businesses run by Republicans in a public-private partnership that controlled both the economy and the government.[9]

Patronage jobs at city hall begat patronage precinct captains who contacted voters and persuaded them to trade their votes for machine candidates in return for favors and city services. Government contracts from city hall

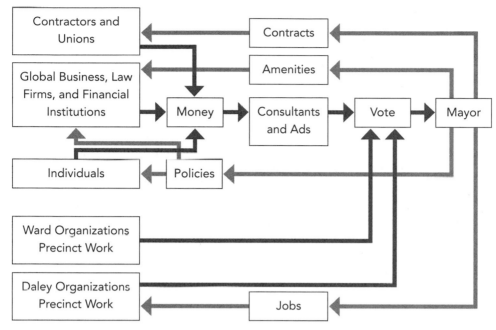

Figure 5.2: Richard M. Daley machine. (Source: Created by the author)

convinced otherwise Republican businessmen to give the election campaign contributions necessary to fund the Democratic Party's campaign literature and walking-around money, also known as street money, to pay off voters who voted for party candidates. These contributions of precinct work, money, and votes won most elections for the Daley machine. With Richard J. Daley winning elections and controlling both city and county governments, he was able to distribute the spoils necessary to keep the machine running. Thus, the Daley machine was characterized by patronage, nepotism, precinct work, favoritism, crooked contracts, and absolute party loyalty.

However, by the end of the twentieth century and the beginning of the twenty-first, the machine modernized. It was transformed by Richard J. Daley's son, Richard M. Daley, during his own twenty-two-year reign and took the more complicated form shown in figure 5.2.

Despite superficial similarities, such as having a Mayor Daley in charge, several aspects of this Daley machine differed significantly from his father's. Patronage and precinct organizations were supplemented with media-based, presidential-style campaigns. Richard M. Daley's, and later, Rahm Emanuel's, campaigns were centered on the candidate more than the party. In the second Daley era, ward organizations were supplemented by Daley political organizations loyal only to him. These Daley organizations—like the Hispanic Democratic Organization—were based on patronage at city hall that provided jobs for the precinct captains who worked the precincts. They got out the vote for Daley and the candidates that he supported.

In the new Daley machine, old-style patronage and corruption of the old machine now coexisted with campaign contributions from global corporations, public opinion polling, and media manipulation. In addition to individuals and businesses who profited from the global economy, city contractors and construction labor unions continued, as they had in the past, to contribute money to the machine campaigns.

However, in a major change from past regimes, rich individuals, global businesses, law firms, and financial institutions contributed millions of dollars to hire national political consultants and to buy public opinion polling, direct mail, and slick TV ads. In the 2003 and 2007 elections, Richard M. Daley raised nearly $4 million, per election, which was the most any mayoral candidate had raised until then. But those records would soon be dwarfed by the money Rahm Emanuel would raise in his mayoral campaigns in 2011 and 2015, which reached as high as $32 million in a single election.

The payoffs in Richard M. Daley's machine also differed from those of his father's time. There were still patronage jobs given to precinct workers and contracts flowing to contributing businesses, as under the Richard J. Daley machine. But now urban amenities—flowers in the parkways, wrought-iron fences, Millennium Park, the museum campus, and, most importantly, a tax structure favorable to the new global economy—were added. As Daley biographer Koeneman concludes, "It is likely that history's judgment will be that [Richard M.] Daley's achievements outweigh his mistakes. It is a reasonable bet that the 'one line of history' for Rich Daley is that he was the leader who helped transform Chicago into a global city."[10] He also transmogrified his father's political machine into one that could work in the twenty-first century.

Mayor Rahm Emanuel, in office from 2011 to 2019, put the Richard M. Daley machine on steroids. He had no political troops of his own to work the precincts. However, some old-time ward bosses in both the Black and White communities supported him and provided precinct workers to carry his message to voters. But his regime was marked by the following:

- awarding city contracts to building trade contractors along with no-bid direct voucher payments to downtown global businesses;
- pursuing global and corporate-centered public policies;
- providing urban amenities, desired by Chicago's wealthy individuals and corporate elite;

- like his machine predecessors, having a rubber-stamp city council to enact his programs and policies;
- the most expensive elections ever held in Chicago; and
- continued control of both elections and government policies.[11]

City Government

Throughout its history, Chicago has been ruled by a regime that included the business leaders, political party/government leaders, and to a lesser extent, leaders of major institutions like hospitals and universities.[12] Boss mayors like Richard J. Daley were supported by business leaders who provided campaign contributions and by ethnic groups and labor unions that helped to deliver the votes necessary for the Democratic Party to stay in power. In return, the businessmen received government contracts for goods and services. Ethnic and racial groups received symbolic recognition and their appropriate share of elected positions and appointed patronage jobs. It was pretty much a quid pro quo exchange that for Whites meant continuing policies of segregation as well.

In the Richard M. Daley and Rahm Emanuel eras, the regime evolved and so did the public policies. Big businessmen and women no longer wanted just to sell their products to city hall, although some of the crooked and inflated contracts for goods and services continued. They wanted instead new public policies appropriate to a global city marked by transnational corporations. Thus, the development of the Loop as the international headquarters for businesses and the production of amenities such as Millennium Park; public safety downtown (but not necessarily in ghetto neighborhoods); shiny new buildings and high culture like a world-class symphony, opera, and art museums. So, Chicago became a global city providing services to global corporations and serving as the global capital of the Midwest.

The political machine was outfitted with a new, modern, urbane attire. But citizen participation in policy making was still unwelcomed. There was more information on the Internet, cable TV channels, and Internet posts, blogs, and tweets. But it was all sound and fury that did not signify democracy.

A more liberal and benign boss sat on the fifth-floor mayor's office in city hall. But downstairs, the city council still had fifty aldermen who were mostly rubber stamps for powerful mayors. Symbolically and practically, the city council gallery can seat only 550 of the 2.7 million Chicagoans. Participatory democracy could not happen in such a small space nor did the city council contemplate that it would.

There were multiple interest groups that created some pluralism in policy making but in the most fundamental decisions, the public was left out in the Richard M. Daley and Rahm Emanuel eras. Additionally, decisions by transnational corporations and the national government continued to be made far away from city hall: the average Chicago voter had no influence over the outcome of those decisions that deeply affected their lives.

As they had over the last one hundred and fifty years, reform movements continued to press for more democracy and for laws and policies that would better serve the public interest. But despite some gains, the "power elite," which in Chicago consists of businessmen and machine politicians, got their way most of the time.

The 2019 Chicago Mayoral Election

Most often, Chicago elections have come down to a contest between reformers and a continuation of the status quo. And so it was in 2019.

Originally, Rahm Emanuel and a majority of the aldermen who had loyally supported him were to stand for reelection. The third term of Mayor Emanuel would continue his policies and complete his legacy in the manner of the Daleys who ruled before him.

Since Rahm had begun to raise millions of dollars and assembled a campaign team, he was fully expected to run for reelection. By the spring of 2018, only a handful of Democratic candidates and no Republicans had announced to run against him. Most well-known alternative candidates, like Cook County Board president Toni Preckwinkle, were running for other offices or were out of politics entirely. Still, several individuals had declared their candidacy for mayor, including Paul Valles, former Chicago Public Schools superintendent; Amara Enyia, who had run unsuccessfully in 2015; and Lori Lightfoot, former head of the police board and former Assistant U.S. Attorney.

The early polls showed Rahm Emanuel with only about 30 percent of the vote and others, like Lightfoot, trailing with no more than 5 percent of the vote.[13]

The race changed dramatically when Mayor Emanuel dropped out just after Labor Day. When he decided not to run for reelection, new candidates jumped into the race, among them Toni Preckwinkle, State Comptroller Susana Mendoza, former school board president and mayoral candidate Gery Chico, and former U.S. Commerce Secretary Bill Daley, who was the son and brother of previous Daley mayors. The field suddenly swelled from seven candidates to twenty-one and included Black, White, and Latino candidates and supporters of both the old-style machine politics and reformers.

There were basically two competing definitions of the race the candidates were selling. Cook County Board of Commissioners president Preckwinkle and State Comptroller Mendoza were among the candidates arguing that their previous experience as government executives best qualified them to be mayor, while Lightfoot and Enyia were among those arguing that change and reform were needed.

Then, in late December 2018, the FBI raided the offices of Fourteenth Ward alderman and powerful finance committee chair Ed Burke.[14] The criminal complaint filed a week later charged that Alderman Burke used his clout and aldermanic privilege to block a driveway permit for a Burger King restaurant in his ward unless the company hired his law firm to handle their property taxes appeals and gave a $10,000 campaign contribution to Toni Preckwinkle's 2018 campaign for Cook County Board president.[15]

These shocking allegations of corruption were soon followed by the news that another alderman, who was guilty of corruption, was wearing a wire, recording conversations for over two years that led to more aldermen and businessmen being charged. At the same time, a third alderman, Willie Cochran (Twentieth Ward), pleaded guilty to corruption charges. All of these events confirmed the corrupt "Chicago Way" and made the election for voters about reform, not experience.[16]

Lori Lightfoot declared her candidacy for mayor in May 2018. In spite of low name recognition and low early polling numbers, her campaign's internal polls showed that there was a path to victory for her if she could attract the voters likely to support her once they knew about her. White, liberal, and gay voters were likely to support her, but she could attract Black and Latino support as well. Of course, a viable campaign to reach these voters couldn't be run without money, staff, and volunteers.

By the end of June, Lightfoot had raised more than $500,000 from seven hundred donors, had 325 volunteers, and hired a young but professional campaign staff. By September, five hundred volunteers and several paid workers were gathering the 12,500 legitimate signatures necessary to put her on the ballot. In the end, knowing that her petitions would be challenged by the other candidates, she gathered thirty thousand signatures.

By July, candidate forums and debates were being held. Because so many candidates were running and sharing the same stage, these were challenging formats. Lightfoot did well enough that she was able to pick up more supporters and gain experience in presenting herself and her issues, but none of the candidates was able to land knockout blows in this format. Debates work best with fewer candidates.

In the meantime, serious work on policy papers was being done. The first Lightfoot position paper released in August 2018 was a nine-point plan on ethics and good government reform.[17] She and her team would release detailed position papers on key issues regularly throughout the campaign. Only Paul Valles would have as substantive a set of policy papers, so Lori was identified by the media and attentive voters as a serious candidate.

By October, Bill Daley had raised more than $1 million and Garry McCarthy (the former police superintendent) had raised $830,000, followed by Lightfoot at $827,000. But half of Daley's funds came from himself, while Lightfoot had hundreds of contributors.

The 2019 Chicago mayoral election followed the pattern of the 2016 Republican presidential primary campaign, in which sixteen candidates ran against Donald Trump, and it was echoed in the high numbers of candidates for the 2020 Democratic presidential nomination. A candidate like Jeb Bush in 2016 would be leading one week, until he was shot down by the media or by investigative news stories, and then another candidate would become the front runner, until Donald Trump eventually pulled ahead. Likewise, in 2020, only after the South Carolina primary did Joe Biden pull ahead of the pack.

In the Chicago case, various candidates would be in the lead, only to be displaced by another frontrunner a week or two later. Toni Preckwinkle was the candidate with the most consistent advantage. However, she was involved in the Burke corruption scandal because Burke had raised money for her 2018 County Board president campaign at an event at his home. In addition to serving as chair of the Central Cook County Democratic Party (i.e., party boss), Preckwinkle had supported the previous party boss, Joe Barrios, in his campaign to be reelected county assessor. In short, she could be portrayed as one of the old political machine candidates. Lightfoot's TV advertising spots linked Preckwinkle, Mendoza, and Chico to Burke, and linked all of them and Bill Daley to the old corrupt machine. That characterization resonated with the voters.

By January 2019 with two months until the primary election, only seven candidates had raised more than $1 million. Bill Daley was leading the way with $4.2 million and Lightfoot had raised a respectable $1.1 million. Some candidates were at the bottom of the fund-raising effort, such as John Kozlar, who had raised only $1,014. The media did not take seriously candidates unable to raise the necessary funds to run an effective campaign and to pay for television advertising.

Not yet well-funded enough to buy TV ads in the expensive Chicago media market, the Lightfoot campaign concentrated on social media. By January, she had thirteen thousand Facebook likes (8,000 by Chicagoans) and was spending $1,500 a week on social media buys to extend her social media contacts. She had a strong webpage and was on Instagram and other sites. The campaign strategy called for mounting TV ads by February 11, the first day for early voting. In the meantime, she took advantage of free media by attending debates, releasing position papers, and commenting on news events like the conviction of White police officer Jason Van Dyke for the fatal shooting of a Black man, Laquan McDonald. She also partnered with three aldermanic campaigns to expand into additional campaign offices and have literature distribution centers throughout Chicago. However, on January 22, *Chicago* magazine still ranked her only the seventh most likely to win the election.[18]

Then on February 8, she got the endorsement of the *Chicago Sun-Times* and released the first of her television ads with a buy of $280,000. From that point on, she was able to continue running TV ads until the end of the election as well as continue her campaign's extensive use of social media. Her volunteers grew in number, and she began to get larger financial contributions as she was seen as having a chance to win.

By the weekend before the primary election, Daley had raised $8.65 million, followed by Preckwinkle at $4.5 million, a few other candidates doing well, and Lightfoot now having $1.54 million. She had raised enough to get her message out. Because she peaked late, the other candidates did not train their negative advertising on her but mostly on one another.

In the February 26, 2019, primary election, Lightfoot led the field, with 17.5 percent of the vote. Preckwinkle came in second with 16 percent. So, the runoff election on April 2 would be between two Black women Democratic candidates who were the top vote-getters, both of whom had progressive reform credentials. Runoff elections in Chicago are held for mayoral and aldermanic candidates who do not get more than 50 percent of the vote in the primary elections.

In the polls the following month, the Lightfoot campaign worried because they showed her with a lead of 30 percent over Preckwinkle. What if the polls were wrong or if Lightfoot supporters became overconfident and stayed home on Election Day? But the polls turned out to be right. Lightfoot got the endorsement not only of the *Chicago Sun-Times* but now also the *Chicago Tribune* and *Crain's Chicago Business* in the general election. She picked up political endorsements from elected officials, organizations, and previous mayoral candidates. In the end, she won the runoff election on April 2, 2019, with 74 percent of the vote, carrying all fifty wards. The landslide was a clear mandate for government reform.

This Chicago mayoral election was an alternative to the polarization, racism, and gridlock of national politics at the time. Chicago ended up almost unanimously choosing a Black, lesbian woman as their mayor along with the most progressive (and diverse) Chicago city council in years. The voters in all wards—separated by wealth, race, and class—all voted overwhelmingly for Lori Lightfoot. If something similar is to happen at the national level, we have to increase citizen participation in politics and government. It is likely that we will have to start renewal of informed citizen participation at the local level if we are to revive our democracy. While participation in the 2020 election and the end of Trump era is cause for hope, the hard work of rebuilding the city and the nation lies ahead.

Representative Democracy

A fundamental problem that we confront in the United States is whether we can create the information and means of participating to allow us to be democratic citizens. It is clear that we will not re-create the conditions of Athens or Republican Rome. There are different requirements for democracy in large modern nation states like America and cities like Chicago.

Robert Dahl, perhaps the preeminent U.S. political scientist of the twentieth century, wrote in 1998 that democracy must provide the opportunity for

- effective participation
- equality in voting
- gaining enlightened understanding
- exercising final control over the agenda
- inclusion of adults[19]

To achieve these goals, Dahl concluded that representative democracies require

- elected officials
- free, fair, and frequent elections
- freedom of expression [especially a free press]
- alternative sources of information [news media, social media and direct face-to-face contact not under the control of the government]
- associational autonomy
- inclusive citizenship[20]

He called this scaled-down version of democracy adequate for our time "polyarchy," derived from the Greek roots of "many" and "rule." Thus, polyarchy is the rule of the many, but not of all citizens all the time in elections and policy making. It differs from the earlier representative democracies of the eighteenth and nineteenth centuries with their restrictive suffrage but also from democracies "in units so small that members can assemble directly and make (or recommend) policies and laws."[21]

As Dahl puts it, for older democracies like ours, "the challenge is to perfect and *deepen* democracy."[22] Yet, fulfilling the requirements for large-scale democracies that Dahl sets in order to achieve polyarchal democracy will be difficult.

It is clear that simply voting in elections every two to four years is insufficient to guide government policy making or to hold political leaders accountable. Especially since income inequality and the flood of money, including dark money, into campaigns tilts election results and wealthy interest groups with their paid lobbyists tilt policy-making in ways that favor them. While there has been continual improvement in suffrage over the last two centuries, there is still voter suppression and gerrymandering, and the Electoral College that bias results to favor incumbents. Finally, lobbying unduly influences officials once they are elected.

Mass and Social Media

Consider, first of all, how we obtain our political information. As citizens, we often lack the information to choose the best representatives and to press for the best public policies. Obviously, for participation to be meaningful, it has to be informed. Our information systems today are radically changed from even a few decades ago. Fewer people now read newspapers. In 2017, weekday print and digital circulation in the United States was 31 million, with 34 million readers on weekends out of a population of 330 million—that means that fewer than 10 percent of us get our news directly from newspapers. Furthermore, that readership continues to decline by about 10 percent a year.[23] The number of journalists has plummeted by 40 percent in the last decade, and the resulting diminished supply of reliable news "is a core contributor to the misinformation society."[24] Reliable information depends on investigative journalism, not simply parroting government press releases or providing entertainment features, comics, advertisements, or horoscopes.

Simply switching to Internet sources like Facebook, Twitter, or Instagram is not adequate to gain the information necessary to hold the government accountable. The average digital visit to a news site is only 2.5 minutes.[25] Thus, most Americans lack the necessary information they need to be responsible citizens, since we don't get it from newspapers, TV, or Internet newsfeeds. In addition, even with cell phones there is still a digital divide as a significant number of people in the United States are without digital access. This became more and more evident during the coronavirus pandemic, when many lower income students could not participate effectively in distance learning and their parents lost their jobs when they couldn't work remotely from home.

In past decades, people watched television networks like NBC, ABC, CBS, and public television to get their news. Now, however, 90 percent of our TV news, including cable news, is controlled by four giant conglomerates: Comcast (including NBC), Disney (ABC), Viacom/CBS, and AT&T (including Warner Media).[26] Thus, mass media is controlled today by a very few corporations that value profits over civic responsibility.

Now with the cable TV expansion, the Internet, and web streaming, people access different sources for their entertainment and news, which means Americans don't have a common set of "facts." In addition, social media sites like Facebook and Twitter provide many people with their principal news source. Approximately one-third of young adults polled said that their primary source of news on the 2016 election came from Facebook and Twitter.[27]

As a result of these changes, we don't share a common source of news. Sixty percent of Republicans now get their news from Fox News, and 65 percent of Republicans trust it for their political and election news. Only 30 percent of Republicans get their news from ABC, and even fewer Republicans trust other media sources. Fifty-three percent of Democrats get their news from CNN, and 67 percent of Democrats trust it, although they also get and trust their news from more sources.[28] But the end result is that Americans get their news from different sources based on their partisan identities. Because of these news silos, we do not share a common set of facts and we don't see or listen to the same opinions.

Since some media sources are ideologically biased, we are confronted with what Donald Trump labeled "fake news." That is, some information presented to voters is false. This undermines Americans' faith in the news reported in the mainstream media. Worst of all, many people cannot tell the difference between factual stories and "fake news" on television and social media.

As a result of this fragmentation and misinformation, citizens are left to choose candidates or support policies without a common factual basis. The ideal for political decision-making remains a focused political debate between candidates or policy advocates on the same stage (or media platform) in which they can answer each other's assertions and by which voters can compare candidates and their policy proposals. The model is the famous Lincoln-Douglas debates in the nineteenth century. Or the Kennedy-Nixon debate on national television in the 1960 election. But debates with ten or more candidates structured to obtain thirty-second answers to rapid-fire or show-of-hands questions make it hard for voters to get the information they need to choose meaningfully between candidates. This was a problem in the 2016 and 2020 presidential elections and in the 2019 Chicago mayoral elections. Voters have even less information to understand complicated public policies, like how to provide health care coverage for all Americans.

At best, most citizens get only headline news for both campaigns and public policy decisions. Even presidential candidates covered on national television news get on average only seven-second soundbites. The news anchors and reporters get longer times, but the entire news story rarely runs over a minute or two.[29] Likewise, in the 2016 election campaign, "policy issues garnered only about 10 percent of the election news coverage compared to 40 percent for horse race stories."[30] That hadn't improved in the 2020 election either.

Nor is social media the solution. According to Victor Pickard,

> Facebook is an algorithm-driven advertising company governed solely by profit imperatives. . . .
>
> Such profound media power residing in one monopolistic platform arguably presents a unique threat. . . . By the end of 2016, 42 percent of referral traffic to publisher sites came from Facebook. Facebook commands 77 percent of the mobile social-networking traffic in the United States; half of all American adults access its platform on a daily basis; and nearly all new digital-ad revenue is captured by it and Google. . . .
>
> . . . Facebook needs international regulatory oversight. Democratic societies must individually and collectively decide on Facebook's responsibilities and how they should be enforced. Self-regulation isn't sufficient.[31]

Pickard is only one of many critics of social media's influence on U.S. politics and policies.

Social media has become a useful tool for organizing and mobilizing campaign support among the public. But it still needs to be regulated to prevent hacking of elections and the spread of false information inciting violence. We did better in the 2020 election in preventing some of the worse social media abuses, but this area will require international regulations. Finally, after the insurrection in January 2021, when a pro-Trump mob stormed the Capitol in Washington, D.C., social media platforms like Facebook and Twitter began to censor then-President Trump's false statement about stolen elections and incitements to riot. But this self-regulation by social media sites themselves is still a work in progress.

We need to ensure that there is reliable information available through BBC-style public broadcasting that both PBS and NPR are beginning to deliver reliably throughout the country. However, they will require much more public funding to do the job we need them to do. In addition, private news media need to be subsidized to provide more extensive and reliable news coverage. A number of newspapers and magazines are beginning to ask subscribers and foundations for funding to increase their news staffs and reporting. Finding a way to raise sufficient funds without the government taking over and controlling all media is one of the issues we need to tackle in the years ahead.

The lack of common news sources, inadequate mass media coverage of issues and candidates, social media bubbles that provide only biased points of view, and the resulting low voter turnout in most elections together undermine the inclusion of all adults. Inclusion and voter participation remains one of the essential characteristics of any form of democracy.

Citizenship Today

Because of these problems, often fewer than 20 percent of the registered voters cast ballots in local elections. In Chicago, rarely do more than a third of eligible residents cast their votes. Even in important national elections, only 59 percent of the eligible population voted in 2016, 53 percent in 2018, and 67 percent in 2020. However we calculate them, our voting rates remain among the lowest of established democracies even with the increase in 2020.[32]

Before the 2020 election uptick, at least thirty countries ranked higher in voting participation than we did, not only including most of Europe, but also South Korea, Israel, and Mexico.[33] Some countries require voting, have national automatic voter registration systems, hold elections on holidays, and use proportional representation. This demonstrates that there are structural solutions to increase voter representation. Of course, most important is providing qualified, distinctive candidates from whom the voters can choose.

One consistent problem has been the low level of youths voting in elections. There is a movement afoot to lower the voting age to sixteen, at least for local elections, while at the same time improving civics education in schools.[34] There are strong reasons for doing so. "Voting is habit-forming. Studies show that people who skip the first election after they become eligible are less likely to turn out for future elections. . . . Nonvoting is a habit too. . . . Sixteen-year-olds are more likely to vote when they first become eligible because they are immersed in their communities and can benefit from education and encouragement from parents, teachers, their high school environment, and community organizations."[35]

Another group who have been disenfranchised in many states are former felons who lost their right to vote when convicted and who may be ineligible to regain it after having served their sentence. As of 2016, "state laws had disenfranchised nearly 6.1 million Americans because of a felony conviction. That amounts to 2.5 percent of the total US voting age population."[36]

Lowering the voting age and restoring the enfranchisement to former felons are two structural reforms that can increase voter participation in the United States. As Joshua Douglas urges, we should "work toward an almost unimaginable goal—something like 90 percent turnout."[37] But the active citizenship gap is a bigger problem than merely voting turnout. There are at least 12 million undocumented immigrants with no current path to citizenship and, therefore, no federal right to vote.

Apart from the issue of participating in democracy by voting, the number of citizens who participate by contributing money, volunteering on campaigns, lobbying, meeting with officials, writing letters, phoning, or sending e-mails about policies is much smaller. Fifteen percent of the public participate in campaign activities and only 17 percent give money to candidates.[38] These forms of participation also strongly reflect social, racial, and income inequalities. Phil Parvin puts it this way:

> The problem facing contemporary democracies is not merely that poorer people are not choosing to participate in politics. It is that contemporary democratic states have reconfigured themselves in ways which exclude the poor. Democratic states no longer provide citizens at the bottom end of the wealth and income distribution with the ability to develop democratic capacity or political knowledge through participation in the civic and associational activities which play a central role in the development of these things. As a result, poorer citizens are losing both the desire to participate and the capacity for effective or informed political participation.[39]

He concludes that "the problem is, at least partly, that individuals of low socio-economic status do not identify as *citizens* (in anything other than a purely legal sense) or participate as such."[40] Beyond institutional barriers such as voter suppression and the lack of a common information source, the poor often do not feel that they are equal citizens with the rights and obligation to participate. It is hard enough for them to get the basic necessities of life for themselves and their families, much less to take the time and effort to become informed and to participate politically. We need to resolve economic and racial inequalities and the status of immigrants as well as providing better information and making voting and citizen participation easier.

There are psychological as well as structural problems. As Dahl puts it, "citizens are not political equals; thus, the moral foundation of democracy, political equality among citizens, is seriously violated. Therefore, market-capitalism greatly favors the development of democracy [only] up to the level of polyarchal democracy."[41] The full representative democratic ideal that citizens would participate in both voting in elections and advocating policies is unrealistic, according to Dahl. In the United States today, most citizens do not participate, and when they do, their participation is usually limited to voting.

As a nation, we don't even meet the standards of Dahl's polyarchy. In a polyarchy, it is assumed that there are multiple parties and interest group organizations that compete in different policy arenas. The winning policies, which are frequently compromises between competing groups, are determined by voters electing officials who carry out their preferred policies. In a polyarchy, voters choose between competing groups and no one group or elite rules on all issues. Yet certain racial and economic groups clearly have more power than others in America today.

Voter Participation and the Turnout Gap

Key to citizen participation is registering and voting. Yet, we know that participation levels are low. How are we to account for the difference between the ideal of high voter participation and the lower levels of voting that occur across the United States and in cities like Chicago?

As political scientists Benjamin Page and Martin Gilens write, "Among advanced democratic countries, the United States is unique in its low levels of voter turnout. . . . The voice of the people in U.S. elections is both *weak* (easily outshouted by partisan activists and campaign donors, especially in low-visibility primary elections) and *biased*."[42]

Economist Anthony Downs was the first to establish a mathematical model of voting behavior in his *Economic Theory of Democracy* (1957). According to Downs, whether or not individuals vote can be explained by the probability of a vote mattering and the utility of voting minus the cost in time and effort of casting a vote. In short, when there is no compelling reason to vote or when an election is not close enough for a single vote to matter, the effort in getting the information and taking the time to vote is too much for many citizens.

William Riker and Peter Ordeshook revised Downs's equation.[43] They introduced the additional variable of the psychological benefit of voting. They sought to quantify the psychological benefits of voting as to whether or not a vote mattered and the likelihood of a vote swinging the election. In practical political terms, the clearer the contrast and attractiveness of candidates, the importance of the issues to be decided, and the closer the election, the more people turn out to register and to vote because they care about the outcome and they know their vote will help determine the outcome.

Of course, some people vote not only because they can calculate a practical, material benefit from voting, but because the process of voting itself provides some psychological benefit to the individual. It often allows them to affirm an aspect of their identity, be it partisan, ideological, or ethnic. In addition, we know that socioeconomic factors such as age and class affect voting. In general, the more educated, wealthier, and higher the social status of voters, the more they are likely to vote. Likewise, older voters are more likely than younger voters to vote.

We also know that different racial and ethnic groups vote at significantly different rates. There is a persistent gap between racial/ethnic minorities and majority White turnout that is not explained just by socioeconomic disparities. This creates a paradox: "America is increasingly Black, Latino, and Asian American, yet at the end of the day the preferences of white voters continue to drive political outcomes."[44] The fundamental reason for this is that Whites are still the majority of the electorate and the most numerous in most electoral districts. Under these conditions, they most often vote at a higher rate because their vote matters. Where racial minorities are the majority in electoral districts, a higher percentage of them turn out because it is clear that collectively their votes matter in these districts.

Of course, different turnout rates can be changed by charismatic candidates or important issues critical to the voters, but in general, the White vote carries the day. In 2016, by one calculation, White turnout of those eligible to vote was 69 percent, Black turnout 51 percent, Latinos 43 percent, and Asian Americans 38 percent.[45] While Blacks have increased their level of election participation, Asian Americans and Latinos continue to have lower turnout rates. "Even after accounting for non-citizenship, in no midterm election have more than 45% Asian Americans or 40% of Latinos voted."[46] There is a racial registration and voting gap still to be overcome in America.

However, there is a more fundamental issue than even the racial differences. The conventional theory of representative democracy holds that the public, through their election of those who govern, determine the policies. However, "most residents of democratic countries have little interest in politics and do not follow news of public affairs beyond browsing the headlines."[47] In addition, "the political 'belief systems' of ordinary citizens are generally thin, disorganized, and ideologically incoherent. . . . Most democratic citizens are uninterested in politics, poorly informed, and unwilling or unable to convey coherent policy preferences through 'issue voting.' How then are elections supposed to ensure ideological responsiveness to the popular will?"[48]

In short, how can we have a democracy if the people often don't vote, and when they do, they have little knowledge of politics or coherent ideological or policy preferences? "Voters, even the most informed votes, typically make choices not on the basis of policy preferences or ideology, but on the basis of who they are—their social identities."[49]

What Is to Be Done?

In the elitist approach, it is enough if citizens have the opportunity to vote with enough basic information for them to do so intelligently. It is acceptable to leave the serious policy making to the elite. In the pluralist approach, we can call ourselves a democracy only if there are competing elites who are able to represent the interests of different groups within the broader public and the voters still have the final vote on who governs. The populist approach demands more people voting, clearer public debate of alternatives, and the ability to hold representatives accountable. Majority policy preferences would be translated more directly into laws and government action.

It is clear that populist or participatory democracy does not exist in our nation today. But much can be done to better meet the other standards of representative democracy. One alternative is automatic voter registration, which would eliminate many of the hurdles voters face to register. We could as well prevent voter suppression, expand the Voting Rights Act, block election hacking, prevent gerrymandering, ensure that votes are fairly counted, and end one-party dominance.

However, uninformed voting, with voters not paying attention to election campaigns, policies, and government decision-making, is unlikely to improve the quality of our democracy. Relatively informed participation is required. Beyond political reforms, we also need to find a way to fund responsible mass media and we will need to place more restrictions on social media in order to better meet citizen needs for unbiased, balanced, and truthful political information. Victor Pickard suggests:

> The philanthropy world should redouble efforts to shore up—and reinvent—struggling newspapers as they transition to nonprofit status.
> . . . Ideally [there should be] a new public-service system supported through a combination of private contributions and public subsidies. . . . Facebook and Google . . . [should] allocate a small percentage of their advertising revenue—which could generate many millions of dollars—toward public-service journalism.[50]

A comprehensive plan to provide political news to citizens needs to be agreed upon and supported along the lines of Pickard's suggestions.

Finally, we need to lessen the racial divisions, rural-urban split, and ideological polarization. This healing needs to occur especially after the divisive Trump era. It will not come easily.

The bottom line for democracy is that there must be more participation and more informed participation. Not only in the occasional election but in monitoring the actions of government officials and, at least, retrospectively voting out of office those who do not represent us well.

In cities like Chicago that have been historically governed by machine politics, that political party stranglehold must be broken.

To achieve more participation, simple exhortations for us to be better citizens and do our citizenship duties are insufficient. We must create the conditions and opportunities for democratic participation.

Lori Lightfoot campaigns in Chicago in 2019. (Photo by Marcus Robinson)

6

Polarization and the Politics of Resentment

While people frequently engage in protest demonstrations in our nation's capital, Congress itself had not been attacked since the British burned down the U.S. Capitol in the War of 1812.[1] Until January 6, 2021, when a mob of Trump supporters stormed the Capitol in an insurrection. Later that night, after the mob had been cleared by Capitol Police, DC Police, and the National Guard, 147 members of the House of Representatives voted against the certification of Joe Biden as the next president of the United States. These events of January 6 were a testament to the deep political divide that continues in our nation.

The election of Donald Trump in 2016, the recapture of the House of Representatives by the Democrats in 2018, and the divisive rhetoric in the 2020 election had already made obvious that political polarization was widespread. This divisiveness was not eliminated simply by the defeat of President Trump in 2020. The divisions so clearly on display during the Trump era are deep-seated. They predate, and have continued after, the Trump presidency.

The 2020 presidential election displayed our continuing racial and ideological divisions. In the end, 81 million people voted for Biden and Harris over Trump and Pence, who received 74 million votes.[2] Many of the battleground states were won by a margin of only a few thousand votes, indicating how closely divided many of them were.

There is still great resentment in the electorate and a widening gap between the political parties, elected officials, and party factions. It appears in the conservative wing of the Republican party and the progressive wing of the Democratic Party. This is not new. Ever since the American Revolution, when we fought a war to separate from Great Britain, and later when the Federalist and Whig political parties first formed, the country was divided. We fought a Civil War, and suffered political splits in the Great Depression when the "New Deal" was instituted. We have had numerous fractious political times in our nation's history.

Nonetheless, there is an extraordinary level of polarization today in which a large number of Americans vote out of resentment rather than from positive feelings. If we are to witness democracy's rebirth, we must find a way to manage these conflicts and to provide a sense of common belonging. What our forebears after the American Revolution called the patriotic Spirit of '76 and Lincoln called in his Gettysburg Address "a rebirth of Freedom." We must find a way to reknit our nation, create a level of tolerance of political differences, and promote civic virtues like active participation. We need to foster loyalty to our nation beyond party, interest, or faction.

Divisions in Chicago

Chicago has undergone a remarkable transformation that offers possibilities for future politics in the United States. In 1983, in a very racially divided election, African American Harold Washington was elected mayor with only 36 percent of the vote in a primary over two White candidates, Jane Byrne and Richard M. Daley. Byrne and Daley split the White vote, and each snared a share of the Latino vote. Harold Washington, who represented Chicago for two terms in the U.S. House of Representatives and had earlier served in the Illinois legislature, garnered a massive Black vote. To his Black support he added strong Latino support and the backing of some Whites. His rainbow coalition won.

The Democratic primary was not only an election about race. It was an ideological election in which voters chose a reform "progressive" administration under Washington over a continuation of the old Democratic political machine under either Byrne or Daley.

Perhaps the racial division displayed in this 1983 election was clearest in the general election, when the White Republican mayoral candidate, Bernie Epton, ran on the theme "Before It's too Late!," which voters understood to mean "vote for the White candidate or the Blacks will take over." Some White Democratic ward committee members instructed their precinct captains to have Democratic voters vote for the Republican candidate in order to preserve party machine and White dominance of Chicago politics and government.

When Washington was sworn into office, he faced a city council divided between twenty-one mayoral supporters and twenty-nine opponents. Thus began the political period in Chicago history known as Council Wars. A local comedian coined the moniker after the popular *Star Wars* movies, and it did seem in many ways to be a clash of good and evil.[3] Titanic struggles in the council ensued in which the mayor and the aldermen seemed unable to agree on anything. Stalemates over budgets, federal grants, and everything else created gridlock. The opposition attempted to block the mayor's progressive agenda at every turn. This was the greatest city council clash since the mid-nineteenth-century civic wars, during which the council was so divided that it could not even raise a quorum to meet for four months during the Civil War.[4]

However, despite gridlock and racial conflict, the Washington administration gave birth to a period of progress featuring freedom of information executive orders and laws providing information on all government decisions, affirmative action in city hiring and contracts, the largest neighborhood infrastructure improvement program in Chicago history, and neighborhood economic development. City council battles weren't pretty, but Chicago was transformed and brought into the late twentieth century.

Polarization and conflict can lead to major policy changes, as in this case of Chicago. Fast forward almost four decades to 2019. Mayor Lori Lightfoot, another African American, was elected and instituted another progressive era in Chicago government. Unlike the racial clashes of 1983, this time the runoff election was between two African American women, Lightfoot and Toni Preckwinkle. As we saw in the previous chapter, they bested nineteen other candidates from various races, ethnic groups, and ideologies. Chicago had changed from its twentieth-century politics.[5]

Racial divisions still matter in Chicago, but, like Harold Washington, Lightfoot won by assembling a rainbow coalition. A major difference between the two election outcomes is that a majority of her support came from the liberal White community.

When the dust settled after the 2019 election, Lightfoot was able to gain an overwhelming majority in the city council, winning a critical voice vote on the adoption of the rules of procedure, committees, committee chairships, and reforms. Her progressive administration began to enact a hundred-page transition team report promising hundreds of improvements, large and small. In the first hundred days of Mayor Lightfoot's government, Chicago witnessed fundamental changes made over a weakened opposition favoring the status quo. In 2019 she settled a contentious Chicago teachers strike without the level of animosity that had occurred under Mayor Rahm Emanuel. She passed her first budget, in which she had to make up a $838 million budget gap without raising property taxes, by a council vote of 39–11. Since then, she provided strong leadership during the pandemic and economic recession.

Her second recession budget during the pandemic addressed a $2 billion gap. It also passed, but by a narrower 28–22 vote.

In 2021, a split in the city council continues in which some members of the old machine still oppose the mayor. On the other side, progressive caucus council members push for more radical action and the Black caucus pushes for more participation in economic development efforts, such as recreational marijuana sales. Still, to date Mayor Lightfoot has not lost a single vote since she took office, and she has been able to overcome the council divisions which have not been as crippling as the Council Wars era. She continues to follow her progressive reform agenda.

There is not a permanent city council racial and political division as occurred during the Council Wars under Mayor Harold Washington in the 1980s. There are instead multiple voting factions, including a liberal faction that supports Mayor Lightfoot and that delivers the council majority needed for her to govern effectively.[6] Most impressively, as of this writing Mayor Lightfoot has been effective during the COVID-19 pandemic and the resulting economic recession, two of the greatest crises during her first term.

In 2020 and 2021, Chicagoans united and mostly complied with city stay-at-home public-health orders during the pandemic. These were more restrictive than in some other parts of Illinois. Certainly, Chicago was more unified than the country was under the Trump administration, which failed spectacularly to provide the leadership necessary to help states fight the pandemic and reopen the economy. Mayor Lightfoot's handling of the pandemic polled at 86 percent positive in June 2020 and remained high.[7] By contrast, polarization across the nation remained, and the Pew Research Center on April 18, 2020, found that 65 percent of Americans thought that "Donald Trump was too slow to take major steps to address the threat of the coronavirus outbreak to the U.S."[8] Even so, he received 74 million votes in his 2020 reelection bid.

National Polarization

We certainly see dramatic political clashes and polarization on the national stage. The wider split between the Democratic and Republican Parties began at least back in 1994 with Newt Gingrich's Contract with America agenda, which helped Republicans win control of the House of Representatives. Some scholars and political analysts trace this polarization further back to Richard Nixon's southern strategy in 1968 in his long-term effort to wrest control of the South from the Democrats.

In any case, the polarization of the political parties was accentuated with the growth of the Tea Party and the successful election of Tea Party Republicans to Congress and state legislatures in the twenty-first century. At the other end of the ideological spectrum, the emergence of Democratic Socialist Bernie Sanders as a major Democratic contender in the 2016 and 2020 presidential primaries signaled the leftward swing of the Democratic Party, as did the election of left-wing candidates like Congresswoman Alexandria Ocasio-Cortez.

This polarization was not just confined to Congress and presidential campaigns. Unfortunately, it also affected judicial selection and judicial decisions at both the state and national levels.[9] It has been highly visible in Congress. For example, Senator Mitch McConnell used Republican control of the Senate to block President Obama's programs, and Congresswoman Nancy Pelosi used Democratic control of the House of Representatives to block President Trump's programs. Thus, polarization has been on full display in the gridlocked Congress for more than a decade.

Polarization occurs among the public as well. During the placid 1950s, many observers had called for more consistent ideological differences between the two major political parties to offer voters a clearer choice in elections.[10] That has occurred in the decades since then, but the result has been a stark polarization, which many Americans are not happy with.

The Pew Research Center poll in September 2019 found that "across all 30 political values, the differences between Republicans and Democrats dwarf all other differences by demographics or other factors."[11] In short, not just politicians, but the public is polarized. Further, Pew Research Center found that there is a 57 percent gap between Democrats and Republicans on gun-control policy, 55 percent on racial attitudes, 48 percent on climate and environment, 43 percent on immigration, and even 27 percent on foreign policy.[12]

Polarization among the public has become dangerous because Trump and Biden supporters no longer disagree just on policies—now they hold very different core values. In a survey just before the 2020 election, the Pew Research Center found that 80 percent of those who supported each presidential candidate said "they fundamentally disagree with the other side on 'core American values and goals.'" Ninety percent said "there would be 'lasting harm' to the nation if the other candidate won the presidency."[13] Such strong opposition to members of the other dominant political party primes the country for violence, not compromise.

Apart from polarization of the public, numerous studies have shown that polarization in Congress has increased during recent decades, creating greater gridlock and inability to get things done.[14] The most conservative member of the Democratic Party in Congress is now more liberal than the most liberal Republican Party member of Congress. And the ideological difference between Donald Trump and his principal 2016 Democratic Party challengers, Hillary Clinton and Bernie Sanders, or his 2020 challenger, Joe Biden, was even greater than the split in Congress.

So how did Donald Trump become the spokesperson for conservatism and get elected to the highest office in the land? He was elected because of deeper trends.[15] There have been fundamental changes in the U.S. economy, society, and politics over the last half-century. Some refer to this as the waning of the golden age. We are in a postindustrial era in which an increase in minorities and immigrants and globalization have reshaped the America of the 1950s. Globalization and automation, in particular, cost workers jobs, especially in small towns and rural America. The economic recessions during the early years of the twenty-first century added to the misery of the working class. Those who lost jobs, housing, and hope, or fell further behind, were justifiably angry. Both parties failed rural dwellers and the White working class.

The resentment and polarization grew so great that the pro-Trump forces (along with White supremacists and other dissatisfied factions) not only believed that the 2020 election that elected Joe Biden president was stolen, but stormed the Capitol while Congress was in session. This insurrection of January 6, 2021, was violent, ending in five deaths and hundreds of injuries to both police and rioters.[16] The intent was to prevent Congress from officially certifying the vote of the electors making Joe Biden the next president. It vividly demonstrates the depth and the dangers of this level of polarization.

Scholars argue that these long-term trends in polarization and resentment more than short-term forces produced Trump's victory.[17] It didn't have to be Donald Trump who was elected in 2016. As political scientist John Campbell writes, "It could have been someone else, perhaps even earlier than 2016 if he or she had been willing to capitalize on the economic, racial, ideological and political trends . . . [but] Trump was an extremist extraordinaire . . . pandering to anti-immigrant racism, while still promising deep neoliberal tax and spending cuts."[18]

One of the forces that has deepened the gap between political parties and factions has been the role of the media. The Pew Research Center reports: "When it comes to getting news about politics and government, liberals and conservatives inhabit different worlds. There is little overlap in the news sources they turn to and trust. And whether discussing politics online or with friends, they are more likely . . . to interact with like-minded individuals."[19] Not surprisingly, conservatives cite Fox News as their main source of political news. For liberals, NPR, PBS, and the BBC are the most trusted news sources. So different mass media and social media information sources make the gap wider and harder to bridge. In short, both mass and social media exacerbate political polarization rather than lessening it.

Political changes that began in the later twentieth century hardened in the early twenty-first and contributed to further polarization and to Trump's 2016 election. One of the remarkable changes in U.S. politics beyond presidential politics was the rise of the Tea Party in the first decade of the twenty-first century, paving the way for Trump's election. Although there have always been conservative members of Congress, like Barry Goldwater during the 1960s, the Tea Party grew after 2010 to influence U.S. elections in three ways:

> First, Tea Party rhetoric primed white working-class Republicans for Trump's inflammatory language during the 2016 presidential campaign . . . Voters were more likely to support Trump if their representatives were already expressing high levels of incivility on Twitter. . . .
>
> Second, during the Republican primaries, the Tea Party's support was split, particularly between Marco Rubio and Ted Cruz, thus affording Trump an opening because Republican Party elites could not coordinate on a single candidate of their choice. . . .
>
> Third, during the general election, voters whose representatives were attached to the Tea Party were more likely to go for Trump than for Clinton.[20]

The Tea Party revolution made conservative candidacies more viable, and normalized incivility in our politics.

Resentment

Objective economic and political forces contributed to the Trump phenomenon. But the politics of resentment further explain why Trump won the 2016 election and received so many votes in 2020. Some analysts write that "this resentment is the 'red thread' even throughout the 2016 campaign and Trump's electoral victory."[21] As Katherine Cramer puts it, this resentment is not just between politicians in Washington: "members of the public are increasingly polarized," summarizing that "the divides are not just about politics but about who we are as people."[22] Cramer writes about Republican Scott Walker's rise to governor of Wisconsin in 2011, presaging the Trump phenomenon. She studies the rural-urban divide in U.S. politics, small-town versus big-city America and notes:

> Many rural residents exhibit an intense resentment against their urban counterparts. . . .

. . . Many rural residents have a perspective I am going to call "rural consciousness." . . . It includes a sense that decisions makers routinely ignore rural places and fail to give rural communities their fair share of resources, as well as a sense that rural folks are fundamentally different from urbanites in terms of lifestyles, values, and work ethic.[23]

Of course, many urban and suburban dwellers who have lost jobs and lost their homes during the Great Recession are equally resentful of big banks and political insiders whom they blame for their suffering. Some of them joined the conservative revolution.

Politics may be partly about issues, candidates, and party platforms, but what Cramer and others point out is that the prime political consideration is one's identity. She writes: "Perhaps issues are secondary to identities. Perhaps when people vote for a candidate their overarching calculation is not how closely does this person's stances match my own, but instead, is this person like me? Does this person understand people like me? The answers to those questions *include* a consideration of issue stances, but issue stances are not necessarily the main ingredient."[24]

While the rural electorate comprise only about 15 percent of the population, both Republican Party conservative candidates like former Governor Walker and President Trump depended on the rural vote as central to their election victories. Added to dissatisfied rural voters are similarly dissatisfied suburban and city voters who also have a deep-seated resentment of the economic and political elites who they believe are responsible for their misfortunes.

The politics of resentment moves beyond polarization. Even when political parties, their leaders, and their supporters differ on policy questions, they may be able to find common ground on issues like infrastructure improvement, funding the Department of Defense, or fighting a pandemic. However, as Cramer puts it, "When arguments about how we ought to allocate resources to each other are made on the backs of our resentment toward each other, what does the future hold?"[25] There is animosity toward government and the rich and powerful because people feel "overlooked, ignored, and disrespected."[26] Rural residents, in particular, feel ignored by the news media and the powers that be. There aren't many in government who represent them, come from their backgrounds and experiences, speak to their concerns, and deal with the problems they face. What do they have in common with, for instance, members of Congress, 70 percent of whom are millionaires? In urban areas, similar divisions occur between rich and poor and racial and ethnic groups. All these divisions and identities contribute to resentment.

Tara Westover has said the political split is because

Democrats and Republican now have a different experience of life in this country. Broadly speaking, the modern economy works well for cities and badly for the countryside. . . . The hinterlands, which rely on agriculture and manufacturing—what you might call the "old economy"—have sunk into a deep decline. There are places in the United States where the recession never ended. . . .
. . . Trump [in 2016] told a more convincing story about what was happening in America than the left did."[27]

Beyond the divide between political parties and the rural/urban divide, if demagogues are able to blame minorities, so-called welfare queens, immigrants, or foreign countries for our problems, the way is paved for some form of tyranny. Autocrats take over and democracy decays.

So, the politics of resentment is not politics as usual. As Cramer puts it, "a politics of resentment stems from and reinforces political differences that have become personal. In a politics of resentment, we treat differences in our political points of view as fundamental differences in who we are as human beings." She goes on to assert that "political divides are rooted in our most basic understandings of ourselves, infuse our everyday relationships, and are used for electoral advantage by our political leaders."[28]

As two major scholars of the decline of our democracy argue, "What makes our polarization so dangerous is its *asymmetry*. Whereas the Democratic base is diverse and expanding, the Republican Party represents a once-dominant majority in *numerical and status decline*. Sensing this decline, many Republicans have grown fearful about the future."[29] This fear was displayed in the desperate attempt by President Trump and his followers to reverse the obvious outcome of the 2020 election and the storming of the Capitol in January 2021. Parties in the past have lost elections and lived to fight another day. But now they believe that losing will bring "ruinous consequences" and that they may not have a chance of winning again in the future. With the demographic base of the Republican party contracting, the likelihood of losing future elections increases and polarization and resentment reach a fever pitch.[30]

Polarization in Elected Officials

Both the electorate and public officials are more polarized than in earlier eras. Andrew Hall and other political scientists hold that the main reason for polarization in government is that it "is already baked into the set of people who run for office." Candidates are already "rigid in their ideological positions" before they run. So, the voters realistically get to choose only between the limited choices of candidates they are offered by the two major parties. And those candidates chosen in party primaries are most often more ideologically extreme than the voters.

The costs versus the benefits for moderate candidates are greater than they are for more ideologically extreme candidates:

> Citizens whose ideological positions range from the far left to the far right face certain costs of running for office, as well as certain benefits of holding office if they win election. But, because the winning candidate gets to influence ideological policies in the legislature, the ideological payoffs of running for office are not equal across the ideological spectrum. More-extreme citizens are more averse to having a representative from the opposition side of the ideological spectrum, while more-moderate citizens are more ambivalent. As a result, when costs of running are high or benefits of holding office are low, more-moderate candidates are disproportionately less likely to run.[31]

Although voters tend to vote more often for moderate candidates when given the choice, polarization in the U.S. House of Representatives in terms of both ideology, issue stands, and voting records has more than doubled since 1980.[32] This is not because voters themselves are voluntarily voting for more extreme candidates, but because only extreme candidates are on the ballot. Andrew Hall estimates that "roughly 20 percent of overall polarization in the House is due to choices voters make among the candidates who run for office. *The other 80 percent of polarization exists no matter which* candidates *voters choose.*"[33] So, the set of people who run is causing most of the polarization.[34]

The costs of running for office have increased because candidates are now required to raise much more money from donors. One result is that "costs and benefits have changed, over time, leading to more polarization in our [state and national] legislatures."[35] Fund-raising has become more difficult, time-consuming, and unpleasant, taking many hours a day for candidates. In addition, the media scrutiny of candidates is greater and many individuals can earn greater financial rewards in the private sector for the same work and skills.

So, during the same time that the electorate has become more polarized, the incentives and disincentives of running for office favor more extreme candidates. To some extent this is a good thing, because these candidates and officials bring a greater commitment to changing the political system. But, as we see in national politics today, the more ideologically committed officials also polarize government, such that "comprise" becomes a dirty word. Gridlock and less public support of the government are the result.

Dissatisfaction with Democracy

The resentments and polarization in the United States are not unique. Populist political parties are gaining support in Europe and around the globe.

In twenty-seven countries polled by the Pew Research Center in 2018, 51 percent of those polled were dissatisfied with how democracy is working in their countries. This dissatisfaction is directly linked to "economic frustration, the status of individual rights, as well as perceptions that political elites are corrupt and do not care about average citizens."[36] Among those who thought the economy was bad in the United States, 80 percent were dissatisfied with the way democracy was working. And because of the politics of resentment, 67 percent of those who disagree with the statement "elected officials care what ordinary people think" are dissatisfied.

E. J. Dionne writes that in the United States we have had a "divided political heart" from the beginning of our nation.

> The United States was born with a divided political heart. The Founders . . . were seeking a balance between liberty and community. . . .
> The Founders understood that self-interest is a fact of human nature, and *also that it is not the only fact*. They tried to build protections against the excess of self-regarding behavior into their framework for our government. But they also sought to build a community that fostered the virtues self-government required.[37]

In the 1990s, these divisions between liberty and community were manifested in the surprisingly strong third-party campaign of Ross Perot, which received 19 percent of the popular vote in 1992.[38] It was a major repudiation of the two major political parties. This was followed by the clash between Democratic president Bill Clinton and Republican Speaker of the House Newt Gingrich, which would bring a total government shutdown and later impeachment proceedings. MSNBC's Steve Kornacki identified this period as the birth of our current political tribalism, but in fact it is merely another manifestation of our divided political heart.[39]

This divided political heart continues to be manifested in the twenty-first-century division between the Tea Party favoring individual liberty and Occupy Wall Street favoring communitarian principles. Both groups, for very different reasons, were dissatisfied with American government and society. They concluded, and many Americans today agree, that our democracy and economy are not working for them. These divisions are still reflected in the differences between Donald Trump, conservative members of Congress, and their backers on the one side and Senator Bernie Sanders and his Our Revolution supporters on the other. Both the public's and our leaders' political hearts remain divided.

Both the left and the right are dissatisfied with our democracy. The Tea Partiers and the Occupiers and Black Lives Matter protesters are polarized in the policies they advocate to solve the problems in our nation. But neither of the long-existing Democratic or Republican Parties are offering solutions to our twenty-first-century issues. As a result, these political and ideological factions have attempted to move the Republican Party to the right and the Democratic Party to the left. As these political divisions have widen, dissatisfaction has also grown. Sometimes it boils over into rioting in the cities or the January 6, 2021, attack on the Capitol.

Polarization in Chicago

The political cleavages in the city of Chicago are different from the national divisions and play out in different ways. While there are certainly liberals and conservatives in Chicago, Democrats have been ascendant since the reign of Mayor Richard J. Daley (1955–76). The Republican Party is simply no longer viable in Chicago politics. No city officials are Republican.[40] In sports terms, there are no Republican A-team players to move up to the majors, no aldermen to make a credible run for mayor or higher offices. Because the local Republican Party has very few active precinct captains within the city, it can't cultivate much voter support. For instance, Joe Biden won 82 percent of the vote in Chicago in the 2020 election and carried some wards by 96 percent.[41] Republican voters have almost disappeared in much of the city.

There is still a Republican Party in the metropolitan region, but Illinois has also changed over the last several decades from more or less evenly divided between the two major parties, a purple state, to a Democratic majority blue state. Instead of an equally divided congressional delegation, both Illinois U.S. senators are Democrats, and thirteen of the eighteen U.S. representatives are Democrats and Republicans are likely to lose one of their five seats after the 2021 redistricting.[42] With the 2018 elections, Illinois got a Democratic governor and an overwhelming Democratic majority in both houses of the state legislature.

That is not to say that there is no divisions in Chicago politics. For over a century, the traditional political division has been between the Chicago

Democratic machine and reformers. A hundred years ago the reformers were Progressives and Republicans, but for the last fifty years they have been liberal Democrats. The machine has traditionally been maintained by patronage jobs, favoritism, nepotism, and crony contracts for businesses that support it. Reformers have long fought to eliminate those aspects of machine politics in order to run a transparent government providing the best government services for the lowest taxes. Modern progressive reformers like Mayors Harold Washington and Lori Lightfoot have sought to provide not only good-government reforms, but also affirmative action, social justice, racial equality, and pro-immigrant policies.

Over the decades, the Richard J. Daley machine has been transformed to include minorities in positions of power, such as African American Cook County Board president Toni Preckwinkle, who doubles as chair of the Central Committee of the Cook County Democratic Party. At the same time, while patronage jobs have been limited by court decrees, the new post-Daley machine has allied itself with businesses in the global economy. Wealthy individuals and corporations now provide the money to run more presidential-style campaigns locally.

Underlying these partisan political divisions are racial divisions in the city. City elections frequently turn on racial identity. For practical political purposes the city is now one-third Black, one-third White, and one-third Latino, with a growing Asian American population. These racial groups frequently divide their support between machine and reform candidates, so racial/ethnic identity politics often determines voting in Chicago, just as it does elsewhere in the nation.

Perhaps the evolving racial/ethnic nature of Chicago politics is best illustrated by the selection of Mayor Richard J. Daley's successor in 1977, the election of Mayor Harold Washington in 1983, the selection of Mayor Washington's successor in 1987, and the election of Mayor Lori Lightfoot in 2019.[43] These successions are windows into the changing racial politics in Chicago.

The 1977 Mayoral Succession

Mayor Richard J. Daley, Chicago's legendary political "Boss," died on December 20, 1976. The power struggle over who would succeed him began almost immediately. Within hours, Daley's corporation counsel, William Quinlan, advised administrators at city hall that under city and state law there was no acting mayor, although many believed that African American Thirty-Fourth Ward alderman Wilson Frost, as president pro tem, should be acting mayor by virtue of his position in the city council.

At city hall, aldermen began holding political caucuses even before Mayor Daley was buried. In all but one case, these were racial/ethnic caucuses because these had been the most fundamental political divides in Chicago politics for decades. Nine Black aldermen met with Wilson Frost in a show of support for his declared candidacy to become acting mayor. Other ethnic groups gathered similarly including a Polish bloc that met in Forty-First Ward alderman Roman Pucinski's office and a seven-member Jewish bloc formed for the first time in the council's history in order to have a role in the process.

One nonethnic meeting that I attended as alderman included reform aldermen and younger machine aldermen who desired to reform the council. In this joint caucus, we discussed the process by which power was to be shifted. But there were too little cohesiveness, too few common interests between the pro-administration and reform aldermen, and too few votes in the combined group to elect the next mayor. After a single meeting, this coalition fell apart.

The administrators in Daley's government, acting for the dominant Irish Eleventh Ward and the business elite of Chicago, moved to contain potential racial and ethnic revolts and to maintain the status quo in city government. The most important meeting was held on December 21, the day after Daley's death, in the office of Tom Donovan, Daley's patronage chief. Joining Donovan in the meeting were Frank Sullivan, the mayor's press secretary; Corporation Counsel Quinlan; Aldermen Bilandic, Burke, Frost, Vrdolyak, Marzullo, and Roti from the city council. Although there was posturing and additional summit meetings of this group before coming to a power-sharing agreement over the next few days, the political forces that had backed Daley, especially the Eleventh Ward crowd and powerful businessmen, quickly settled on Eleventh Ward alderman and Finance Committee chair Michael Bilandic, as Daley's successor. In the end they would prevail.

Bilandic as finance committee chair and floor leader under Daley knew how the government was run. As a corporate lawyer, he was certain to follow traditional and financially conservative policies acceptable to the business community. His problem was that he wasn't well liked by the aldermen. They preferred someone like "Fast Eddie" Vrdolyak, with whom they could make political deals. Most of all, if Bilandic were elected, the Eleventh Ward and the Irish would still run the Democratic Party and the city. This meant that other aldermen and ethnic groups would not gain much power in the transition.

The ethnic caucuses, phone calls between aldermen, and backroom deals led to five potential candidates for mayor. They were Polish alderman Pucinski, who had only his own vote; Irish Fourteenth Ward alderman Ed Burke, with slightly more support; Croatian alderman Ed Vrdolyak, with ten to twelve votes; African American alderman Frost, with a wavering thirteen Black votes and support of three White reform aldermen, including me; and Alderman Bilandic, with just short of the twenty-five votes needed to be elected. Then Vrdolyak agreed to support Bilandic if he could have Bilandic's current job as finance committee chair.

These behind-the-scenes negotiations did not go unchallenged. On the evening of December 22, more than two hundred African American leaders rallied to back Wilson Frost for acting mayor at a unity meeting at the Roberts Motel, the site of civil rights gatherings in the past. However, the next day when Alderman Frost attempted to hold a press conference at Daley's fifth-floor office to declare himself acting mayor, the city hall administrators had the police bar the door to the mayor's office.

On Christmas Eve and Christmas Day, Alderman Burke acted as a go-between for Bilandic, Frost, and Vrdolyak. Frost agreed to withdraw from the race for acting mayor to become finance committee chair, Vrdolyak settled for president pro tem, so Bilandic now had the votes needed to be elected mayor. The final city council vote was 48–2, with only Forty-Third Ward alderman Martin Oberman joining me in voting no.

In its editorial following the 1976 election in the city council, the local NBC affiliate, WMAQ Channel 5, reported that "the formation of ethnic and racial coalitions to bargain for slices of power following Mayor Daley's death made Chicago look like a last bastion of old style of backroom, horse-trading politics. . . . Picking political figures on the basis of race and nationality is wrong. It polarizes the city."[44]

The 1983 Election

By the 1983 election, race trumped ethnic politics and would continue as a major force in the Council Wars that followed. The divisions were no longer among the Irish, Polish, and Jews but primarily a racial split among Whites, Blacks, and Browns. At the same time, the reform versus political machine battles continued.

As noted earlier in this chapter, in the Democratic mayoral primary, African American Harold Washington benefited from a heavy turnout in the African American community, more than 90 percent of whom voted for him. He picked up a third of the Latino vote and more than 10 percent of the White vote. This rainbow coalition let him win the primary with only 36 percent of the votes cast. This was a big change since the 1977 selection of

Mayor Bilandic. While Whites were still the largest racial group, they were no longer the majority. When they split their votes, they no longer prevailed. Because of the unified Black vote and the split White vote, Harold Washington became the first Black mayor in Chicago history.

This was an election decided primarily on race and political ideology. Washington's campaign and his government defined a reform agenda composes of three parts:

1. good government reform (honesty and efficiency in government);
2. empowerment (affirmative action to bring minorities and women into the highest level of government and to redistribute government jobs and contracts); and
3. citizen participation and control (decentralizing government decision-making, empowering neighborhood organizations, and providing government accountability).[45]

Washington's first reform promises satisfied White, lakefront constituencies; the second satisfied minority groups; and the third gained support of community organizations and organizers throughout the city, including in White ethnic sections.

The racial nature of this election was laid bare when alderman and Democratic Party chair Ed Vrdolyak, who was supporting Jane Byrne, spoke to White precinct workers on the Northwest Side, bluntly telling them that "a vote for Daley is a vote for Washington. It is a two-person race. It would be the worst day in the history of Chicago if your candidate . . . was not elected. It's a racial thing. Don't kid yourself. I'm calling on you to save your city, to save your precinct. We're fighting to keep the city the way it is."[46] His speech before the election, which was immediately front-page newspaper and TV news, had the opposite effect from what he hoped. It mobilized the Black and reform vote and further split the White vote between Byrne and Daley.

In the runoff election, Harold Washington was pitted against former Republican state legislator Bernie Epton and the campaign continued to be explicitly racial. In the end, Washington won with only 52 percent of the vote because a number of White Democratic machine ward committee members and their precinct captains worked openly for Republican Epton. Better a White Republican than a Black reform Democrat as mayor, they concluded. Both the primary and the runoff election were filled with racial slurs such as "It's our turn now. . . . We want it all, we want it now. . . . Go get-em Jewboy. . . . [and] Epton! Epton! He is our man. We don't want no Af-ri-can."[47]

The 1987 Mayoral Succession

With the sudden death of Mayor Washington in office on November 25, 1987, the problems of mayoral succession that had occurred when Mayor Richard J. Daley died were repeated but with a different outcome. There were new laws governing succession, but the same racial political divisions remained. By this time, there were more Latino aldermen who would, as a bloc, have a role in the succession process, just as they played a prominent role in Washington's 1983 and 1987 elections, providing the margin of his electoral victories.

Even before Fourth Ward alderman Tim Evans—the chair of the finance committee and Mayor Washington's floor leader—returned from Northwestern Memorial Hospital, where Mayor Washington had just been pronounced dead, the succession maneuvering at City Hall had begun.

> With one eye on the television set that was delivering the grim news to his third-floor City Hall office, [African American] Ald. William Henry (24th)—who had made no secret of his disdain for elements of [Mayor Washington's] reform agenda—began calling other aldermen into his office and started to line up their ward-organization armies.
>
> "There was an appropriate sadness," said one alderman of the gathering in Henry's office during those tense afternoon hours Wednesday. "On the other hand, it seemed like, 'Hallelujah, we're free.'"
>
> A few hours later, as Evans . . . returned from the hospital, he was grabbed by Ald. Bobby Rush (2nd). "I asked him if he wanted to be mayor and he said, 'Yes,'" Rush recalled. "I told him what was going on [in Henry's office]. And we started making calls that night."[48]

Evans and his supporters were too late. Alderman Henry had already lined up six Black aldermen to support Eighth Ward alderman Eugene Sawyer for mayor, and he had talked to all the other Black aldermen. In the meantime, White Northwest Side alderman Dick Mell (Thirty-Third) was telling reporters that he had lined up twenty, mostly White, aldermen. He offered spoils, power, and committee chairships to the other council members in an attempt to get the necessary twenty-six votes to be elected, but he couldn't break the council's racial barriers to get a majority.

The four Latino aldermen (two Mexican Americans and two Puerto Ricans) decided to vote as a bloc to maximize their influence. They eventually decided to vote for Evans. However, their unified support was insufficient to elect him.

Meanwhile, twenty-four White aldermen met at the Northwest Side home of Alderman Joseph Kotlarz (Thirty-Fifth). At the meeting, both Alderman Mell and Northwest Side alderman Terry Gabinski (Thirty-Second) attempted to marshal enough support to be elected mayor. Yet, even if they could command unified support from the White machine aldermen, they still had to obtain the support from White lakefront reformers or a couple of Latino or Black aldermen to win. When it became clear that neither Mell nor Gabinski could line up the requisite votes, Mell began meeting with Sawyer to see if a winning coalition to elect either of them could be assembled. Finally, in a clandestine meeting in a restaurant parking lot, Mell was convinced that Sawyer had the necessary Black support. If Mel swung the White ethnic aldermen, Sawyer could be elected and so he was.

After a marathon session of the city council a few days later that lasted until the early morning hours of December 2 and was attended by several thousand former Washington supporters who backed Alderman Evans, Sawyers was elected by a vote of 29–19. Sawyer was chosen as mayor because the city's elite feared that race riots would ensue if a White alderman was selected to replace Harold Washington.

In 1987, the selection process was carried out by secret caucuses, just as they had been a decade earlier when Bilandic was selected as mayor. However, the earlier ethnic caucuses evolved to racial groupings—White, Black, and Brown. When the Black aldermen and community split between the more progressive faction supporting Evans and the machine faction supporting Sawyer, the White aldermen were able to determine the outcome of the election even though they couldn't elect one of their own race.

The 2019 and 2020 Elections

After Sawyer, two Whites, Richard M. Daley and Rahm Emanuel, would follow as mayor before a Black woman lesbian, Lori Lightfoot, would overcome the racial splits to be elected in 2019 as the first Black woman mayor of Chicago. However, her largest base of support was in the White and LGBTQ community. Nonetheless, like Washington she would assemble a rainbow coalition, which in the runoff enabled her to win 74 percent of the vote and to carry all fifty wards.

Throughout the end of the twentieth century and into the twenty-first, race polarization and racial voting would remain a major force in Chicago politics. This polarization began to be partially overcome with Lightfoot's election in 2019. Nonetheless, racial resentments and identity remain a powerful force in Chicago as well as national politics. The 2020 national election continued to showcase racial, ideological, class, and rural-urban divisions. Joe Biden obtained massive support from the Black community and majority support from Latino and Asian American voters. Whites remained the principal support base for President Trump. The politics of resentment in many ways deepened those divisions in the country. President Biden won by partially bridging the racial divide. But race and ideology still divide the nation.

United We Stand

Polarization and the politics of resentment must be healed if American democracy is to be reborn. Mark Edmundson describes the guidance of our most American poet, Walt Whitman, who saw the importance of healing divisions after the Civil War:

> Whitman speaks to our moment in many ways. One of them is quite simple: At a time when Americans hate one another across partisan lines as intensely perhaps as they have since the Civil War, Whitman's message is that hate is not compatible with true democracy, spiritual democracy. We may wrangle and fight and squabble and disagree. Up to a certain point, Whitman approved of conflict. But affection—friendliness—must always define the relations between us. When that affection dissolves, the first order of business is to restore it. . . .
>
> Perhaps what Whitman mainly offers is hope—the hope that this new form of social life can prosper and give people access to levels of happiness and freedom that they have never enjoyed.[49]

We need this spirit of democracy and level of civic cohesion to provide the motivation for us to sacrifice private interests for public good. The Chicago successions and elections over the last fifty years do suggest that deep divisions can be overcome. We can reach across racial and ideological divides in a recognition of a greater loyalty: being Chicagoans and Americans before anything else.

Divisions in U.S. politics must be overcome. Not to end all conflict, for the contestation of ideas is the very basis of democracy. But to stop a politics of resentment that leads to the election of autocratic leaders or mob rule. We must become friendly combatants. Often, the clash of our ideas can produce a third way—a compromise or a balance in pendulum swings of public policy that are inevitable in a democracy.

Chicago is an example of how this can occur. The century-long battle between order and innovation, political machine and reform movements, ethnic and racial divisions has swung toward progressive reform. The fierce combat of election has ended this time not in Council Wars but in the normal tug and pull of democratic political factions as Chicago faces the challenges of being a global city, rides the waves of a turbulent economy, copes with a deadly pandemic, deals with a still racially divided society, and reforms an antiquated government as it is brought kicking and screaming into the twenty-first century. Continuing problems of crime, violence, police misconduct, poor schools, lack of affordable housing, too few good jobs, unemployment, and all the rest of Chicago's ongoing problems remain to be overcome. There is no one right answer for these problems, but in the normal push and pull of democratic politics, we find partial answers. Chicago is taking a step forward into a more positive future. So now must our country.

This was demonstrated in the election of Lori Lightfoot as mayor, in the gradual unraveling of the rubber-stamp city council, and in Chicago's unity in confronting the COVID-19 pandemic. While previous racial and political divisions have not magically disappeared, political polarization has decreased and support for Chicago government has increased.

Chicagoans elected a Black, woman, lesbian mayor in 2019.[50] The city council has begun to act more like a legislative body while providing Mayor Lightfoot a governing majority. This is unlike the racial and political polarization and council wars of the Harold Washington administration.[51] Chicagoans, after some difficulties in the first days following the official social distancing and stay-at-home orders, cooperated with city and state government instructions in 2020 and 2021. The end result was that, while there were still many COVID-19 cases and a regrettable number of deaths, the city was able to "bend the curve" and dramatically decrease cases and deaths by the summer of 2021. In a time of crisis, polarization and resentment was partially overcome in Chicago even as political divisions continued nationally.

The banding together that happened in Chicago, in which everyone sacrificed during the pandemic for the greater good, can be extended. And, the level of polarization and resentment nationally must be lessened if we are to preserve our democracy.

Then-President Donald J. Trump and Chicago alderman Ed Burke were both involved in political corruption. As alderman, Burke secured property tax reductions for the Trump businesses in Chicago. (Courtesy AP Images)

7

Corruption

Income and racial inequality, the corrosive effect of money in elections and lobbying, and the lack of citizen participation in politics and government lead to political corruption that further undermines our democracy. As Larry Diamond writes, "nothing more readily saps democracy of its legitimacy than the widespread perception that government officials are mainly there to enrich themselves, their cronies, and their parties rather than to serve the public."[1] This especially applies to Chicago and the United States today.

While there is considerable debate about its precise definition, political corruption is the use of political or governmental office for the private benefit (usually economic) for oneself or one's family and friends.[2] In the simplest cases, corruption takes the form of outright bribes to public officials, but there are many subtle forms of both financial and moral corruption. In the case of corruption, the benefits to officials, their families, and friends can be anything of value. Moreover, institutional corruption can occur in which the individuals may act morally but the institutional outcomes are biased and corrupted. Whichever form corruption takes, it is never in the interest of the public.

The problem of political corruption is well illustrated by the Trump administration, which was one of the most corrupt in U.S. history. President Trump—pictured with indicted Chicago alderman Ed Burke in the photo that opens this chapter—is a self-proclaimed billionaire who bragged about bribing public officials with campaign contributions before running for office himself.[3] His most troubling conflicts of interest came during his presidency. Indeed, "because of the corrosion by omission and commission at the top [by President Trump], the United States is far more corrupt than it was a decade ago."[4] This chapter describes that corruption at both the local and national levels and sets forth cures for it. Chicago is especially familiar with corruption, and its battles against corruption hold lessons for the nation.

Corruption takes many forms. The emoluments clause in Article 1 of the Constitution is meant to prevent even small gifts from foreign powers that might influence federal officials.[5] While president, Trump violated that clause by enriching himself with foreign guests staying at his hotels and properties.[6] Many U.S. businessmen and lobbyists also stayed at his hotels and played golf at his resorts to win his favor.[7]

He promoted and profited from his business interests overseas, such as Trump Hotels and Condominiums around the world; his companies received loans from foreign banks and nations.[8] He even proposed holding the 2020 meeting of the G7 leaders at his Trump National Doral Miami golf resort until public outcry caused him to recant petulantly.[9] In short, the presidency materially enriched Donald Trump and his family while he was a sitting president.

While president, Trump claimed to be friends with autocrats and dictators, among them Russia's Vladimir Putin and North Korea's Kim Jong Un, and he praised dictators like Iraq's Saddam Hussain and Syria's Bashar al-Assad.[10]

This is evidence of his moral as well as financial corruption.

Beyond emoluments, many leaders of Trump's presidential campaign staff pled guilty to a laundry list of public corruption charges after lying to cover up their actions. Evidence of this malfeasance was documented by the report by Special Counsel Robert Mueller in 2019.[11] According to the *New York Times*, as of November 15, 2019, and Reuters as of August 20, 2020, eight people among his campaign leaders have been found guilty of crimes in the 2016 campaign that elected Trump. They were proven corrupt in court.[12] Those convicted included Trump's campaign manager, Paul Manafort, along with his campaign advisers, Roger Stone, and Steve Bannon. Other campaign officials were charged with crimes, many of whom Trump pardoned.[13] In the final weeks of his presidency, he pardoned former campaign manager Paul Manafort, campaign advisor Roger Stone, and a number of other campaign and government allies.[14]

It is clear from Trump's public statements during the campaign that he invited the Russians to interfere in the 2016 election by hacking and releasing Hillary Clinton's and her campaign's e-mails.[15] And his campaign took advantage of the WikiLeaks releases provided by Russian hackers to win the general election in 2016.[16]

After Donald Trump became president and the Mueller report was released, President Trump engaged in new acts that resulted in his impeachment by the U.S. House of Representatives on two articles: for bribery and wire fraud in pressuring the president of Ukraine to investigate a political opponent, and for obstruction of Congress by withholding documents and preventing individuals from testifying in the impeachment inquiry. In short, the president was charged with seeking to force Ukraine to undermine a political opponent by withholding a White House state visit and necessary military support in Ukraine's war with Russia. Although on December 18, 2019, the House of Representatives voted—mostly along party lines—to impeach him on two articles, ultimately the U.S. Senate failed—mostly along party lines—to muster the sixty-seven votes necessary to convict President Trump and to remove him from office.[17]

David Bennett writes, "history teaches that there are three kinds of corruption in national politics: money, power, and sex. Amazingly, in less than one term, Trump has racked up ample material for impeachment on all three."[18]

Nor have the conflicts of interest been just with President Trump himself. In the first two years of his term, twenty-four notable government officials quit or were forced to resign. Four members of his cabinet—Health and Human Services Secretary Tom Price, Veterans Affairs Secretary David Shucklin, Environmental Protection Agency Executive Director Scott Pruitt, and Secretary of the Interior Ryan Zinke—were among them. These members of Trump's cabinet were forced to resign because of their misuse of their public offices, funds misspent on their travel, redecorating their offices at exorbitant cost to taxpayers, and using federal employees for personal tasks rather than government work.[19] In addition, Secretary Ryan Zinke was involved in a land deal in his hometown of Whitefish, Montana, with the CEO of Haliburton, one of the largest U.S. energy companies. Zinke had in his official capacity opened additional public lands to oil drilling and eliminated many protections against environmental damage by such drilling.[20]

Housing and Urban Development (HUD) Secretary Ben Carson was not convicted and did not resign, but he spent more than $30,000 redecorating his office—$25,000 above the $5,000 limit. He told his staff that "$5,000 will not even buy a decent chair."[21] These redecorating expenses occurred at the same time the Trump administration was proposing cutting HUD's budget for affordable housing by $6.2 billion.

The 2020 election revealed a moral corruption that was even more dangerous to our democracy. After losing the popular vote 81 million to 74 million and the Electoral College 306 to 232, Donald Trump falsely argued that the election had been stolen.[22] Even though contested state recounts were done by hand to confirm results, more than three dozen lawsuits failed in the courts, and even key federal officials declared that the election was one of the most secure ever held in the United States, Trump and his most devoted supporters attempted to argue that it was stolen.[23] Both the U.S. Cybersecurity and Infrastructure Agency and the attorney general at the Department of Justice said so.[24]

President Trump continued to attempt to overturn the results and thus undermine democracy and the rule of law. On January 13, 2021, President Trump was impeached for a second time by a vote of 232–197 in the U.S. House of Representatives for inviting his followers to storm the Capitol while Congress was in session.[25] The article of impeachment also included the charges that he instigated the insurrection of January 6 and attempted to intimidate Georgian public officials to steal the 2020 election for him.

Level of Corruption

Even before all President Trump's actions were publicly known, Transparency International on its Corruption Perception Index ranked the United States as the twenty-second least corrupt nation out of 180 nations studied.[26] By the time Trump left office in 2021, we had fallen to twenty-fifth. We fall far behind less corrupt countries like Denmark and New Zealand. Based on international standards, the United States is riddled with corruption.

Corruption didn't occur only in the Trump administration, however. Many other local and national political and governmental officials continue to be convicted on corruption charges. Over the two decades from 1998 to 2019, the Department of Justice charged 22,075 public officials with public corruption. In the same period, 19,953 officials were convicted, with thousands still awaiting trial. In the single year of 2019, the last date for which we have figures, 780 public officials were charged with public corruption, 734 were convicted, and 451 were awaiting trial.[27]

A study by the Carnegie and Knight Foundations on election fraud documented 2,068 instances in which there were criminal prosecution for such fraud in the twelve years between 2000 and 2012.[28]

With all these corruption and election fraud cases occurring, there is no sign of this level of corruption changing. Public corruption in U.S. politics and government seems to be a constant.

Most corruption convictions over the last several decades have been at the state and local levels of government. Corruption does not happen only on the national stage or with a single administration, but is endemic throughout our political system. It will not be eliminated simply by electing a different president or other individual public officials.

As an example of this corruption, consider Chicago. It is the most corrupt city in the country, with the most federal corruption convictions over the decades that systematic records have been kept since the 1970s.[29] Illinois, in turn, is the third most corrupt state, with more than 2,100 corruption convictions from 1976 to 2019 and averaging thirty federal corruption convictions each year.[30] Chicago and Illinois corruption cases are not only numerous but often among the most outrageous as well.

Although chapter 4 touches on this, it's relevant to revisit a couple of particularly egregious facts about Chicago and Illinois corruption, namely that four of the seven Illinois sitting and former governors elected between 1960 and 2006 were convicted in federal court of political corruption. This is more than any other state in the country. Again, as we saw in chapter 4, from 1972 to 2020, thirty-five Chicago aldermen and former aldermen were convicted of public corruption, as were nineteen judges and five members of Congress representing Illinois districts.[31]

Some scholars using different methods and measurements come to similar but slightly different conclusions. For instance, the Center for Public Integrity (CPI), in its assessment of government accountability and transparency, relying on reports from journalists and other state political experts, lists Illinois as only the thirteenth worst in transparency because it enacted some good ethics laws and procedures after major corruption scandals, but the CPI still gives the state an overall D+ for its ethics laws and transparency.[32]

An argument is also made that Chicago and Illinois aren't necessarily the most corrupt city and state, only that the U.S. Attorneys' offices in Illinois are more active in prosecutions. I argue that the U.S. Attorneys' offices in Illinois, and particularly in Chicago, have more investigators and prosecutors working on corruption because there are so many cases to prosecute there.

The effect of this high level of corruption is recognized by the public as well. In February, 2016, Gallup released a poll on Americans' confidence in their state governments. Illinois ranked last, with only 25 percent of the population reporting that they felt confident in the state. The next lowest was Rhode Island, with 33 percent. The state with the most public confidence was North Dakota, with 81 percent. Even more disappointing, this is the second time Gallup took this poll with similar results: in 2013, Illinois also ranked as the least trusted government, with only 28 percent of the residents reporting that they trusted the state government. Over the years, Illinois residents have become even more cynical and jaded about their elected officials. In 2014, Gallup research showed that 50 percent of Illinois residents would leave the state if given the opportunity, more than any other state in the nation.[33]

An Egregious Case

In the early part of the twenty-first century, the poster child of Illinois corruption was Governor Rod Blagojevich. He was one of four Illinois governors in recent times to be convicted of public corruption. Blagojevich was convicted on seventeen counts, including wire fraud, attempted extortion, and conspiracy to solicit bribes in a wide-ranging set of shakedown schemes to gain bribes for some gubernatorial appointees and to get campaign contributions for himself.[34] He also had the distinction of being the only governor in Illinois's two-hundred-year history to be impeached and thrown out of office before being convicted in federal court.[35]

FBI wiretaps recorded Blagojevich blatantly detailing his corrupt deals. Putting private gain over the public good, we hear him trying to sell a U.S. Senate seat that was vacated when Barack Obama became president in 2008 to the highest bidder because, as governor, he had the right to make the appointment. He declared over his wiretapped phone, "I've got this thing and it's fucking—*golden*. And I, I'm not giving it up for fucking nothing."[36]

Blagojevich, one of the youngest people to be elected Illinois governor, liked to comb his hair in Elvis Presley style, adopted a folksy campaign approach, was charismatic and easy to like. While he had faults, as governor he promoted some progressive ideas like negotiating affordable drugs for seniors and raising the minimum wage. Perhaps most ironically, he promised to end the corruption of the previous Governor George Ryan's administration. Even progressive reformers like myself supported him in his first gubernatorial campaign.

He was convicted not only for trying to sell a U.S. Senate seat. What he did with considerable frequency was appoint his people to state boards and commissions who then used their positions to rig contracts in return for payoffs for themselves and campaign contributions for the governor. After all, Blagojevich had to raise more than $20 million for each of his gubernatorial campaigns, and he needed much more to achieve his grander goal of running for president. It was a massive shakedown scheme in which many of his fellow conspirators also went to jail. One Blagojevich friend and coconspirator, Christopher Kelly, committed suicide rather than face prison.

Blagojevich was shameless in shaking down anyone, including CEOs of hospitals needing state government permission to expand their services, including a children's hospital.

It was a pay-to-play system of government contracts and bribes. Everyone in on the deal—contractors and fixers—made a lot of money. And the governor got the campaign contributions needed to run for reelection, and maybe, president one day.

Rod Blagojevich's personal story is representative of machine politics in Chicago. After graduating law school in California, he returned to Chicago and began his legal and political career with former Alderman "Fast Eddie" Vrdolyak, who would later also be convicted of several corruption offenses. Blagojevich served for a while as an assistant state's attorney in traffic court and then married Patricia Mell, daughter of Chicago alderman Dick Mell. From being a low-level member of the Chicago Democratic machine, Blagojevich quickly moved up in the political world after his marriage.

After joining his father-in-law's alderman's staff, he was elected by Alderman Mell's patronage precinct workers as a state representative. With Mell's political support, he was soon elected to the state legislature, then the U.S. Congress, and eventually governor. Despite his rise to becoming governor, he was impeached, removed from office, and ended up with a federal prison sentence of nearly fifteen years for his crimes. On February 19, 2020, after Blagojevich had served only eight years, President Trump commuted his sentence, saying that the sentence was too long for the corruption he had committed.[37] A corrupt president commuted the sentence of a corrupt governor who had previously appeared on his *Celebrity Apprentice* TV reality show and whose wife, Patti, made appeals for the commutation on Fox-TV that the president watched.

Corruption is an inevitable part of machine politics in Chicago and Illinois, and Governor Blagojevich was a part of the political machine that elected him. The ever-necessary requirement of raising more money to run for higher political office only increased the pressure for greater levels of corruption on his part.

History of Corruption in Chicago and Illinois

Rather than catalog all the corruption scandals in our nation's 250-year history, including famous scandals like the Teapot Dome Scandal in the Harding administration of the 1920s, the robber baron period, or the Watergate break-in, it is easier to focus on Illinois' almost equally long history of corruption.

The first stolen election was at Chicago's incorporation in 1833. Those present at the town meeting decided to incorporate by a vote of 12–1 even though two of the voters didn't meet the residency requirement. Later that year, they recorded a vote of 28–1 to elect a slate of town trustees—even though there were fewer than twenty-eight citizens living in the town at the time.[38]

Illinois was similarly corrupt in its early state history. One of the first governors, Joel Matteson, who served from 1853 to 1856, left office owing the state a quarter of a million dollars. The governor and his conspirators received cash for scrip issued by the government as an IOU in order to build the Illinois and Michigan Canal. However, those costs to build the canal had already been paid by an issue of federal government land. Essentially, the state and the taxpayers paid twice for the same project and the profits were simply pocketed by the governor and his allies. A civil lawsuit eventually forced the governor to pay back the money, but no criminal trial was held.[39]

One of the most notorious cases of state corruption in the early twentieth century was the election to the U.S. Senate of William J. Lorimer whose supporters paid $100,000 in bribes to forty Illinois state legislators. "Bribes of up to $2,500 per bribed lawmaker were split as pre-vote payments and then as part of a post-session 'jackpot' of payments. . . . At the time a Model T Ford cost $850."[40]

In 1912, Lorimer was expelled from the U.S. Senate for winning his seat by bribery. Public outrage over this scandal propelled forward the Seventeenth Amendment (1913) to the U.S. Constitution, which provides for the direct election of senators. In Lorimer's case, corruption in Illinois spawned national reform.

Another famous practitioner of corruption was Illinois secretary of state Paul Powell, noted among other things, for saying "I smell the meat a-cooking."[41] Meaning he smelled the opportunity to get a bribe. When he died in 1970, he had an unexplained $800,000 in his hotel room closet in a shoebox, two leather briefcases, and three strongboxes. Much of this money came from state contracts awarded without competitive bidding to friends and political allies. He made even more money from the secretary of state's power to name horse racing dates for which he received bribes and racing stock in return for doling out the best dates to racetracks.

The rest of his loot came from unrecorded campaign contributions and pocketing checks when people paid for their driver licenses. Powell, who served five years as Speaker of the Illinois House of Representatives and six years as secretary of state, died with an estate worth $4.6 million, although he never earned more than $30,000 a year in his elected positions. He didn't accumulate his millions by thriftiness but by bribery, extortion, and corruption of the old-fashioned kind.[42]

The overall lessons of Chicago and Illinois corruption are clear. Corruption is fostered by machine politics in both Democratic and Republican political parties that, in turn, is characterized by patronage, favoritism, nepotism, and corrupt government contracts. A culture of political corruption developed over time in which Illinois and Chicago citizens expect to pay bribes for government services in one form or another and officials expect to be bribed for doing their job.

The defense of the corrupt public officials, including Rod Blagojevich, has been that "everyone is doing it." But everyone isn't doing it, and corruption undermines representative democracy in which elected representatives are supposed to act on behalf of the public interest, not for their private gain.

There is a real cost to this corruption. For example, one obscure public official, Dixon comptroller and city treasurer Rita Crundwell, stole over $53 million from this small Illinois town where President Ronald Reagan was born. Her outright theft took away funds needed for police protection and road repairs.[43] In this case, corruption made local government less effective and prevented citizens from getting the government services they deserved.

Overall, it is estimated that corruption in Illinois costs taxpayers on average more than $500 million a year.[44] For instance, over $100 a year for a decade was paid for the police torture that gained false convictions under the infamous Chicago commander Jon Burge.[45] Jon Burge and the police officers under his command on the South Side of Chicago tortured over a hundred innocent Black men to make them confess to crimes they didn't commit. The financial cost of all forms of corruption, including police torture and police corruption, in Illinois has caused a significant part of the budget deficits in city and state government. But the cost of corruption also includes lost lives and property, such as the deaths caused by then Secretary of State George Ryan's employees selling licenses to unqualified truck drivers, whose incompetence killed people on the state highways. Or the corrupt building inspectors who took bribes that led to nightclub fires or porch collapses that killed college students.

Illinois's high level of endemic corruption also undermined citizens' faith in their government, which is an even greater cost than the monetary losses. Corruption, along with the city's and state's inability to adequately fund government, is why Illinoisans trust their governments less than citizens of any other state. While there is partial machine democracy in Chicago and Illinois consistent with corruption, neither true representative nor participatory democracy can be achieved when there are such high levels of corruption.

Human beings are fallible and some individuals will always succumb to greed, but consistent corruption is incompatible with democracy. Our founders knew this from the examples in Europe. Just as they sought to avoid the tyranny of King George III, they hoped to avoid the corruption they saw overseas. However, today in Chicago and nationally, corruption has become systemic.

Corruption in the United States

Unfortunately, the story of corruption is not new in the United States. Our founding fathers tried to build protections against it, having witnessed its effects in Europe before the Revolution. Zephyr Teachout describes our founders as seeing France as a nation that was "essentially corrupt, a nation in which there was no true polity, but instead exchanges of luxury for power; a nation populated by weak subjects and flattering courtiers." In Britain they saw a "corrupted republic, a place where the premise of government was basically sound but civic virtue . . . was degenerating."[46] They wanted to avoid the fates of these European nations.

Therefore, our founders strove in the Constitution and the laws they adopted to create structures to prevent and contain corruption. They sought to promote the democratic spirit on which the nation was founded.

The Constitution is replete with checks and balances as well as prohibitions against emoluments and titles of nobility. The founders sought to prevent any actions that could undermine officials acting in the public interest. They created competition between branches of government, and with federalism they established a division of power between national and state governments, in order to check the ambition of government officials and would-be tyrants. Later laws would explicitly prohibit bribery and extortion.

Corruption in the discussions at the 1787 Constitutional Convention and the ratification debates in the states afterward referred primarily to the use of public office for private gain, just as we use the term today. The intent in the Constitution was to erect structures "in order to discourage self-serving behavior in public life."[47] But structures were not enough; civic virtue in the public and public officials was also needed so that "in the execution of public duties, the public good ought to be sought first" over private interests.[48] In the convention and ratification debates, references to "corruption" as merely quid pro quo bribes "constituted less than one-half of 1 percent of the times [the term] corruption was raised."[49] Thus, the founders had a much broader understanding than the twenty-first-century U.S. Supreme Court held in decisions like *Citizens United* (2010) and *McCutcheon v. FEC* (2014). Our nation's founders understood that corruption in the sense of putting private interests above the public interest could take multiple forms. Therefore, the people themselves had to have integrity for the nation to survive, but the founders believed that a proper structure of the government could help prevent corrupt acts.

Unfortunately, our long history is replete with examples of corruption: from gifts of the French king to American diplomats in the eighteenth century; to bargain basement sales of lands to individuals and the railroads in the nineteenth; to the more common bribes and campaign contributions today like those in the Rod Blagojevich scandals and conflicts of interest by President Trump and members of his campaign and administration.

Outright corruption and unethical behavior have insidious effects. If there is a corruption tax—that is, if corruption in government steals our tax dollars—then, why should we pay our taxes if they are only to be stolen or pocketed by corrupt officials and their business allies? If public officials don't obey the laws, why should citizens? Corruption among officials inevitably leads to a corruption of the body politic, and a corrupt public elects corrupt officials in a vicious cycle.

Moreover, when there is moral decay in the public, there will be unethical behavior in our public officials. Finally, when officials are corrupt, the citizenry will no longer possess the virtue to support a democratic republic. Therefore, in the United States today, it is no longer an issue of a few rotten apples that can be plucked out and removed. A more accurate image is that of a rotten apple barrel that must be totally cleansed.

Former U.S. Representative Jill Long Thompson makes two further points about why ethics is important in politics:

> I saw [Donald] Trump was undermining the very principles of democracy: the lack of transparency, the issue with emoluments, his unwillingness to reveal his tax returns, having his daughter sit next to a foreign leader at the White House and then she gets an opportunity to sell her line of products in that country. . . .
>
> We need [instead] people of integrity, people who are there to serve the public and not enrich themselves. . . .
>
> If our leaders are not speaking the truth, then it makes it more difficult for the citizenry to get accurate information. If the citizenry is not getting the truth, then we are not making the right decisions.[50]

Corruption by public officials enriching themselves undermines faith in government. This, in turn, leads to hiding the truth from citizens, which makes democracy—or rule by the people—in any sense, impossible.

Institutional Corruption

Corruption does not only take the form of "individual corruption." It is also present in "institutional corruption." Lawrence Lessig, in his *America, Compromised*, argues that "we have allowed core institutions of America's economic, social and political life to become corrupted."[51] He goes on to say that

When we speak of corrupt institutions, only sometimes do we mean that an institution is filled with corrupt individuals. . . .

. . . We could imagine an institution that is corrupt even if no one within that institution was also corrupt.[52]

When an individual gets caught taking a bribe to pass a law or to take an administrative action favoring a private party and is fired, fined, or jailed as a result, that is a case of an individual act of corruption. The preverbal rotten apple in an otherwise honest government. However, there have been more than 2,100 people in recent decades convicted of public corruption in Illinois, more than 1,800 of whom were in metropolitan Chicago—this is clear evidence of institutional corruption. It is a rotten political system, not a single bad apple, or actor.

In my book *Corrupt Illinois*, I detail the corruption in the Chicago City Council, the Cook County court system, agencies of the state government, and various branches of local government.[53] Despite similarities in the corruption, the methods used, the ways and levels of payoffs, and the results, from a crooked zoning change, permit, contract, or rigged murder trial, all differ across these different governments. But each undermines the institutions of government and any faith citizens may have in their government.

When institutional rules and norms promote corruption and a common pattern of multiple cases exists in the same institution, then institutional corruption flourishes. Lessig gives as an example of institutional corruption that goes beyond individual corruption the Greenback Primary, in which political candidates must first raise a lot of money from rich individuals and corporations before they can become viable candidates for Congress. Both candidates running for office and their campaign contributors may be personally honest, but having to raise large sums of money inevitably makes the candidate beholden to special interests or wealthy individuals. As we saw in chapter 4 regarding money in politics, the wealthy contribute more money to these campaigns than average voters whom the elected officials are supposed to represent. Once elected, officials then naturally give more access to those who contributed the funds necessary for them to win their election and who will be key in the next election.

The founders understood corruption as institutions and individuals being responsive to the wrong influences. James Madison in Federalist Paper 52 on Congress wrote that it should have an "immediate dependence on, and intimate sympathy with the people," having recognized that instead the British Parliament at the time was overly dependent on King George III.[54] Unfortunately, today members of both houses of the U.S. Congress are overdependent on businesses and wealthy individuals.

Other examples of institutions that can become corrupt even if individuals within them are not include corporations that become too big to fail or regulate in the financial sector; journalists and news media who report what is most entertaining and profitable, rather than news citizens most need; academics who are paid for public testimony that support claims of the companies that pay them; and lawyers who conform with business interests of their clients rather that what they personally know is right.[55]

There are many other examples of institutional corruption in which "institutions with a presumptive [positive] purpose finds itself diverted by incentives that compromise its purpose."[56]

Thus, the test for government is whether its officials serve the public interest, the interests of the officials themselves, or the interests of private individuals and groups.

It is difficult to correct institutional corruption. We have criminal law, ethical standards, and rules to curb individual corruption. In general, greater transparency, better ethical training, investigations by inspectors general and oversight by the legislative branch can limit cases of individual corruption. However, curbing institutional corruption requires changing the norms and overall political culture. For instance, institutional corruption in Chicago is unlikely to end until the political machine is finally destroyed.

We can make legal and structural changes to improve our government and political system. However, when there are institutional problems, no one change will be a silver bullet to fix the system. What will be required are structural changes and more fundamental changes like elimination of the culture of corruption. It requires eliminating machine politics and ending the history of corruption. Beyond corruption, our transformation in the post-Trump era requires a rebirth of democracy.

Curing Corruption

By implementing laws and by structural changes, we can deter some individual corruption by posing heavy penalties for those who participate in corrupt schemes to defraud the public. But as the Illinois and Chicago cases demonstrate, past corruption creates a corrupt political culture. Therefore, any cure also requires a change in our societal norms as well as specific laws and regulations.

As former member of Congress Jill Long Thompson writes:

Without ethics, democracy cannot survive. . . .
. . . I have long been concerned that too many of our people, including government and corporate leaders, pay too little attention to the ethical

aspects of conducting the people's business. . . . I have grown even more troubled by a lack of character and ethics among many who hold positions of leadership in both public and private sectors. It is also troubling that the public outcry has not been more widespread.[57]

Historian and activist Mary Frances Berry notes the importance of the public taking action:

> The good news is that all of us who want clean elections with better candidates and accountability can effect change by taking concrete steps. We can work against voter suppression and help citizens who do not have government IDs get them. . . . Ending the disenfranchisement of felons who have served their time, and joining in the mobilization against the influence of donations in politics, are also crucial. And certainly, supporting officials . . . who try to punish vote buyers who exploit the poor is a worthwhile cause.
>
> . . . Combined with voter education and organization, and accountability devices such as a recall, incentives could make the disaffected see that voting matters and beats [bribes] of five dollars and a pork chop sandwich. And casting a ballot might become a real, rather than rhetorical, civic virtue.[58]

Corruption can be rooted out only by implementing a multipronged program over many years. Certainly, among the necessary steps going from the easiest to the most difficult are:

1. **Facilitating greater transparency.** Government transparency involves more than just doing a massive government data dump on the Internet. Information must be provided in more usable forms, alongside strong freedom of information laws guaranteeing the rights of individuals and organizations to demand and receive government data in a timely fashion. Currently, transparency most often means that the needed information is buried somewhere on a website. However, the information, such as voting records and details of government contracts, must be provided in a form that allows the public to hold public officials accountable. For instance, the voting records of Chicago aldermen are posted on the city clerk's website as raw data. Proper software and website design could, however, crunch recorded votes into graphs, charts, and dashboards so that voters and civic organizations could see at a glance how each elected official has voted over time on controversial issues on which divided roll call votes were taken.

2. **Requiring civics courses.** All educational institutions above grade school should make civics courses a condition of graduation. These classes must provide students not only with structural political knowl-

edge, like the differences in the three branches of government, but also with civic engagement experiences and information on the causes, costs, and cures of corruption. The purpose is to train a new generation of civic-minded citizens with the necessary knowledge, skills, and motivation to bring about renewal.

In 2021, the Civics Secures Democracy Act was introduced in the U.S. House and Senate [HR 1814 and S. 879] to give civic education the same priority as STEM (science, technology, engineering, and mathematics) education in K–12 schools. It would reorganize and appropriately fund civics education.

Along with its passage, granting sixteen-year-olds the right to vote would make a difference. Voting is habit forming, and this is an age when there would be the most support in school and in the new civics courses to encourage voting.

3. **Eliminating gerrymandering and enacting term limits.** Gerrymandered districts protect incumbents and political parties. Noncompetitive districts empower extreme partisans to elect officials who increase polarization. Eliminating gerrymandering can be accomplished by creating a nonpartisan redistricting commission for all elected officials. Modern computer software allows district maps to be made compact, contiguous, racially fair, and to protect communities.

   It will also be necessary to enact term limits and limit outside employment of elected officials to prevent conflicts of interest. Currently elected officials control the districts in which they run, and incumbent advantages mean they stay in office indefinitely. Too many use their clout to lobby other units of government for favorable decisions for their private clients. Finally, a revolving door in which officials leave office only to lobby for the companies they formerly regulated is far too common.

4. **Creating and strengthening the position of inspectors general and establishing anticorruption commissions.** This is especially critical in governments that do not have them. Inspectors general have the authority to investigate fraud, corruption, and waste, and their reports make government more effective and efficient. Their investigations are often the first step in uncovering and prosecuting corruption.

   A related step in cities and countries that have moved from corrupt to non-corrupt has been the formation of anticorruption commissions like those in Hong Kong and Sydney, Australia. Some U.S. cities and states have established ethics commissions to ensure that public officials understand anticorruption laws by which they must abide.

5. **Reversing unhelpful court decisions.** Under the *Citizens United* decision, the courts currently allow unlimited campaign contributions and require an explicit quid pro quo to prove corruption. A constitutional

change may be needed and creating fairer elections certainly requires new laws. Contribution limits and campaign expenditure restrictions will be resisted by current elected officials as well as by wealthy individuals and businesses that are currently able to buy access.

6. **Providing public funding of political campaigns.** Public funding with full disclosure of contributions and limits on spending is essential. Public funding is being used in some states and cities, but expanding public funding of campaigns to all levels of government is needed. While a majority of voters don't like the rich having too much influence, many don't want their tax dollars spent on politicians. A shift in public opinion is required to bring about more widespread public funding.

   A good reform strategy is to increase the number of cities and states using public funding of campaigns. As the public gets used to this at the local level, they will be more willing to push for further public funding of national elections.

7. **Electing public officials who carry through on their promises of ethics reform.** Many candidates run on a platform of reform, but, once elected to office, often continue old corrupt practices. One such example is Governor Rod Blagojevich of Illinois, who was elected as a reformer but wound up in prison for political corruption.

8. **Destroying political machines.** This is accomplished by eliminating their foundations of political patronage, corrupt government contracts, and favoritism. Some states also need to consolidate local units of government. For example, in Illinois there are seven thousand separate units of local government, each with their own governing boards, employees, and ability to tax. This sheer multiplicity creates many nooks and crannies in which small-time political bosses can flourish.

   Patronage is now illegal in the United States and corrupt contracts have always been illegal, but bid-rigging and bribes continue. Enforcing these restrictions requires constant vigilance.

9. **Increasing citizen participation.** We can increase participation in elections and government by methods such as universal voter registration, neighborhood government in urban areas, changing legislative procedures to promote citizen involvement, and strengthening the democratic legislative process. Too often governments lock citizens out from any meaningful form of participation except voting every two or four years.

   Very specific steps that can be taken to increase participation include automatic voter registration; granting the vote to sixteen-year-olds; re-enfranchising former convicted felons; ending voter suppression; extending early voting; and utilizing mail-in ballots. We should consider the option used in twenty-six other countries, which fine those who fail to vote. The higher the level of citizen participation, the less room there is for corruption.

For these changes to be enacted, the public must understand the problem of corruption and how political corruption undermines our democracy. Moreover, we will have to demand these changes consistently over a long period of time. Usually, reforms occur piecemeal and episodically because of a major scandal. Examples include the Watergate scandal that prompted the campaign finance reforms of the 1970s and the Blagojevich scandal in 2008 that prompted new Illinois ethics laws. Perhaps the heightened level of corruption and the challenges to democracy by the Trump administration will inspire the election of new public officials and cause an aroused public to pass the laws and constitutional amendments necessary to curb corruption.

A new president has been elected. But the transformation of America has only begun.

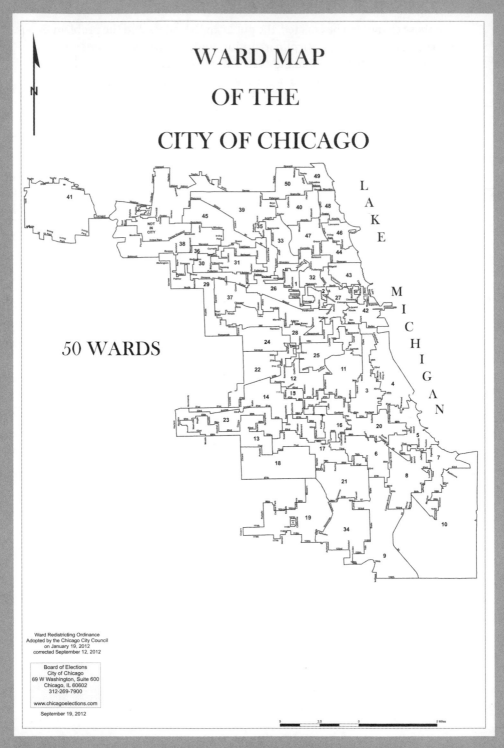

WARD MAP

OF THE

CITY OF CHICAGO

50 WARDS

The fifty gerrymandered wards of Chicago.

8

Structural Problems

Indicted Fourteenth Ward alderman Ed Burke was fond of telling the story of an Indiana woman who lived in a small town. She went to her lawyer to make a change in her will so she would be buried in Chicago. Her lawyer asked her why she wanted to do that, since she had lived her entire life in the small Indiana town. She said, "Well, as you know, I have always been a strong Democrat. I want to be buried in Chicago, so I can continue to vote after I am gone." This apocryphal story always got a good laugh from Chicago audiences. But, in truth, dead people and people who no longer lived in Chicago have voted in Chicago elections. Vote fraud was rampant, and it was worse when paper ballots were still cast. Switching to having votes counted by scanners and computers has lessened vote fraud. As the Chicago election experience illustrates, while there are structural barriers blocking democracy, they can be partially cured with structural solutions. Increased voter participation through automatic voter registration, early voting, and greater use of mail-in ballots, along with a clear paper trail so contested elections can be recounted by hand, have reduced the instances of election fraud.

There are many obstacles to democracy's rebirth. Some are entrenched problems, like income and racial inequality, money in politics, low levels of citizen participation, and corruption. Beyond these fundamental societal problems, however, are a series of structural deficiencies that create barriers to the practice of democracy. These are more easily solved. These deficiencies can be cured by simple legal changes. In short, there are defects in our laws, institutions, and political practices that can be corrected. But correcting them will require overwhelming public support and the enactment of new laws. Some authors call these necessary laws, norms, and practices the guardrails of democracy.

I had my first personal encounter with these problems more than fifty years ago. In Chicago in 1969, I had just founded the Independent Precinct Organization (IPO) with those who had backed Eugene McCarthy, Robert Kennedy, or George McGovern (who had lost the Democratic Party nomination to Hubert Humphrey, who then lost the 1968 presidential election to Richard Nixon). Our goal as an organization was to fight the Chicago Democratic machine headed by Boss Richard J. Daley. Rather than bringing change from the top down, as we had hoped to do in the 1968 presidential election, we were going to build a better democracy from the bottom up, through our grassroots election and issue campaigns.

As a part of our early efforts, we backed two independent aldermanic candidates in March 1969 elections: William Singer, who was successfully elected to represent Chicago's Forty-fourth Ward; and John Stevens, who narrowly lost the aldermanic election for the Forty-Second Ward. Singer's Forty-Fourth Ward covered the Lincoln Park and Lakeview communities. Bill Singer's win set off a series of independent Democratic victories over machine candidates on the North Side of Chicago for the next several decades. Those victories allowed us to remake Chicago political history.

The story was different in the Forty-Second Ward, which ranged from the Magnificent Mile along Lake Shore Drive and Michigan Avenue, where wealthy Whites lived, to the Cabrini-Green Chicago Housing Authority projects on the west end of the ward, where poor Blacks were packed tightly together.

The Democratic machine ran as their Forty-Second Ward aldermanic candidate, Raymond Fried, a White precinct captain who had cancer and didn't make a single public appearance during the campaign. Because the machine was so powerful, he was able to win without campaigning. After being elected in March 1969, he died in office in January 1970. In that 1969 aldermanic election, IPO backed a charismatic candidate with deep ties to the community, African American social worker John Stevens.

It was an intense campaign. Our Forty-Second Ward campaign headquarters was firebombed in the dead of night—fortunately, none of our volunteers was hurt, but our headquarters was destroyed. A nearby church offered us space, where we completed the campaign with at least some protection from arson and physical attacks. As they say in Chicago, "politics ain't bean bag"—it isn't a game, but political warfare with no holds barred. That 1969 aldermanic campaign in the Forty-Second Ward was hard fought. Voters were intimidated and election fraud defeated our efforts at reform.

One of the structural problems that we faced in the election was that Chicago had recently switched to using voting machines. Of the sixty precincts in the Forty-Second Ward, four still voted by paper ballot—and all four paper-ballot precincts were in the African American Cabrini-Green area, whereas the wealthier White precincts all had voting machines. Although our candidate, John Stevens, was a well-known social worker in Cabrini-Green and was backed by many community leaders, the Forty-Second Ward Democratic organization under Ward committeeman and Cook County Board president "Gentleman" George Dunne was one of the strongest machine ward organizations in Chicago.

When the primary election was over, Fried avoided a runoff by a mere 742 votes out of more than 10,000 cast. We lost all four paper-ballot precincts by massive margins but won much of the rest of the ward. Our worst loss was in one paper-ballot precinct that tallied 400 votes for Fried to only 12 for Stevens.

Unlike voting machines and, later, punch cards and computer screens, paper-ballot voting provided an easy way to steal the election in the Forty-Second Ward. Two methods were used.

One was perfected by a precinct captain nicknamed "short pencil Pete," a legendary precinct worker from earlier in the twentieth century. He hid a short pencil between his fingers and marked the ballots for the party's preferred candidate as the voters came into vote. If somehow voters cast a vote for the "wrong" candidate, he simply marked an X on the paper ballot to vote for the machine candidate as well, canceling out the offending vote. His favored candidate won by a landslide every election.

More commonly, a party precinct captain stood outside each paper-ballot polling place. Having taken the first ballot when the polls opened, he marked the stolen ballot for the machine candidate. As voters entered the polling place, they were given a ballot already marked for candidates favored by the machine. When they signed in, one of the election judges handed them a blank ballot, which they took to the voting booth. Behind the balloting curtain, voters pocketed the blank ballot and instead inserted into the ballot box the precinct captain's pre-marked ballot. When they returned the unmarked ballot to the precinct captain, they were given a $5 IOU to be cashed at a grocery store or bar, usually for liquor.

The precinct captain then marked the blank ballet for the next voter to use. And the voter who cast the fraudulent vote went off to cash in their reward. In Louisiana, they might receive a pork chop sandwich for their vote instead. Other states used other forms of walking-around money to bribe voters.[1]

Without reliable poll watchers representing reform candidates at each polling place, it was impossible to catch these forms of voter fraud or unscrupulous precinct captains voting in the name of deceased voters, as the story by Alderman Burke memorializes. Chicago overcame these crude forms of election fraud by changing laws and regulations governing elections. Today, Chicago has a broad-based coalition of more than twenty reform organizations under the umbrella of Just Democracy that continues the advocacy for election reform that groups like IPO began fifty years ago. And victories continue to be won on automatic voter registration, extended early voting, mail-in voting, and safer voter methods that leave a paper-ballot trail. Unfortunately, at the same time, there are voter suppression efforts, with more than seventeen other states with restrictive voter identity laws and a number of states passing more restrictions on voting since the 2020 election.[2]

Broader Structural Problems

Still in the twenty-first century, structural problems inhibit and constrain representative democracy in the same way that earlier political machine practices defeated reformers. These are beyond the practical problems of outright voter fraud, income inequality, money in political campaigns, and illicit lobbying. While some voter suppression and voting fraud methods used in the paper-ballot era have been remedied, new ones have emerged in our electronic age. Democracy is still being subverted by structural flaws.

Tom Ginsburg and Aziz Huq identify five mechanisms by which democratic erosion unfolds and undermines liberal constitutional democracies:

- making constitutional amendments that alter basic governance arrangements,
- eliminating checks between different branches,
- centralizing and politicizing the bureaucracy,
- contracting or distorting the shared public sphere, and
- eliminating effective political competition and rotation out of elected office[3]

These trends are happening all over the world, and unfortunately they are beginning to occur in the United States.[4] We need to act now to prevent democratic erosions like these before it is too late. Here are some obvious structural reforms to be undertaken.

The Electoral College

Emblematic of these broader challenges to representative democracy is the Electoral College. The Electoral College is a body of electors established by Article 2 of the Constitution that convenes every four years for the purpose of electing the president and vice president.

If we were writing the American Constitution today, we would not include the Electoral College as the method of determining the outcome of presidential elections. Here's why: while the Electoral College was meant to ensure the election of eminently qualified candidates and prevent the election of unqualified demagogues, it is patently undemocratic. Smaller states are overrepresented, electors are chosen by the presidential campaigns in practice, and the winner-take-all system of electing the electors in the states can skew the outcome.

There have been five times in our history when the Electoral College vote did not match the popular vote, resulting in the election of a president who did not receive the popular majority. This occurred with the election of John Quincy Adams in 1824, Rutherford Hayes in 1876, Grover Cleveland in 1888, George W. Bush in 2000, and Donald Trump in 2016.[5]

Our founding fathers expected voters to select electors who would exercise their own good judgment in selecting the best president for the country rather than necessarily voting for the popular favorite. In practice, however, most voters today do not personally know any of the elector candidates and so cannot select electors for their judgment. Rather, they vote for the slate backing the presidential candidate they prefer, and those electors are, in turn, pledged to vote for that candidate. Thus, the idea that the electors would vote independently for the best candidate is undermined in practice. For instance, efforts to convince electors not to vote for Donald Trump to whom they were pledged because of fears of how he would govern failed dramatically in 2016.

Since the number of electors is equal to the total number of members of Congress in both houses, and because each state has two senators, less-populous states are overrepresented in the Electoral College. Moreover, since in all but two states (Maine and Nebraska) winning a plurality delivers all of the state's electoral votes to the winning candidate, the number-two candidate is not represented by a proportional vote.

The current Electoral College has 538 electors, and a majority of 270 is needed for a candidate to be elected president. In 2016, as a result of the plurality rule by which the candidate with the most popular votes wins all the electors in most states, Donald Trump received 306 electoral votes, compared to Hillary Clinton's 232. This happened even though Clinton won the popular vote by nearly 3 million votes.[6] Four years later, because he won by more than 7 million votes, Joe Biden reversed the result and received 306 electoral votes to Donald Trump's 232 votes.[7]

The nature of the winner-take-all vote for electors in nearly all states, and the way the Electoral College math works, mean that the presidential election usually turns on the electors from only a handful of states that currently include Arizona, Florida, Georgia, Michigan, Ohio, Pennsylvania, and Wisconsin—not on the vote across the nation. One practical consequence is that these states receive most of the campaign attention, while voters in other states don't get as much information on the candidates. "For example, in 2012 Democrat Barack Obama spent a total of $404 million on television ads; of this total, $173 million was spent in Florida where hundreds of thousands of ads aired. . . . In 2016, 94 percent of general election campaign events from July through November 8 (Election Day) occurred in just twelve swing states, and two-thirds of all candidate events occurred in just six highly contested states."[8] The same pattern was repeated in 2020.

Added to this is the fact that nearly four million Americans in U.S. commonwealth territories of Puerto Rico, Guam, Northern Mariana Islands, American Samoa, and U.S. Virgin Islands do not get to vote for electors. These U.S. citizens are disenfranchised. If their votes counted, presidential candidates, and the federal government, would be forced to deal with their issues. As it is, Americans living in these territories are more likely to be left to cope with economic problems, hurricanes, and rising sea levels on their own without either a vote for president or the representation that other states have in Congress.

Eliminating the Electoral College altogether would take a constitutional amendment and is unlikely to succeed in the near future. There have already been hundreds of proposed amendments to change or eliminate the Electoral College, which is more than any other constitutional change. None has yet been adopted.[9] Supreme Court justice Ruth Bader Ginsburg suggested that such a change to the Constitution is "more theoretical than real. It's largely a dream because our Constitution is . . . hard to amend."[10]

In addition, eliminating the Electoral College is blocked not only by the least-populous states in order to maintain their advantage but also by the political parties and southern states, where politicians want to preserve the region's White supremacy in the twenty-first century.[11] An alternative solution is for each of the states to distribute the electors based on something other than a winner-take-all formula. Currently, in forty-eight states, a candidate who wins a state by 51 percent of the popular vote wins all of that state's electors. Rather, electors could be distributed on a proportional basis. So a candidate with 51 percent of the vote would get approximately 51 percent of the electors. This solution has already been adopted by a few states such as Maine (1972) and Nebraska (1996).

In the Electoral College we have a clear example of a structural problem in our representative democracy that has been recognized for decades, but for which we have not found the political will to resolve. Election results often reflect the majority will of the voters, but not always. As the 2000 and

2016 elections indicate, the problem is becoming more acute and occurring more often with significant consequences.

A common reform proposal is eliminating the Electoral College and deciding the presidency by popular vote. But that would take a constitutional amendment that, in turn, would require overwhelming popular support over decades. (For instance, the Equal Rights Amendment to the Constitution has failed to pass after more than three decades of support by a majority of states.)

An alternative solution that can be more easily achieved requires only changing the election laws in a few states. The National Popular Vote, as it is called, is supported by nonpartisan and progressive organizations like Common Cause. As of this writing, fifteen states and Washington, D.C., have already adopted it as law, bringing to 195 the total number of electoral votes so committed.[12] These states have signed an interstate compact to allocate all of their state's Electoral College votes to the candidate who receives the most votes nationwide. This is possible because states, not the federal government, control election procedures. This change comes into force only after enough states sign on to the pact that the total number of Electoral College votes committed is at least 270.[13] With the National Popular Vote legislation, future presidential elections will be decided solely by the national popular vote as soon as a handful of new states with 82 electoral votes collectively join the compact.

Some scholars argue that we should *not* change the Electoral College either by constitutional amendment or by interstate compact. They suggest that the National Popular Vote is unconstitutional and that such a constitutional amendment is unwise. One conservative advocate puts it this way: "One danger of all these attacks on the Electoral College is, of course, that we lose the state-by-state system designed by the Framers and its protections against regionalism and fraud. . . . The more fundamental danger is that these attacks undermine the Constitution as a whole. Arguments that the Constitution is outmoded and that democracy is an end in itself are arguments that can just as easily be turned against any of the constitutional checks and balances that have preserved free government in America for well over two centuries."[14] I cite these arguments because it is important to realize that proposed structural changes have wide-ranging, and often unintended, consequences.

I think, however, that the effect of elections won by candidates who did not receive a majority vote has in undermining faith in democracy outweighs fears of weakening the Constitution. After all, there have been twenty-seven amendments to the Constitution adopted so far without destroying it. Most importantly, despite arguments by critics, a majority of Americans support the change.

If we don't have the political will to make a relatively simple change in the laws and procedures such as eliminating the Electoral College, which a vast majority of people agree inhibit representative democracy, it seems unlikely that we will muster the strength to fix the other structural problems that impede democracy.

Gerrymandering

One consistently identified problem in our representative democracy is gerrymandered districts from which we elect our U.S. Representatives, state legislators, aldermen, and city council members, a situation that allows incumbents to stay in office for decades. This contributes to the more than 90 percent reelection rate for members of Congress. Not only do gerrymandered districts keep incumbents in office too long without meaningful competition, but they provide the party drawing the maps more seats than it deserves based on the vote it received. Since winning the party primary in gerrymandered districts means winning the election, the resulting partisan districts make it more likely that party extremists who can motivate their base will be elected. So, officials become more extreme and polarizing.

The term "gerrymandering" goes back to 1812, so it is scarcely a new concept. Simply put, it means to draw electoral districts to advantage political parties in order to help them win elections, and often, to protect the incumbents. It derives its name from the drawing of legislative districts in 1812 to favor the Democratic-Republican Party that was signed into law by Massachusetts governor Elbridge Gerry. The name is a hybrid of Gerry's name and "salamander," which is what the resulting map of one of the legislative districts looked like.

The maps of the First and Second Wards of Chicago vividly illustrate the way in which districts can be gerrymandered. They cut across unrelated communities and across racial groups. They can be seen visually to have holes and weird configurations.

The practice of gerrymandering has grown more common today as legislators "crack" (split away party supporters from a district), "pack" (cram all party supporters in a single district so they can't win in others), or "hijack" districts (put two legislators from the same party in the same district to compete against each other). In 2016, the congressional districts were redrawn in North Carolina so that gerrymandered districts caused the North Carolina congressional delegation to be represented by ten Republicans to three Democrats, which is a much greater partisan imbalance than in the electorate.[15] The 2020 elections, with court redrawn districts, changed the

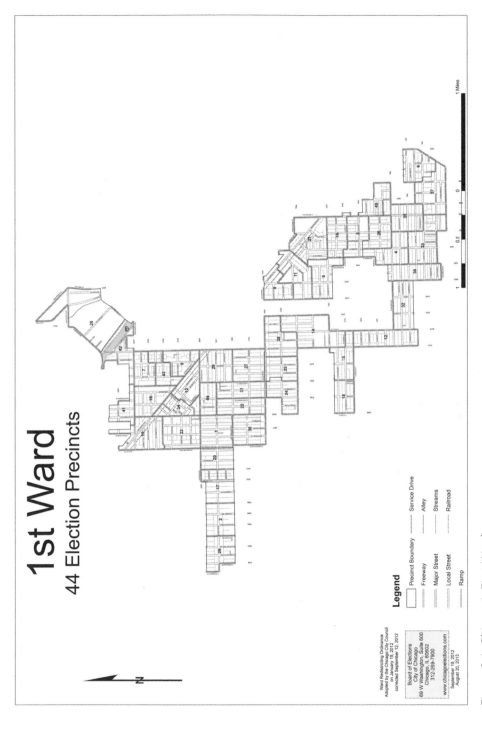

Figure 8.1: Chicago's First Ward.

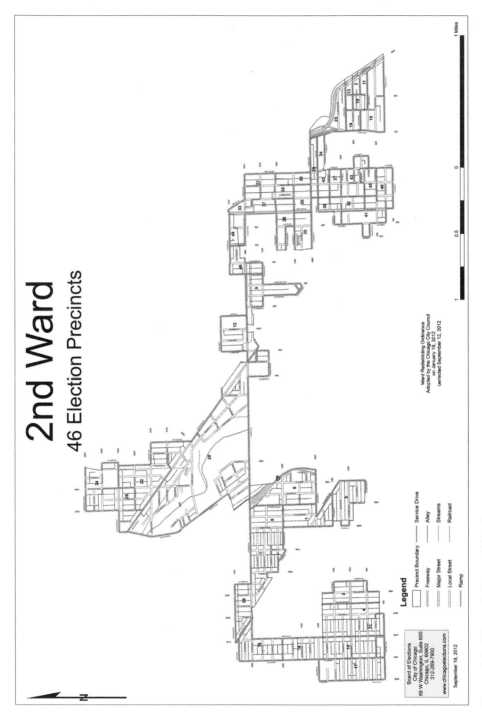

Figure 8.2: Chicago's Second Ward.

congressional balance to eight Republicans and five Democrats. Electoral maps matter.

There are now statistical tests such as the Chikina-Frieze-Pegden mathematical test to determine whether or not a district has been gerrymandered. Wendy Cho and Simon Rubinstein-Salzedo explain: "The Supreme Court has declared that partisan gerrymandering is unconstitutional. However, it has yet to identify a manageable standard for adjudicating partisan gerrymandering. That is, the Court does not know how to distinguish a partisan gerrymander from a constitutional electoral map. It has stated that partisan information may be used in the construction of a map, and that '[t]he central problem is determining when political gerrymandering has gone too far.' That is, 'the issue is one of how much is too much" (Vieth v. Jubelirer, 541 U.S. 267 2004).[16] Simply put, we can now answer the court's question of when has partisan gerrymandering gone too far. However, in recent Supreme Court cases, such as the consolidated cases of Rucho v. Common Cause and Lamone v. Benisek in 2018, the court ruled that, until these statistical tests are accepted by the courts, "partisan gerrymandering claims present political questions beyond the reach of the federal courts."[17]

However, as Nonpartisan Vote argues, the severe consequences of gerrymandering still need to be corrected: "Indeed as modern targeting technology has made redistricting a partisan science, there has been a steady drop in Congressional seats where the outcome is in doubt and voters have a meaningful choice. In 2014, only 39 out of 435 seats were considered competitive. 2016 was even worse. Just 37—less than 10%—of U.S. House races were seriously contested[—]the lowest in five decades. Safe districts limit voter choice. They fuel hyper-partisanship. Incumbents of either party need only appeal to their base. There is less incentive to broaden their message, compromise or have meaningful debates on issues."[18] Reformers argue: "voters are supposed to select their elected representatives," but with gerrymandering "legislators use their power over the process to pick their voters."[19] Since as many as one-third of the uncompetitiveness of congressional districts since the early 1980s are due to gerrymandering, this is not a trivial issue.[20]

Like the Electoral College, the problem of gerrymandering has a simple solution: appoint a nonpartisan redistricting committee to redraw the electoral districts using computer technology after each decadal census. In the 2000s for instance, Arizona and California voters took the redistricting power away from their state legislators. Six other states already use bipartisan commissions to draw district maps: Hawai'i, Iowa, Idaho, Montana, New Jersey, and Washington.[21] Of course, legislators resist having their power to control their own districts for reelection taken away from them. So, for this reform to succeed in most states, it is going to have to be adopted by binding referendum. However, many states don't have binding referendums by citizen initiative, and where they do, the requirements to get a proposed change on the ballot may be difficult to overcome.

Beyond having nonpartisan commissions rather than politicians draw their own reelection district maps, it is important to have objective standards for how those districts should be drawn. Current standards, which unfortunately are not consistently applied, emphasize compactness and contiguousness. Additionally, because our society is still plagued by institutional racism and racial bias in voting, the federal courts have required that some districts be drawn to guarantee minority group representation. A supermajority of 65 percent of the constituents in heavily minority districts should be minorities, and local elections, such as city council elections, should be held in districts rather than at-large to insure that minorities have some representation in local government.

A further standard in constructing districts should be that, to the extent possible, communities are protected so that their elected representatives reflect community views and interests. In Chicago, the Englewood community is divided between five wards and represented by five aldermen. For each alderman, Englewood is only a small portion of their ward and not their primary focus.[22] Similarly, Chinatown, the most concentrated residential area of Chinese Americans in Chicago before the 2010 census, was divided into four wards and had four aldermen.[23] These kinds of divided districts make it hard for elected officials to consider the interests and shared views of a community and to be held accountable for representing it.

Term Limits

In addition to the nonpartisan redistricting, another popular reform proposal is term limits for public officials. The effort to impose term limits on office holders has been more successful than nonpartisan redistricting. Term limits were imposed on some officials in both Athens and the Roman Republic. In the United States, the most notable limit on terms of office has been restricting the presidency to ten years in office. Thirty-seven states have some limit on the terms of the governors, while fifteen state legislatures impose term limits. However, six states that previously adopted term limits have had them overturned by either the courts or legislatures.[24] Most public officials fight against the imposition of term limits, thereby slowing additional adoptions of the reform.

New York, Houston, Los Angeles, and Philadelphia are among the cities that have adopted term limits on their mayor and city councils. This issue is being discussed in many big cities and term limits have been adopted in many suburbs. Term limits are useful tools to keep mayors from becoming too autocratic and to curb corruption of long-serving city council members. In Chicago, Mayors Richard J. Daley and Richard M. Daley both served over twenty years in office, and I personally observed how they became more dictatorial the longer they stayed. Similarly, Fourteenth Ward alderman Ed Burke served for more than fifty years in that position before being indicted for public corruption.

Term limits' effect on state public policy, such as budgets and spending, has been more limited than its advocates have hoped. The scholarly consensus seems to be that, while term limits may cause turnover in office holders, and thereby, increase the number of women and minorities in office, the public-policy implications are less definitive. Term limits do not offer the silver bullet to reform representative democracy that some of its more avid supporters claim. To obtain better representation, we have to elect better public officials. While ending gerrymandering and adopting term limits for public officials may make government more representative, these solutions are not a panacea.

Voter Suppression and Automatic Voter Registration

Voter suppression is the attempt to limit voting by groups such as minorities and former felons by making registering to vote more difficult and by purging the voting roles to partisan advantage. The American Civil Liberties Union, one of many organizations fighting against voter suppression, reached this conclusion: "Voting rights are under attack nationwide as states pass voter suppression laws. These laws lead to significant burdens for eligible voters trying to exercise their most fundamental constitutional right. Since 2008, states across the country have passed measures to make it harder for Americans—particularly black people, the elderly, students, and people with disabilities—to exercise their fundamental right to cast a ballot. These measures include cuts to early voting, voter ID laws, and purges of voter rolls."[25]

While much of the attention has been on voter suppression efforts in the South—to prevent minorities, who are likely to support the Democrats, from voting—efforts to prevent students and others from voting in northern states has occurred as well. The general strategy to prevent voter suppression has been to contest these efforts in court. And there has been some success in overcoming voter restrictions, but efforts to restrict the vote continue.

A broader response has been the movement to reinstate provisions of the Voting Rights Act. Ever since this act passed in 1965, there has been an effort to eliminate barriers to voting by making voting easier, lowering the voting age to eighteen (Twenty-Sixth Amendment, 1971), and stopping racial discrimination by the poll tax or constitution tests, which were commonly deployed in southern states after Reconstruction more than a century ago.

The House of Representatives voted to reinstate the Voting Rights Act on December 2019 and again in 2021.However, the bill was killed in the Senate in 2019 and would have been vetoed by President Trump should it have passed. It or the broader For the People Act (HR 1) ideally will eventually be adopted now that President Biden has been elected. Yet, it will take major public pressure to overcome the filibuster that is used in the Senate to block voting rights legislation. Still as a matter of fairness, justice, and protection of our fundamental rights as citizens in a democracy, adopting at least the John Lewis Voting Rights Act is necessary. But, as of this writing, it has not occurred.

Another alternative to countering voter suppression is automatic voter registration (AVR), which would make the states responsible for registering all eligible voters unless the voter actively opts out. Fifteen states and the District of Columbia have instituted AVR. Other states have introduced legislation to enact AVR.

The Brennan Center for Justice explains why AVR makes such a difference:

> Automatic voter registration (AVR) is an innovative policy that streamlines the way Americans register to vote. AVR makes two simple, yet transformative, changes to the way our country has traditionally registered voters. First, AVR makes voter registration "opt-out" instead of "opt-in"—eligible citizens who interact with government agencies are registered to vote or have their existing registration information updated, unless they affirmatively decline. Again, the voter can opt-out; it is not compulsory registration. Second, those agencies transfer voter registration information electronically to election officials instead of using paper registration forms. These common-sense reforms increase registration rates, clean up the voter rolls, and save states money.[26]

The idea of registering all citizens to vote is common in other democratic countries that register everyone when they are born or when they get the equivalent of our Social Security number. Of course, most other democratic countries also have a higher level of voting than we do. In many ways, AVR is simply a way to begin to narrow that difference between us and other democracies.

Decades ago, states began to make voter registration easier with motor voter laws that let citizens register when they applied for drivers' licenses. However, those still tended to be opt-in situations in which the citizen had to request registration and, usually, fill out a paper form. Still, motor voter increased voter registration by making registering easier.

States at the same time began to allow mail-in ballots without requiring a specific reason for needing to vote by mail such as illness or travel. And many states began to set up early voting polling places as early as a month before the election to allow citizens to vote at times more convenient to them than Election Day.

AVR, coupled with expansion of early voting and easier absentee or mail-in voting, have simplified the registration and voting process in a number of states. Thus, the 2020 election had the largest number of Americans ever to vote in an election and the highest percentage since 1900.

At the same time, efforts at voter suppression by limiting early voting, requiring multiple forms of identification to be able to vote, preventing former convicted felons from voting, and reckless purging of voting rolls continue to occur. Republicans, in particular, have wanted to prevent minorities from voting because they are more likely to vote Democratic. Republicans are especially concerned about state legislative, congressional, and national elections where minority voting can change the balance of power between the political parties.

A related issue is the restoration of voting rights for convicted felons who have served their sentences. Many states are currently enacting stricter laws, but at the time of writing, in the District of Columbia, Maine, and Vermont, felons do not lose their voting rights, while in nineteen states their rights are automatically restored on release from prison. In eighteen states, former felons lose their voting rights while they are on parole or probation; "former felons may also have to pay any outstanding fines, fees or restitution before their rights are restored." In eleven states, felons lose their rights indefinitely if they have committed certain crimes.[27]

The general trend, highlighted by the passage of a citizen-initiated referendum in Florida in 2018, has been to restore the voting rights of former felons. This single reform can potentially increase the voting rolls by hundreds of thousands of voters in more populous states. However, this does not always happen easily or quickly. For instance, Florida requires that all fines and fees must be paid before a former felon can register to vote. As a result, in 2020 only about 31,000 of the potential 418,000 inmates released since 1997 (or about 8 percent) registered to vote.[28] This helped the Republicans to win in Florida in 2020, since the former felons, who were heavily minorities, registered as Democratic at about twice the rate as Republican.

At the other end of the spectrum from voter suppression is a movement to expand the electorate by letting immigrants, who are not yet citizens, vote in local elections. One in ten, or more than 25 million, people in the United States are foreign-born noncitizens. In some communities, the proportion is much larger.

Political scientist Ron Hayduk argues that letting noncitizens vote is an issue of fairness and of practicing democracy:

> It is only fair that persons who are a part of a local community and contribute to its tax base and economy should have a say in the formulation of laws and policies that have a direct bearing on their well-being. . . . [Allowing immigrants to vote] will help politically integrate individuals and groups who have a vested interest in our collective future. . . .
>
> . . . Restoring voting rights to all residents would update democracy for these global times.[29]

In general, structural impediments to voting undermine democracy. The general direction over the two and a half centuries of U.S. politics has been to allow ever more people to vote. For instance, the property requirement to vote has been struck, and women, minorities, and eighteen-year-olds have been added to the voting roles. Currently, there is serious discussion of allowing sixteen-year-olds to vote.

There is widespread agreement that free, fair, and vigorously contested elections in which all votes are counted equally are the hallmarks of democracy. While there have to be some limits as to who can vote, enfranchising as many people as possible has been the goal. That requires removing undue structural barriers to voting.

Electoral Integrity and Electronic Voting

We usually assume that our elections are the best, the gold standard of the world. However, measured across a variety of standards, such as electoral laws, electoral procedures, media coverage, campaign finance, and voting process, we come in 32nd among 163 nations in the Perception of Election Integrity. This index is maintained by the Electoral Integrity Project and supported by agencies like UNESCO and the International Political Science Association. One month after each national election, experts are surveyed to determine how the country did in election integrity an election integrity score. The United States scores only 70 on a 100-point scale, and thus, we are tied with countries like Barbados and South Africa, far below countries with the best electoral integrity, like Norway, Costa Rica, and Germany.[30]

Obviously, many structural improvements are needed to improve the election process in the United States. Certainly, this is true in Chicago, with its long history of rigged and crooked elections.

However, we need to move beyond simply preventing fraud and making elections fair. A number of nations require citizens to vote or pay a fine if they don't vote. Even if we aren't ready to take this step yet, we should consider technological advances and how elections might better be held in the future. Certainly mail-in ballots increased voting in the 2020 election, with more than 65 million votes cast by that method.[31] However, with our extensive use of electronic devices and the Internet, shouldn't we shift mostly to electronic voting? Why do citizens have to physically go to their precinct polling place, or to an early voting site, when they could vote on their computer in the same way we take surveys, pay our bills, and communicate with friends and groups around the world? While there is still a significant digital divide that might prevent some people from voting electronically even from a smartphone, that divide has begun to close significantly during the pandemic.

Furthermore, most states already use some form of electronic voting at their polling places such as punch cards, optical scanners, and specialized voting kiosks with direct-recording electronic voting systems. The results of those votes are then transmitted electronically to a centralized vote tabulating center. In these cases, each voter is certified and the computer links are secure. Moreover, there is usually a paper trail so the ballots can be recounted if the election outcome is disputed.

However, there have been broader experiments in electronic voting. In Arizona, the Democratic Party ran the 2000 party presidential primary entirely by Internet voting. Each voter was sent a personalized identification number (PIN) in order to vote. That election went off without a hitch and was popular with the voters.

Various forms of electronic Internet voting have been used in other countries. However, due to Internet security concerns, some countries like the Netherlands and Germany have stopped using Internet voting. So, the transition to electronic voting does need to be made carefully.

There is especially a concern with possible election tampering and voter fraud. Particularly because Russia hacked Ukrainian elections and attempted to do so with the 2016 and 2020 U.S. presidential elections, as detailed in the Mueller report.[32] Currently, the best protection against electronically rigged elections is to require a paper trail so that the elections can be monitored and recounted if necessary. This can't be done with Internet voting from computers at home or on smartphones even when safeguards are used to reduce fraud.

Given how much of our lives is now conducted online—credit card purchasing, banking, buying stocks and bonds, Facebook posts, Tweets, and seeking dating partners—it is likely that we will move to electronic voting within the next decade. The issue, therefore, is not whether we will have voting by Internet, but how to make it accurate, safe, secure, and verifiable.

There will be an up-front cost to switch to a secure electronic system, but, as we determined after the problems with the punch cards in the 2000 election, there is really no choice but to make the investment to update our voting systems. This is especially the case because the voting equipment purchased in the aftermath of the 2000 election fiasco is now approaching the end of its useful life—it will have to be replaced in any case. In the 2020 election, states were able handle the switch to mail-in voting, and now more than one-third of us vote that way. So, we should plan in future elections to move to voting systems that encourage greater voter participation.

Voting Systems

Beyond electoral integrity and electronic voting are issues of how our votes should be counted, how presidential candidates should be chosen, and whether we should have more uniform electoral procedures.

There are those who advocate major changes, such as that instead of our winner-take-all system we use proportional representation and ranked-choice voting.[33] In proportional representation, three to five candidates, instead of just one, are elected from each district. Each party elects the number of candidates based on the vote they receive. For example, if Republicans receive 70 percent of the vote and Democrats receive 30 percent, then in a district with three elected officials, the Republicans would elect their top two candidates on the ballot and Democrats would elect one. Many parliamentary democracies use this system, but it will not easily be adopted in the United States because we are not used to using it.

A somewhat easier reform to get adopted, which Maine has instituted, is ranked-choice voting. In brief, voters don't just vote for their first choice. Instead, they rank candidates in their order of preference. If no candidate receives a majority, the candidate who receives the fewest first-place votes is dropped, and whichever candidate received each voter's second-place vote, is awarded their vote. This process is continued until a candidate receives a clear majority and is declared elected. Thus, the strength of voters' support is registered and recognized in the outcome.[34]

Implementing either proportional representation or ranked-choice voting will have to overcome the fact that they are unfamiliar to most Americans. However, Maine voters have been satisfied with their ranked-choice voting system and have resisted all attempts by the legislature to end it. However, there have been multiple attempts both to expand Maine's ranked-choice voting to the presidential election and to repeal it. Even in Maine, it remains a controversial system.[35]

Even if alternative electoral systems are not adopted and elections continue to be run by state and local governments, eventually passing a broader Voting Rights Act, such as HR 1, which is pending at the time of writing, with uniform national standards for registration, voting, and tallying the vote is essential. It is also important to allow the U.S. Department of Justice to intervene when voters' rights are denied. The current hodgepodge of laws and practices across the country means that, in practice, not all citizens have equal voting rights.

An Undemocratic Congress

We have many structural problems that go beyond our electoral systems. For instance, the U.S. Congress, which is meant to be the heart of our representative democracy, has become undemocratic in both its structure and in its procedures.

The U.S. Senate is undemocratic because it represents small states and rural areas proportionally more than big states and urban areas. Large states and cities are not fairly represented. Page and Gilens put it this way: "Over the years as our population has concentrated more and more heavily in metropolitan areas, the small-rural-state bias of the Senate has become a more and more serious problem. Equal state representation in the senate, a relic from political compromises made two and a half centuries ago, has now become the most undemocratic single feature of our Constitution. [We can change that] by Constitutional amendment."[36] These authors recommend that states vote to create a constitutional convention to consider a broad package of "democracy amendments" that might cause Congress and the states to adopt a narrower constitutional amendment to democratize the Senate. However, since it takes thirty-eight states to ratify constitutional amendments, it would mean that some states that would lose power in the Senate would have to vote for it, which is not an easy sell.

The House of Representatives, which is often called "the people's house" because it is more representative than the Senate, poses a different problem because each of the 435 representatives now represents more than 750,000 people. The limit of 435 members was set in the Permanent Apportionment Act of 1929. It would be possible by a simple amendment to that act to create a larger legislative body, but the larger the body, the more unwieldy it becomes. It is hard to believe, for example, that a body of 900 or more members would function very well. And even if the House of Representatives were doubled in size, it would be difficult for House members to represent even 400,000 or so people effectively.

As already discussed, worse problems in the representativeness of Congress are the gerrymandered districts from which member of the House are elected and the need to constantly raise huge amounts of money to run their campaigns. Both gerrymandering and the current campaign finance system undermine Congress.

This situation is worsened by the two-year terms of office for members of the House of Representatives. Michael Golden writes that

> the U.S. House of Representatives is the only federal legislative chamber of any advanced country in the world that carries two-year terms. . . . The time crunch of the two-year terms puts restrictive leashes around the necks of our representatives in two major ways. First, members of Congress cannot let their focus wander very far astray from their next election. . . . Secondly, with the heavy lift of job responsibilities that U.S. representatives are expected to perform both in Washington, D. C. and back home in their districts, the constant campaign . . . steals countless hours from our leaders.[37]

The two-year terms were originally meant to keep House members close to their constituents by having them rejected or reelected often. Four-year terms would better suit our twenty-first-century conditions. I found the four-year term best when I served in the Chicago City Council. Not having to stand for reelection every two years gave me time to create neighborhood government institutions and attend frequent community meetings, which in turn kept me better in touch with the needs and desires of my constituents.

Beyond structural limitations such as a rural/small state bias, size of congressional districts, and two-year terms for members of the House, serious procedural problems make Congress less democratic, less responsive, and interfere with democratic lawmaking. Some of the hamstringing arises from formal rules that would require Congress's agreement to change, but it can also arise from informal precedence that there is little political will to change yet. But that may be changing as frustration with the gridlock of Congress grows.

In the Senate, filibuster rules allow unlimited debate until sixty senators vote for cloture. It is used to block action on controversial legislation and has been used more frequently in recent years. Rules amendments in 2013 and 2017 have allowed cloture on presidential appointments by majority vote, but filibusters still require sixty votes to provide cloture to vote on substantive legislation. Often even the threat of filibuster can kill legislation.

Two suggested filibuster reforms are "insist[ing] that filibusters actually' engage in debate, not just threaten it" and insisting that "all debate be germane" to the legislative issue.[38] Many people have suggested that the filibuster be outlawed altogether, but others point out that during our history it has sometimes been used to protect minority rights. Therefore, it ought to be regulated and limited, but not eliminated.

A similar undemocratic procedure to the filibuster is the hold that allows any senator to hold up presidential nominations until they release it. As Page and Gilens argue, "We know of no coherent argument in favor of the hold. It should simply be abolished. . . . It is just a traditional practice . . . that could be overturned by Senate majority leaders and chairs of the committees that vet appointments."[39]

In the House of Representatives, the informal Hastert rule prevents bills coming to the floor for a vote unless a *majority* of the *majority party caucus* favors it. Thus, controversial measures often die in committee. This means that even a small and ideologically extreme minority of the House can block legislation they oppose, as the Tea Party Republicans did repeatedly during the Obama administration.

This requirement of a majority of the majority has now been partly modified by adoption of the "290 rule," which requires that any measure that has been in committee too long can be brought to the floor for debate and vote if 290 members or more (three-fifths of the House) cosponsor the legislation. This change, advocated by the Problem Solver Caucus in the House, illustrates that it is possible to change rules that inhibit representative democracy. It would be better if it didn't take as many members of the House to discharge legislation from committees and onto the floor for a vote, but this is a positive step forward.

At the time the House of Representatives is at least partially modifying the Hastert rule, the U.S. Senate has become procedurally less democratic. Senate Majority Leader Mitch McConnell at the end of 2019 had more than three hundred bills that had passed the House of Representatives on his desk, but he refused to send them to Senate committees for consideration. This situation actually worsened in 2020, when he blocked most key legislation without any democratic process. It remains a problem in the evenly divided Senate after the 2020 election, when there are fifty Democratic-caucusing and fifty Republican senators. Although some major Biden legislation funding COVID-19 vaccines and economic recovery measures have become law, much legislation is still blocked.

Thus far, undemocratic rules and procedures have worsened gridlock in Congress, which in turn has undermined the public's faith in the institution. Gallup public opinion polls record that 7 percent of Americans say that they have a great deal or quite a lot of faith in Congress, dramatically down from 42 percent in 1973, when Gallup started asking the question.[40] As Michael

Golden writes, "these backwards Senate [and House] rules allow for a massive distortion and skewing of the system. It is time to put a stop to all of the stopping."[41]

Structural Barriers to Democracy in Chicago

Chicago is in many ways an extreme case of the defects in democracy. Just as in national politics, Chicago, and Illinois more generally, have gerrymandered legislative districts. Since the 2010 census, many states with Republicans in control of the state legislature and the governor gerrymandered districts to their party's distinct advantage. This is happening again in 2021. But in Illinois, it is the Democrats who do the gerrymandering.

The process in 2010 was led by long-time Illinois General Assembly speaker Mike Madigan, who redrew districts to make it easier to elect more Democrats to Congress and the state legislature. As a result, in 2020 Democrats controlled 13 of the 18 congressional seats, 73 of 118 seats in the legislature, and 41 of the 59 seats in the state senate. Even after Madigan resigned because of corruption scandals, the process continued in 2021 without him at the helm. It is hard to estimate how much of this Democratic dominance in Illinois can be assigned to gerrymandering, since the state has generally been becoming more Democratic in recent elections. But there is no doubt that at least some of the Democratic dominance is due to unfair drawing of districts.

The Chicago City Council has also been gerrymandered for decades. From 1960 until 2020, lawsuits have been filed after every decade's redistricting except one. I have been an expert witness for the plaintiffs opposing the gerrymandering in most of those lawsuits that occurred like clockwork every decade. In most of those cases, the courts concluded that the Chicago wards were racially gerrymandered unfairly by the Democratic Party. I have thus had a front-row seat to this gerrymandering and to the court cases that followed.

In general terms, lawsuits that succeed in forcing redistricting do so because this form of racial discrimination shortchanges Black and Latino minority populations. These redistricting lawsuits have also proved gerrymandering had the political purpose to protect incumbents, boost the control of the Democratic political machine, and promote the election of White machine aldermen in racially divided districts purposely drawn to provide a White majority in the city council.

The most consequential gerrymandering lawsuit was filed after the redistricting of 1981. In 1986, federal courts held that Chicago wards had indeed been racially gerrymandered and ordered new elections in seven of the fifty wards. Winning the majority of those special elections changed the balance of power in the Chicago City Council from a 29–21 stalemate known as the Council Wars in which White, old-guard machine aldermen opposed African American mayor Harold Washington. After special elections were held, there was 26–24 aldermanic support of the mayor. By the next 1987 election, Harold was able to muster a 40–10 majority in the council. Redistricting allowed the mayor and his new city council majority to pass a progressive reform agenda long bottled up in the machine-dominated council.

Of course, the Chicago machine used more than gerrymandering to maintain its ironfisted control. For instance, it failed to countenance term limits. So, Mayor Richard M. Daley served twenty-two years; his father, Richard J. Daley, twenty-one years; and long-serving aldermen like Ed Burke more than fifty years. Illinois state legislators served similar lengths of time, with Michael Madigan serving as legislator since 1970 and as Speaker for nineteen two-year terms, until he was defeated in the attempt to hold onto his position in 2021. He was still the longest-serving speaker of a state legislature in U.S. history when he resigned his legislative seat.

Yet, these were not the only methods used to control elections and government in Illinois. A few of the political machine's other tactics are described below.

Election Dates

The Democratic Party has persisted in holding elections on dates most likely to suppress voter participation. In fact, many state and local elections around the country are held separately from the national presidential and congressional elections. While the intent may have originally been to separate local elections from national political forces and partisanship, the net effect is to depress voter participation. In many municipal elections in cities and suburbs, fewer than 20 percent of registered voters participate. Even in Chicago, the participation rate is normally in the 30 to 40 percent range, at least 20 percent lower than in national elections.

Worse, Chicago primary elections for city offices are held in February, while presidential and nonpresidential national primary elections are held in early March. With Chicago winters typically lasting until April, any direct door-to-door canvassing (along with petition gathering and voter registration drives) has to be conducted during the harsh Chicago winter, frequently in snow and below-zero temperatures. Often, Election Day is a cold and snowy winter day that suppresses voter turnout.

These elections could just as easily be held in the spring when contacting voters was easier and Election Day was warmer and more hospitable for treks to the polls. In fact, the 2022 primary election has been rescheduled for June because the delay in census data has made the redrawing of congressional districts later, but this is an exception.

The mayoral, aldermanic, and key state elections, like the elections of the governor and key executive officials in the state, could easily be moved to the presidential cycle, or at least to the off-year congressional election cycle, which would increase voter turnout. Instead, the political machine continues this tradition of winter primary elections to hold down the vote since it can rely on the party faithful to show up and keep the machine officials in office despite the weather.

Sham Candidates

Another tactic used by the Chicago machine and candidates elsewhere in the country is putting up fake or fraudulent candidates. Sham, fake, satirical, and ghost candidates remain an ongoing feature of U.S. electoral politics. In recognition of this, the Federal Election Commission has begun to punish individuals who file as fake candidates in federal elections.[42] During the 2016 presidential election, "Deez Nuts," "Butt Stuff," "Master Alexander Soy Sauce," "Taters Gordh First," and "Limberbutt McCubbins" all filed as potential candidates; similar names appeared for fake candidates in 2020. While some sham candidates mock or satirize America's electoral system, other sham candidates are deployed as a means of manipulating the electoral process. This is a covert form of voter suppression: attempting to confuse voters, creating a spoiler effect in order to elect another candidate, and keeping an incumbent official in power.[43] Sham candidates succeed because their names appeal to the subjective biases of a portion of the electorate such as ideology or ethnic identity or as a means of exploiting loopholes in electoral systems.

There are numerous examples of sham candidates in recent elections.[44] The single district plurality system makes it possible to win if sufficient votes can be siphoned off from opposing candidates. For instance, in 2020, Florida sham candidate Alex Rodriguez helped to defeat a strong incumbent candidate: "Alex Rodriguez, the shadow candidate, ran against an incumbent with the same last name, Democratic Sen. José Javier Rodríguez, and appropriated the senator's signature issue: climate change. Though he had no website and no noticeable campaign, the ghost candidate managed to nab 6,382 of the more than 215,000 votes cast in the race—enough to tip the balance to Republican Ileana Garcia, founder of a group called Latinas for Trump, who won by just 32 votes after a manual recount, according to the county canvassing board."[45] Sham candidates like Alex Rodriguez undermine democracy.

As one would expect, because of culture of machine politics and corruption, there have been many examples in Illinois of the use of sham candidates.[46] One that was litigated was the case of Michael Madigan, the long-serving Speaker of Illinois General Assembly. He was opposed by Latino reform candidate, Jason Gonzales, in the 2016 primary election. Madigan's campaign put up two sham candidates to help guarantee his victory.[47] However, the court ruled in this case that even if the voters could have known about the sham candidates and their collective votes added to those for Gonzales, it would not be enough to defeat Madigan.[48]

This use of sham candidates, as alleged in the 2016 Madigan election, creates voter confusion, undermines elections, and weakens representative democracy. The fundamental test of democracy is free, fair, and frequent elections. The use of sham candidates makes elections unfair and alters the outcome to protect the incumbent or the dominant political party. It happens all too frequently in Chicago, in Illinois, and in too many cities and states.

Judicial Elections

A further problem in Illinois is the *seemingly* democratic process of electing judges. In this case, more candidates on the ballot harms justice. Chicago voters are faced with a bedsheet ballot, which in some years has as many as a hundred judicial candidates on it. Although a plethora of lawyer organizations and some newspapers make endorsements, the end result is a list of possible candidates that most voters have no information about. To make matters worse, since 2014, the Republican Party in Cook County has not even offered candidates in the general election because they have no hope of winning. So, voters are faced with no real choice in judicial elections. As in too many one-party-dominated elections around the country, only the primary matters.

In 1970, Illinois voters defeated a referendum that would have instituted merit selection of judges. Although two-thirds of the states and the District of Columbia now select some or all of their judges by merit selection, in Illinois, merit selection was defeated at the polls.[49] The political parties thus maintained their clout in nominating and electing judges.

In rural areas with smaller populations and only a few judicial positions, voters are more familiar with the candidates. In such situations, there may be good reasons to elect judges. In dense urban areas, however, with a hundred candidates and more than forty judges to be elected or retained, the system is unworkable.

One modest reform, which was enacted more than a decade ago, was to switch some judicial districts from county-wide to smaller and racially homogenous districts. This meant that the persistent problem of too few underrepresented minorities on the bench could be partially overcome. As a result, the Circuit Court of Cook County is now more diverse than it has ever been. And women have gained more representation as judges as well. But a bad Black, Latino, or woman judge is little improvement over a bad, unaccountable, White male judge.

The election of judges was originally pursued as an attempt to prevent cronyism and to wrestle the judiciary away from local machines.[50] A better system, however, is merit selection of judges. Under merit selection, a nonpartisan commission of lawyers and nonlawyers recruits and evaluates applicants. The commission then submits the names of usually three of the most qualified applicants to the governor, who makes a final selection. At least for urban areas and statewide courts, merit selection is a superior way to guarantee the impartially of the judicial system.

Unfortunately, the judicial selection process has become more politicized at the federal level. More partisan judges are being appointed by presidents and confirmed by the dominant political party in the U.S. Senate. Recommendations by the bar associates carry little weight. The last two Supreme Court appointments, Neil Gorsuch and Brett Kavanaugh, were selected by a president who only won a minority of the popular vote, and both judges were confirmed by Senate Republicans who received just 43 percent of the total Senate vote share in the 2016 election.[51] Thus, the appointments were not only partisan, but they were made by a party with minority electoral support.

According to Gallup public opinion polls, while 54 percent of the public approves of the way the Supreme Court is doing its job, only 16 percent have a great deal of confidence in the judicial branch, headed by the Supreme Court.[52] It appears that reforms are needed at the national level as well as adoption of merit selection at the state and local level.

There is also discussion of imposing term limits of perhaps ten years rather than appointment of federal judges for life. As federal judicial appointments become more partisan, there is clearly a need for reform.[53]

The Need for Reform

There are many other structural barriers to representative democracy. Not only do we face grand challenges to our democracy like income inequality, money in politics, and corruption, but we are beset with structural problems. Some are obviously undemocratic institutions like the Electoral College or the apportionment of the U.S. Senate. Others are procedural legislative rules like those in the U.S. Congress. We have gerrymandering, sham candidates, and a lack of term limits as well.

Structural solutions used in other countries might be adopted to make our elections more competitive and representative. They include ranked-choice voting, open primaries, and fusion voting, in which more than one party backs a candidate.[54] Perfecting our representative democracy requires constant reforms and experimentation.

These reforms will be adopted only if political movements mobilize citizens to demand changes. The obvious democratic failures and poor policy choices (such as the chaotic federal response to the pandemic) of the Trump era should provide the motivation for structural reforms at all levels of government. They are likely to begin at the most local level and get enacted at the national level as they are proven successful.

Ganesh Siatarmann reminds us in *The Crisis of the Middle-Class Constitution* of an anecdote from the twentieth century: "There is a story about Franklin Roosevelt meeting with some reformers who outlined an aggressive agenda for change. Roosevelt said he agreed with them and wanted to act. But he then then told the reformers, 'Now make me do it.'"[55] We cannot expect the economic elites and their political allies to act to bring about major structural reforms for us. We must mobilize and force those in power to act.

While most structural problems can be solved incrementally, some are so serious as to require constitutional amendments or even calling a constitutional convention. However, a constitutional convention in the current polarized political climate dominated by cries of fake news is not an ideal atmosphere for the calm consideration of the future of our democracy. We should, instead, experiment at the local level while enacting what reforms we can at the national level now. We might begin by enacting the overdue Equal Rights Amendment to the Constitution to at long last guarantee women full rights with men.

As we consider structural reforms, it is important to be very clear about the goals we seek to achieve. Do we want maximum democratic participation, or do we seek to improve representation along with suitable checks and balances to prevent mob rule or hasty and ill-informed decisions by a passionate majority swayed by emotions and demagoguery? It is clear to people of various political persuasions that we need structural reforms, but we must first decide exactly why we are reforming. Then we must be cautious and careful in enacting reforms to prevent unintended consequences. Finally, we must be ready to reform again as needed. However, the faults are glaring in our present system and the guardrails of our democracy are serious weakened. Reform, we must.

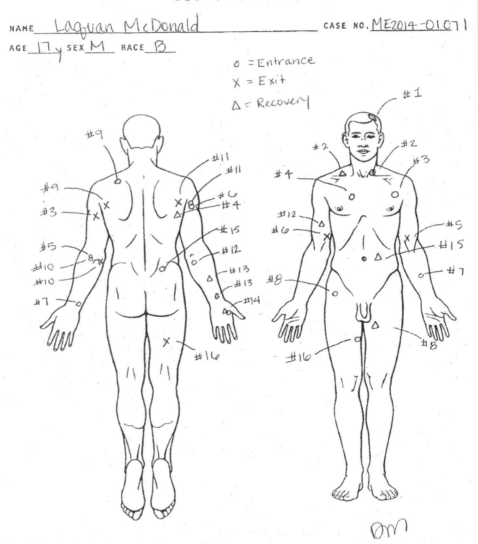

Autopsy report of the sixteen gunshot wounds that killed Laquan McDonald in 2014. (Source: Invisible Institute, https://invisible.institute/news/autopsy-of-laquan-mcdonald)

9

Cascading Crises

During the last few years we have faced exceptional crises. First, there were the continuing problems of police accountability, crime, and the criminal justice system. Institutional racism was again exposed in the shooting death of African American teenager Trayvon Martin in 2013 and the subsequent acquittal of George Zimmerman, who shot him. Then came the shooting of Michael Brown by White police officer Darren Wilson in Ferguson, Missouri, in 2014.[1] Additional cases of police killing African Americans included Eric Garner, Breonna Taylor, and George Floyd, and too many others. The Black Lives Matter movement arose from these tragic deaths.[2]

The photograph that introduces this chapter comes from the autopsy report on the shooting of Chicagoan Laquan McDonald by White police officer Jason Van Dyke in 2014.[3] His murder was caught on videotape. The police said that he had lunged at them with a knife, but the videotape showed that he was not a threat. The lawsuit against the city and its police department was eventually settled for $16 million, and Officer Jason Van Dyke was convicted of second-degree murder.

In addition to the institutional racism and Black Lives Matter protests that shook the nation, a COVID-19 pandemic began in 2020, followed by the deepest economic recession since the Great Depression, the critical 2020 presidential election, and the insurrection at the Capitol on January 6, 2021. All these cascading crises as President Biden named them in his inaugural address on January 20, 2021, placed great pressure on our political system. However, they also offer the opportunity for major transformation rather than continuing incremental changes inadequate to these challenges.

Black Lives Matter

The shooting of Michael Brown in the St. Louis suburb in 2014 has been followed by a continuous series of shooting deaths of African Americans by police and White vigilantes.

Racism in America has existed for more than four hundred years, beginning with the slavery that existed at our founding and the near-genocide of the Native Americans who were here long before Whites arrived. Even after the Civil War provided emancipation, legal segregation continued until it was eliminated in the 1960s by the civil rights movement, court cases, and the passage of national civil rights laws. Unfortunately, racial discrimination and institutional racism continue today. One manifestation of it is the police shootings of minorities, and another is the disproportionate minority deaths during the pandemic.

In response to continuing racism, people organized under the broad umbrella of the Black Lives Matter movement (BLM). Protests continued, often peacefully in marches and demonstrations and on the Internet under the hashtag #BlackLivesMatter. While most protests were nonviolent, sometimes they resulted in violence and store looting. One example was the looting and vandalism that occurred in Chicago's downtown business district and the posh Magnificent Mile shopping area after a police-involved shooting in August 2020.[4]

Not only Africa Americans supported the BLM movement. Some Whites joined the protests, posted signs of support in their yards, signed petitions, and joined calls for government action. Whereas fewer than 20 percent of Whites supported the civil rights demonstrations in the 1960s; in 2020, more than 20 million people participated in BLM protests. As of June 2020, 60 percent of Whites supported BLM, although White support has lessened somewhat since then.[5]

Black Lives Matter began as "an ideological and political intervention in a world where Black lives are systematically and intentionally targeted for demise." By 2018, BLM's goal had evolved into the broader purpose of "build[ing] the kind of society where people can live with dignity and respect."[6]

Those efforts brought counterprotests by conservatives, such as the White supremacist rally in Charlottesville, Virginia, in August 2017.[7] In the period from that Unite the Right march in 2017 until 2019, the Anti-Defamation League calculated that White supremacists murdered at least seventy-three African Americans around the nation.[8] The number continues to grow as the murders continued in 2020 with cases like the White teen, Kyle Rittenhouse, killing two African American protestors in Kenosha, Wisconsin.[9] Then in

2021, the White supremacist and pro-Trump organizations mounted an insurrection in which the Capitol was attacked while Congress was certifying the outcome of the 2020 election.

Despite opposition by White supremacists and conservatives, the Black Lives Matter movement continued to grow. Between 2013 and 2018, the hashtag #BlackLivesMatter was used 30 million times. The BLM movement has spread around the world, but the underlying problem of institutional racism continues here and elsewhere.

Chicago's Torture Machine

The problem of systemic racism did not begin in Chicago. But Chicago, like the rest of the United States, has a long history of racism. Despite the city lying north of the Mason-Dixon Line, and thereby spared much of the history of slavery, and despite fighting on the side of the North in the Civil War, racial segregation and racial discrimination were common there.

Racism and racial clashes in Chicago were highlighted by the terrible race riot of 1919. After the end of the thirteen-day riot that began with the killing of a Black youth who swam across an informal racial boundary in Lake Michigan, "38 were dead (23 Blacks, 15 whites), 537 injured, and 1,000 Black families made homeless."[10] Unfortunately, this was not the last racial violence nor the last race riot in Chicago.

The *Encyclopedia of Chicago* summarizes more recent racial history this way:

> The aftermath of World War II saw a revival of white attacks on black mobility, mostly on the city's South and Southwest Sides, but also in the western industrial suburb of Cicero. Aspiring African American professionals seeking to obtain improved housing beyond the increasingly overcrowded South Side ghetto, whether in private residences or in the new public housing developments constructed by the Chicago Housing Authority, were frequently greeted by attempted arsons, bombings, and angry white mobs often numbering into the thousands. The 1951 Cicero riot, in particular, lasting several nights and involving roughly two to five thousand white protesters, attracted worldwide condemnation.[11]

Theoretically, racial conflict was to have ended in the 1960s with passage of civil rights laws and affirmative action programs. But, of course, it didn't. There was a Latino race riot in West Town and Humboldt Park on Chicago's Northwest Side in the summer of 1966 and an African America race riot on the West Side of Chicago after the assassination of the Reverend Dr. Martin

Luther King Jr. in 1968.[12] Meanwhile, Chicago continued to be one of the most residentially segregated cities in the country, with a segregation index in the 1960s of 94 percent, declining to about 72 percent today. This means that, even today, 72 percent of Chicagoans would have to move to live in neighborhoods with the same racial mix as the metropolitan region as a whole. Not only are Black neighborhoods separated from White neighborhoods, but Latinos and Asian Americans also live in segregated neighborhoods and suburbs.[13]

There is a direct link between race, income, and wealth in Chicagoland. Inner-city Blacks tend to be poor, whereas White suburbanites after all this time still tend to be richer.[14] This led to what William Julius Wilson calls the permanent underclass, where poor Blacks tended to bequeath the same poverty to their children and their children's children.[15] Poor Black communities were transformed into permanent ghettoes even after high-rise public housing was torn down and those poor Black residents dispersed.

To top all, crime was greater in African American neighborhoods, as were police abuse and a lack of police accountability. One of the most extreme cases was "the torture machine" created under Chicago South Side police commander Jon Burge.[16]

Police violence against African Americans in Chicago has been a constant. The famous murders of Black Panthers Fred Hampton and Mark Clark in a raid by States Attorney police in the 1960s is one well-known case. But blatant police abuse continued for decades afterward. Between 1972 and 1991, Commander Jon Burge directly participated in or approved the torture of over a hundred African Americans. This continued with tacit approval of the police department and the Chicago political machine. For instance, it was ignored by States Attorney Richard M. Daley, who would go on to be elected mayor and remain in office for twenty-two years despite the coverup of the Burge police abuses.[17]

A key case occurred in 1982, when two uniformed Chicago police officers were murdered. Jon Burge was assigned to solve the case.

> Under Burge's command, incensed [Chicago Police Department] officers, kicked in doors, ransacked homes, beat up numerous residents, and once suspects were in custody, tortured the Black men they suspected of being involved in or having knowledge of the crime. Several had bags placed over their heads in what is known in the international torture lexicon as "dry submarino," at least one man was beaten on the bottoms of his feet and testicles, and another was taken to police station roof, where one of his hands was placed in a bolt cutter. Upward of two hundred complaints were filed against the [Chicago Police Department] by abused persons,

ranging from mothers and a fireman, and a taxi cab driver and alleged street gang members.[18]

Brothers Andrew and Jackie Wilson confessed to the crime, after being beaten and tortured, including by electric shock to their testicles by a torture machine the cops under Burge frequently used. Their coerced confessions caused them to be found guilty of these police murders. Andrew was sentenced to death but released before his execution, while his brother, Jackie, was given a double life sentence, even though both were innocent, as would be proven in court decades later.

It took until 1991 for the City of Chicago to admit that Jon Burge and his men had tortured hundreds of Blacks. Over the following decades, the city would pay more than $170 million in restitution and over twenty Black men would be freed from death row and prison because their confessions, which played a major role in their convictions, had been obtained by torture.[19] Later evidence, such as DNA evidence, proved them innocent of the crimes with which they had been charged.

Police abuse, from unfair traffic stops to unjustified shootings on the street and torture at the hands of police officers, fueled the racial clashes and protest marches that would become a prominent feature of twenty-first-century America. They increased as social and economic conditions in African American neighborhoods declined. Crime in minority communities continued to increase. There were 774 homicides in Chicago in 2020 alone, which was 50 percent more than the 506 murders in 2019.[20] When the year ended, beyond the murders nearly four thousand people had been shot; many were civilians caught in the crossfire. Most of those shot were minorities.

Structural Racism

African Americans and other minority groups have made significant gains since the civil rights movement's success in drawing attention to racial segregation and discrimination. However, despite civil right laws dating back to the 1960s, structural racism remains. As the BLM demonstrations since 2013 have highlighted, there is still much to be done. To resolve this continuing crisis, simply electing a few more African Americans, women, and other minorities to positions within the government is insufficient.

One positive effect of the BLM protests has been that they have caused discussions in universities, corporations, and other institutions about what can be done to lessen structural racism. There are louder calls for reparations for slavery and to defund the police today. New laws have been passed ending monetary bail policies in some states and restoring voting rights to former felons. Yet the mechanisms by which institutional racism can be undone more broadly are in dispute. It is clear that a more systematic response to structural racism is needed. The possibility of some form of reparations for past slavery and discrimination is beginning to be considered.[21] In 2021, Evanston, Illinois, became the first town to officially adopt reparation payments for Blacks.[22]

The Black Lives Matter movement has given voice, raised consciousness, and focused public attention on police abuse and the carceral prison regime. It has focused attention on broader structural racism. However, earlier political movements such as the Occupy movement, which similarly utilized protests and raised consciousness, failed to provide the necessary organizational strengthen and coherent strategy to change society. Will the Black Lives Matter movement be more successful?

Cedric Johnson writes: "Black Lives Matter protests have popularized an anti-racist perspective on this contemporary mode of stress policing or 'warrior policing,' how it emerged historically and who are its primary victims. Black Lives Matter protests have also advanced equally wrong-headed assumptions about politics, namely the sense that the renewal of militant black ethnic politics, focused on unity and black empowerment is sufficient to the historical task of ending police violence and mass incarceration. . . . [This] will never happen without achieving broad popular support."[23]

Johnson argues that broad popular support is needed not only within the Black community, as nostalgic calls for the 1960s Black Power movement have suggested. Instead, there must be alliances with progressive Whites, Latinos, and Asian Americans. As Johnson puts it, a movement that can change the racial situation in the United States must be "hewn from hard rock of the society as it exists."[24] Alliances across racial lines must be built if structural racism is to be ended.

Those have at least been begun in Chicago with the election of Mayor Lori Lightfoot by a rainbow coalition. But tensions remain between progressive organizations and aldermen and the mayor over the pace of social and economic reforms.

It is critical that we make strides to overcome structural racism if there is to be a rebirth of American democracy. We must have justice and democracy not just for some people, but for all of us. The Black Lives Matter protests are a challenge to act, but as Johnson writes, it will be necessary to build a movement of change from the "hard rock of society as it exists" today.

The COVID-19 Pandemic

As Americans we face multiple challenges. As this book is being written, we have passed the third wave of the COVID-19 pandemic. By June 2021, over six hundred thousand lives had been lost to the virus in the United States alone.[25] The death toll will rise even higher before an effective vaccine can be distributed to defeat the virus. The worldwide death toll reached 3.76 million.[26] In Illinois alone, more than 15,000 people died from among the more than 900,000 who were infected by the end of 2020.[27] The number of people who caught the disease and who may suffer permanent health effects are many times those who died (who were generally only about 5 percent of those who are infected).

This is the greatest U.S. and worldwide health crisis since the flu epidemic of 1918 and the polio outbreaks of the 1950s. It has changed lifestyles in the United States and around the world. Most governments have imposed isolation, social distancing, quarantining, frequent hand-washing requirements, and closed schools and businesses to try get the pandemic under control. We moved to distance learning in schools and online commercial interactions using software programs like Zoom. Instead of doing our shopping at local businesses, many of us shifted to online shopping. Jobs were lost. Hospitals and medical personnel became overwhelmed, and frequently we didn't have enough hospital beds to treat all the sick. There was a shortage of personal protective equipment (PPE). People couldn't go to restaurants, movies, or sporting events for over a year. Even after the pandemic is over, we will not just return to the patterns of the pre-pandemic period. Like the Great Depression and World War II, the pandemic has permanently affected this generation and is reordering society.

There was also a racial aspect of this crisis. By the first six months of the pandemic, it was "well-established that Black residents and Hispanic residents [were] roughly 2.5 times more likely to get the virus than white residents, [and] more likely to die from it."[28] There was racial injustice even in this pandemic.

The pandemic also affected the election of 2020 and politicians' careers. While Chicago mayor Lori Lightfoot and Illinois governor J. B. Pritzker had approval ratings of over 70 percent for their handling of the pandemic, President Trump's approval rating for handling the pandemic was only 37 percent.[29] It is most likely that President Donald Trump was defeated in the November 2020 election because of his mishandling of the pandemic. However, the fact that he still got 71 million votes indicated that Americans were not united in their response either to the former president or to the pandemic. Many Americans refused to wear masks and take basic health safety precautions. This accounted for the high rate of inflection and a death toll higher than many other countries. Then when vaccines became widely available for free, many Americans refused to take them.

Even when politicians had positive approval ratings, public support, and won reelection, governing problems worsened. For instance, the City of Chicago had an $800 million gap in the 2020 city budget and an additional $1.2 billion gap in 2021 in a $13 billion budget. Taxes had to be raised and services cut as a result of the pandemic.

Like the BLM protests, however, the pandemic could force major changes. "The response to COVID-19 could be similarly far-reaching. . . . The responses could start with a guarantee of universal health care."[30] Our experiences with the pandemic could cause us to redesign our cities and our country to limit pollution, ease climate change, prevent future health crises, ease inequality, and rebuild our democracy. There are moments in history that are "plastic hours," when an "prolonged statis gives way to motion. . . . They require the right alignment of public opinion, political power, and events—usually a crisis."[31] A crisis like the pandemic provides the motivation to get more radical things done if we have the political will to do them.

Economic Recession

As this book is being written, the full extent of the economic recession is still unfolding. We know that we have been in the greatest recession since the Great Depression of the 1930s. It was worse than the recession caused by the terrorist attacks of 2001 and the Great Recession caused by the housing market collapse of 2008, even though there was beginning to be an economic recovery in 2021.

This recession caused by the pandemic produced losses in gross domestic product (GDP) and, more importantly, a loss of jobs and income for millions of Americans.[32]

> Total nonfarm employment fell by a staggering 20.8 million jobs in April [2020], largely erasing the gains from a decade of job growth. Despite increases in the months since, there were 10.7 million fewer jobs on private and government payrolls in September than there were in February [2020].
>
> Private employment rose by 877,000 jobs in September but remain[ed] 9.8 million below its February level. Federal government employment fell by 34,000 . . . ; state employment fell by 48,000 . . . ; and local employment fell by 134,000.[33]

The debate as of the end of 2020 was whether there would be a V-shaped, sharp recovery or a much longer, drawn-out U recovery. But either way, it was expected that as many as 50 percent of bars and restaurants would permanently close before the pandemic ended, that millions of small businesses would go bankrupt, and that unemployment for millions of Americans might be permanent. It is unlikely that we will return to the pre-pandemic economy. New patterns of work seem inevitable.

In the early months of the pandemic, the full economic effects were partially muted by a federal stimulus package that provided individuals with a one-time $1,200 payment and increased levels of unemployment benefits. State and local government shortfalls meant higher taxes, fewer government services, and lost government jobs as well.

By 2021, there were still more home foreclosures, renters unable to pay their rent and being evicted, and utility shutoffs for millions of homes. Travel and convention spending plummeted, devastating the hospitality and travel industries despite some federal assistance. Essential services like public safety, hospitals, grocery stores, and pharmacies remained open and employment of their "essential workers" even increased, but their greater contact with infected individuals also meant that many of these workers contracted the virus and died.[34]

Covid-19 vaccine distribution began in the United States on December 14, 2020.[35] By June 2021, 172 million people had been vaccinated, or about 64 percent of the population.[36] Because of the negative effects of the pandemic, the economy could not fully recover until the pandemic was under control. We must now decide how to rebuild the economy, since vaccines to prevent the virus are being distributed to the public and cases and deaths are dropping.

It is clear, however, that rebuilding will take years. During the pandemic, the pattern of work itself changed as more of us worked remotely. Even when the pandemic is finally brought under control, automation, particularly in the form of artificial intelligence, will eliminate more jobs in the new economy that will follow.

Particularly in this period of economic recovery, changing patterns of work, and automation, it will be necessary to extend government regulation of the economy in order to guide it in a more humane direction while allowing technological innovation to continue. We may have to experiment with new programs like guaranteed employment, and we will clearly have to provide better continuing education for citizens as their job requirements change. We will have to be able to regulate transnational corporations, control international trade, and promote rapid economic development for nations that have been left behind in the previous century. In short, we need to rebuild our economy in a way that facilitates overcoming the challenges to democracy outlined in this book.

The 2020 Presidential Election

Many prayed that the 2020 election would resolve all our problems, lead directly to the reinvigoration of our democracy, and provide solutions to all our society's issues.

The good news was that participation increased in the election. More than 155 million people cast their ballots. Voting increased, even among segments of our population like voters eighteen to twenty-five years old, who traditionally do not vote in high numbers. And Donald Trump was defeated as the incumbent president who was undermining our democracy. The election of the Biden-Harris ticket gives us the opportunity to begin rebuilding America. However, while Donald Trump may have failed in critical ways—such as failing to provide positive leadership during the pandemic, further polarizing our country and coming to symbolize our democratic failures—most of our problems existed long before he became president.

The bad news of the 2020 election was that it was the most expensive election in our nation's history costing $14 billion.[37] The cost of successful campaigns and the role of the wealthy and powerful interest groups greatly outweighed the contributions of average citizens once again. While as citizens we voted in record numbers, we do not yet control the direction of the country. Money still speaks with a loud voice in government and gridlock is still the basic condition in Washington, D.C.

In the aftermath of the 2020 election, President Trump claimed that the election was stolen. As newspaper columnist Steve Chapman writes, "Donald Trump, it has long been clear, is an aspiring despot who resists all checks on his power and greed and undermines the rule of law at every opportunity. Even so, his wrathful attempt to overturn the results of a free and fair election qualifies as shocking. . . . We couldn't have imagined that he would use his position so relentlessly to try to disenfranchise millions of voters.[38] Trump's opposition would lay the groundwork for the later insurrection as Congress was certifying the election.

Still, Joe Biden became president after the 2020 election. But the Democrats lost seats in the House of Representatives and held only a bare majority. Gridlock in Washington has mostly continued. President Biden is not able to get his more radical policies adopted even as major changes are needed to overcome the challenges we face at the end of the pandemic.

The 2022 elections will once again be about the direction of the nation, and no party is likely to win decisive majorities in Congress. Because of national gridlock, much of the slow work of rebuilding our democracy will necessarily have to begin at the local level—the building of social and political movements for change and experimenting with solutions to our problems in order to build the necessary base of support and knowledge. Our work was not done with the conclusion of the 2020 election. Instead, the election has given us the opportunity for change and rebirth. It does not guarantee it.

Insurrection and Attempted Coup

On January 6, 2021, a mob of Trump supporters, including white supremacists, QAnon activists, and right-wing extremists, stormed the U.S. Capitol. They were, at President Trump's urging, there to demand that Congress reject the election of Joe Biden as president by failing to certify his election. They overwhelmed the Capitol Police and interrupted congressional proceedings. Four hours later, they were finally cleared from the Capitol by the police and National Guard troops so Congress could continue the certification process.

The insurrection was a violent attempt to prevent the new government from taking office and was meant to allow Trump to continue as president. In the ensuing battle, five people were killed and dozens injured.[39] As of June 2021, over five hundred people have been charged with crimes for their participation in the insurrection.[40]

Although there have been many demonstrations in the past, the last time the Capitol was overrun was the War of 1812, when the British attacked and burned the building. So this was not politics as usual or a peaceful protest. But it is a sign of how divided the country has become. Congress is still so divided that it was unable to create an independent commission to report on the insurrection as the 9/11 Commission reported on the terrorist attacks of September 11, 2001.

One result of the insurrection was that President Trump was impeached for a second time by the House of Representatives, but once again, he was not convicted by the U.S. Senate when the mostly party-line vote was taken.

Despite this attempted coup, the inauguration of Joe Biden and Kamala Harris as president and vice president occurred as scheduled on January 20, 2021. However, more than twenty-five thousand National Guard troops were needed to protect the city so that it could occur without violence.

Former President Trump and his Republican and conservative supporters have continued to claim that the election was stolen and that Trump is the rightful president. So, while the pandemic is beginning to be under control and economic recovery has started, our democracy is not yet secure.

The Effect of Crisis

While Donald Trump failed to provide positive leadership during the pandemic, polarized the country, promoted an insurrection, and continues to deny the outcome of the 2020 election, he is not alone the cause of our democracy's crisis. He may symbolize our democratic failures, but most of our problems existed long before he became president and must still be overcome now that he is not in office.

The slow work of rebuilding our democracy will necessarily have to begin at the local level. It is there that we will build the social and political movements for change and experiment with solutions to our problems. It is there that we will build the necessary support and the knowledge needed for major reforms to occur at the national level. Democracy's rebirth has not been completed simply with the 2020 election and the installation of a new administration in Washington, D.C. Rather, the election has given us an opportunity to rebuild, it does not guarantee its success. These crises provide both danger and opportunity.

There is no doubt that systemic institutional racism, police abuse, the pandemic, and the resulting economic recession have strained not only our social but our political system. There is no doubt that the 2020 election and the following insurrection challenged our politics and government. In chapter 10, I discuss building a more deliberative democracy, and in chapter 11 I introduce a broader theory of change. But I begin by reflecting on one of Chicago mayor Rahm Emanuel's favorite sayings which is usually attributed to Winston Churchill: "You never let a serious crisis go to waste. And what I mean by that is it's an opportunity to do things you think you could not do before."[41]

As terrible as these cascading crises have been, they provide an opportunity for us to make a great leap forward. They change public opinion, create movements, and build momentum despite fierce opposition from those who favor the status quo. Because of the crises we have suffered together, many more Americans now recognize that something must be done. More of us realize that we are all harmed by institutional racism, lack of police accountability, a failure to deal with systemic social and economic problems, the pain and death that the pandemic brought, the harm from the economic recession, and the threat of our polarized and contentious politics. The idea that something must be done, that radical steps and solutions are necessary, is in the air.

However, we must still develop a consensus on exactly what must be done. Our first task is to develop the vision of the society we want and the first steps in a plan to achieve that vision.

The Forty-Fourth Ward Assembly, 1972. (Photo from author's collection, photographer unknown)

10

Deliberative Democracy

In previous chapters we have explored the many problems facing our representative democracy. These include structural problems, polarization, and weaknesses exposed by the crisis of the COVID-19 pandemic. As we find the "new normal" after the pandemic and the end of the Trump era, we have the opportunity to make our democracy more participatory as well as more deliberative. This will require a combination of direct participatory democracy and improved representative democracy.

In 2017, Bright Line Watch conducted a national survey of 1,571 political scientists to determine the qualities most essential to democracy and how experts rate the state of democracy in the United States. Not surprisingly, like many of us, they ranked fraud-free elections, free speech, equal access to the vote, equal political and legal rights, and safeguards for political opposition and dissent as crucial features in a democracy.[1]

As to the state of our American democracy, these same experts agreed that our country mostly or fully meets the fraud-free election standard despite attempts by Russia to interfere with the 2016 elections. Later, there were breakdowns of the electoral process during the pandemic of 2020 that the 2017 survey did not anticipate. Much more damaging was the refusal to accept the 2020 election results by then President Trump. This, in turn, led to the insurrection and takeover of the Capitol in January 2021. When political science experts surveyed again in 2021, they overwhelmingly rated "the January 6 insurrection and President Trump's pressure on state-level officials to overturn the election as among the most abnormal and important events of the Trump presidency. . . . [They] regard these events and the votes by a majority of Republican lawmakers in Congress not to certify the presidential election results as grave or serious threats to American democracy."[2]

The Bright Line Watch study revealed that most political scientists surveyed thought the United States also did well in open-party competition and in allowing free expression. But a majority of them did not think that our elections were free from foreign influence, that our government was free from corruption, or that we had achieved the basic democratic norms of debate and deliberation.[3]

In 2020, Bright Line Watch repeated the expert survey with 776 expert respondents. Overall perceptions of the performance of U.S. democracy continued its decline, reaching the lowest point since the surveys began. The declines the experts saw were greatest for protections of free speech, tolerance for peaceful protest, and protection from political violence. Experts by 2020 agreed that there was considerable decline of "democratic principles concerning limits on government power and accountability for its misuse."[4] While few experts expected significant fraud in the 2020 election, despite President Trump's claims before and after the election, "two-thirds do not trust that citizens have an equal opportunity to vote or that all votes have equal impact."[5]

Extending the same survey to the public, Bright Line Watch found the following:

> The public is more discouraged about American Democracy than the experts.
> ... They are, for instance, less sanguine about the administration of elections and about protections for free speech and less certain that political parties can compete freely and that people's rights to protest are protected.[6]

Historically, experts suggested that there had been an overall upward trajectory of American democracy until it stabilized in the 75–80 range on a hundred-point scale during the period 1975–2015. Unfortunately, it dropped to a low of 61 during the Trump administration before rebounding slightly to 64 at the start of the Biden administration.[7]

Since the 2020 election, both expert and public opinion has a slightly more positive view of America surviving this stress test of our democracy. "The mean rating on a 1–100 scale nudged up from 53.1 to 53.7 among the pubic from October to November [2020] and from 60.6 to 64.4 among experts. Unsurprisingly, though, this pattern differed sharply between members of the public who approve of Trump and those who do not."[8] As these surveys show, we survived the 2020 election, but restoring our democracy is an ongoing task.

In short, both experts and the public believe that we still have a democracy, but in a very shallow form. It does not even meet the standards of

Robert Dahl's polyarchy that requires competing interest groups and the public through elections determining the winners from among the competing groups; and therefore ultimately, government policies. Instead, we have what Benjamin Barber has called a "thin" form of democracy because people are not actively encouraged to participate in their government.[9] Too many of us don't register to vote, and only about half of registered voters actually vote in most elections. Fewer than 10 percent of us engage in political activities beyond voting. Can a system in which less than 10 percent of the people meaningfully participate be a democracy?

Thus, what we have is mostly a democratic facade. Despite our boasts of democracy, in practice we have a government with only some democratic features. Experts give our system only a score of only about 60, while the public give a lower score of 50 out of 100. Critics conclude that we have an economic and political oligarchy that became an "antidemocracy" under President Trump.[10]

Public opinion polls show that citizens have a negative view of the level of democracy in Chicago and Illinois as well. The deadlock in state government from 2013 to 2019, the long history of political-machine dominance, high levels of corruption, and the low level of citizen participation in state and local politics make this inevitable. A 2016 poll showed that only 25 percent of Illinoisans had faith in their state government, the least of any state in the nation.[11]

The clearest proof of citizen dissatisfaction is that, since the 2010 census, Illinois is one of only three states to lose population, dropping by more than eighteen thousand.[12] This is the first time Illinois lost population since it joined the union in 1818, and the exodus caused it to lose one congressional seat. People are showing their attitude toward the state by voting with their feet and leaving.

Faith in government at both the local and national levels deteriorated in the Trump era.[13] This has begun to change in Illinois, however. After the election of a new governor and a new Chicago mayor in the elections of 2018 and 2019 and their leadership in confronting the COVID-19 pandemic, a large majority of voters approved of their leadership.

While the pandemic forced low voter participation in Illinois's March 2020 primary and in states like Wisconsin, participation rebounded to 73 percent in the November general election in Illinois.

Nonetheless, in both Illinois and the nation during the Trump era, we had only a thin form of democracy. Can a higher level of deliberative democracy be achieved in the post-Trump era? And if so, can Chicago lead the way?

To become a better democracy, we have to become more participatory and improve the representative aspects of our system. We need to become a deliberative democracy. According to James Bohman and William Rehg, "deliberative democracy refers to the idea that legitimate law-making issues from the public deliberation of citizens . . . [and] evokes ideas of rational legislation, participatory politics and civic self-governance."[14] To consider how this might be achieved, we begin with a discussion of experiments in deliberative democracy in Chicago.

Neighborhood Government in Chicago

For many decades now, there have been experiments around the world in neighborhood government. These include elected neighborhood councils with authority over some government spending and veto power over zoning, building, and economic development in their neighborhoods. Currently, some form of neighborhood councils or government exist in Los Angeles, Washington, D.C., and Honolulu, among other U.S. cities.

Neighborhood government experiments overseas are even more advanced. For instance, Florence, Italy, is divided into five separate districts. Each of these districts manages its own local services, such as public works, dealing with uninhabited buildings, social services, and schools. They are governed by district councils elected at the same time as the city government, and they control their own local budgets. These district councils were created by a national law adopted in Italy in the 1970s.[15]

Neighborhood governments have at least two characteristics in common. They represent a neighborhood, community, or ward and they possess some official governmental powers. The strongest control budgets, advise on city-wide policies, and have veto power over zoning, which determines what may be built in their communities. There is currently no international standard for neighborhood governments, although participatory budgeting efforts are the most widespread around the globe currently.

Forty-Fourth Ward Government

In 1972, after being elected alderman the previous year, I created my own experiment in neighborhood government in the form of a ward assembly in the Forty-Fourth Ward in the Lakeview neighborhood of Chicago. The assembly pictured at the start of this chapter was followed by auxiliary participatory government mechanisms, including a community zoning board, a traffic review commission, and a Spanish-speaking *asamblea aberita*. I had originally run for alderman on a three-part platform: If elected, I promised to open a full-time aldermanic service office to provide city services as a right rather than as political favors; to vote as dictated by my conscience and constituency rather than be a rubber stamp for Boss Mayor Richard J. Daley: and to create a ward assembly to allow citizens direct participation in government policy making. By 1972, I was able to fulfill my platform promises.

The preamble to the ward assembly's charter that Forty-Fourth Ward citizens and I created together set out its purpose: "We seek to restore a sense of trust and mutuality in public life. We seek to create a forum for the broadest possible exchange of views among the people themselves and between them and their Alderman. We seek to open up the political process within our Ward to all its people."[16] The brochure announcing the election of the first delegates to the ward assembly explained the goal in very practical terms: "The purpose of the Ward Assembly is to make possible direct citizen participation in shaping the plans and priorities for the 44th Ward and in directing the Alderman in introducing legislation and casting his vote in the City Council."[17]

Delegates were elected from the sixty-four precincts and the more than sixty community organizations in the neighborhood. Two delegates were elected from each precinct, and one delegate was chosen from each community group with more than twenty-five members in the ward.

For any neighborhood government to work, it has to have some real power. That is to say, to get citizens to participate in deliberations, they have to control some government action.[18] This guarantees that the payoff for assembly participants will be greater than the costs of getting elected and participating in the meetings of the neighborhood government.

To make this clear, I signed this covenant with the assembly: "I . . . hereby pledge that I will be bound by the decisions of the 44th Ward Assembly on important issues before the city council and on projects undertaken to promote the welfare of the citizens of this ward and this city, provided that those decisions are either unanimous or approved by a 2/3's vote as outlined in the Assembly's Charter."[19]

When I later attempted to pass a neighborhood government ordinance to create by law ward assemblies in any Chicago ward that wanted them, my proposed ordinance was voted down in the machine-dominated city council by a vote of 44–4.

To create the new instruments of neighborhood governance in the Forty-Fourth Ward required me as alderman to pledge my city council vote and aldermanic authority to the outcome of their deliberations. It required as well, the tacit approval of community organizations and their leaders. By signing it, I pledged to bind my city council vote to the deliberations of the assembly and my power over zoning, traffic, parking, and Latino issues to the more specialized units of our neighborhood government.

Moreover, the creation of neighborhood government in the Forty-Fourth Ward had to be supported by a political organization of campaign volunteers in order to have the many volunteers necessary to conduct the ward assembly elections. In addition, I had to be willing to dedicate aldermanic staff time and financial resources to coordinate the election of delegates, staff the ward assembly committees, and provide the necessary government information for the assembly to have the facts necessary to deliberate on government proposals and pending city council legislation.

Finally, this neighborhood government was founded, as U.S. governments have often been, by the signing of a covenant and the drafting of a constitution. In essence, this covenant and constitution was a public contract guaranteeing that if members of the assembly got elected, deliberated, and decided by vote, then I would carry out their decisions. I would share my power with them.

The assembly continued for a decade from 1972 until 1981, when election of an alderman by the Democratic machine caused it to be disbanded. The Chicago machine and its leaders wanted no part of neighborhood government. Giving citizens more power would undermine the hierarchical control of the Democratic Party and its party bosses.

The ward assembly and later instruments of neighborhood government with which we experimented successfully for a decade were important because it was impossible to consult the entire ward on critical issues to be voted on in the city council or about projects that we might undertake in the ward under my leadership. The assembly was given authority because my successor and I were bound to the outcome of their deliberations and vote. I did not believe that citizens would be willing to participate actively in the assembly if its vote was only advisory and its views could be ignored. By sharing my power, my successor and I were able to get people to sacrifice the time and effort to participate.[20]

And citizens in the Forty-Fourth Ward did participate. At the first meeting of the ward assembly on January 9, 1972, sixty of the sixty-four precincts were represented by 105 delegates. In addition, there were fifty-five delegates elected by some sixty community organizations; thirty official observers including party representatives, public officials, and representatives from non-Forty-Fourth Ward organizations; and more than a hundred ward residents present. The average attendance at ward assembly meetings over the next nine years ranged from eighty to a hundred assembly delegates. It was higher just after the annual election of delegates or when particularly controversial issues were to be decided.

In the 1977 elections for ward assembly precinct delegates, most of the thirty thousand families in the ward were notified by a flyer under their door or in their mailbox. More than 420 people attended the precinct meetings at their neighbors' homes over coffee and cookies to discuss the problems of the community and to elect delegates. More than 1,500 residents signed petitions to certify those to be elected, since any precinct meeting with less than twenty-five people could only nominate delegates, who then had to get at least twenty-five neighbors to sign petitions attesting that they wanted this person to represent them. Hundreds of community organization members also participated in selecting their organization's delegates to the assembly. At different times, as many as seventy-five community organizations had official delegates.

Since most delegates served only a year or two in the assembly, more than a thousand Forty-Fourth Ward residents served during its years of existence and thousands more elected them and participated in discussion of the ward and city issues in that process. In addition, several hundred more participated in hearings each year by the more specialized units of neighborhood government, such as the community zoning board and the traffic review commission. A special effort was made through the *asemblea abierta*, whose meetings were conducted in Spanish, to get participation from the Latino community that might otherwise have gone unrepresented because of language and cultural barriers. Pure participatory democracy of all citizens was not achieved, but much greater participation occurred than in our usual system of government.

Eventually, the ward assembly and units of neighborhood government were destroyed by the political machine. Yet, the experiment lived on in different forms in various wards with community zoning boards that held public hearings on zoning changes and the participatory budget process. The broader ward assembly was never tried again in Chicago, but similar experiments like the Twenty-Fifth Ward Independent Precinct Organization (IPO) with the Twenty-Fifth Ward alderman have begun and may one day evolve into a more complete neighborhood government.

Participatory Budgeting

In 2009, a new experiment in participatory budgeting began in Chicago. Originally, $1 million of "aldermanic menu money" that aldermen could use to spend on city services and repairs in their wards was turned over by Alderman Joe Moore of Chicago's Forty-Ninth Ward to a vote by residents to determine how the money should be spent. Over time, with assistance from the University of Illinois at Chicago's Great Cities Institute, some twelve wards participated in the project that engaged more than thirteen thousand Chicago residents who decided how to spend over $18 million in public dollars by 2019. The experiment has since been expanded to some public schools, allowing students to vote on how to spend dollars from the Chicago Public Schools budget in their schools.[21]

The original participatory budgeting process began in Porto Alegre, Brazil. In 1989, the Workers' Party won the mayoral election on a social justice platform. Each January since then, people's assemblies are held in sixteen districts to deliberate and to elect delegates to determine spending priorities. In 2003, fifty thousand residents took part in the budgeting process, and these budgets over the decades have greatly improved the lot of Porto Alegre's residents. In addition, to involving the entire city, the Brazilian version of participatory budgeting included spending on both infrastructure and social services, while Chicago's participatory budgeting process only involves infrastructure expenditures. Also, lower-income people participate more in Brazil. The participatory budgeting process since its beginning in 1989 has spread to cities and schools around the world, including New York and Chicago.[22]

The participatory budgeting process begins in Chicago wards with community representatives working with aldermanic staff and city agencies to develop proposals for spending funds with specific information from city agencies about possible alternatives and their cost. In the Forty-Ninth ward, in 2018, there were eight community meetings that developed eight proposals for the ballot on how to spend the $1.3 million in city funds. More than 2,378 residents then voted on the winning projects that included the following:

> street resurfacing, sidewalk and alley repair ($626,000)
> 100 trees to be planted ($80,000)
> new bus benches ($33,000)
> artistic murals ($44,000)
> a public plaza/stage or Zócalo in Touch Park ($60,000)
> partial funding for high school artificial turf field and running track
>   ($157,000)[23]

Most years, at least eight wards and their aldermen used this participatory budgeting process each year. Supporters advocate expanding the participatory budget process to all fifty wards, but that will require an ordinance passed by the Chicago City Council and support from the city administration.

Transition Team

Another example of participatory democratic processes in Chicago government was Mayor Lori Lightfoot's transition team, that began its work a week after she was elected in April 2019. The team delivered its final 110-page report filled with several hundred recommendations on May 17, a month and a half later. It was presented to the new mayor for her endorsement, given full media coverage, and published on the Internet.[24] Since then, many of the transition team recommendations have been implemented.

There were more than four hundred members and forty co-chairs of the ten committees of the transition team. It considered 315 policy memos from committee members, civic leaders, and community residents before adopting the final report after two three-hour committee meetings to finalize each of the ten sections of the document.

I served as one of the four co-chairs of the Good Governance Committee. Its members included former public officials, such as former alderman and County Clerk David Orr; leaders of more than a half-dozen civic organizations, such as the Better Government Association; and representatives of ethnic and community organizations throughout the city. Our committee was staffed by a lawyer from Mayor Lightfoot's former law firm and by a paid transition team staff member. They took minutes of our proceedings and drafted the final report with input and editing by all four committee co-chairs.

Because so many of our transition team members were experienced, and our own organizations had developed recommendations that had been rejected by previous city administrations, we were able to produce a comprehensive report in such a brief time period. In our Good Governance Report, we called for city council rules changes, such as requiring regular meetings; preventing aldermen from having outside conflicting employment representing private clients before other units of government; livestreaming and cablecasting council and committee meetings; and better reporting of roll call votes to hold aldermen accountable for how they voted.

Our report also called for better lobbying disclosure, public funding of city elections, eliminating patronage hiring, and ending aldermanic privilege by which aldermen could veto permits and zoning changes, a practice that had frequently led to corruption in the form of bribes to obtain zoning or permits. We also recommended reform of the tax increment financing (TIF) districts.

Amazingly, many of the recommendations of the Good Governance Committee were carried out during the mayor's first year in office before the COVID-19 pandemic hit. There have been transition teams for mayors in the past, but none had been so inclusive or comprehensive. On the day Mayor Lightfoot was sworn into office, she signed an executive order limiting aldermanic privilege, following our recommendation. In the future, aldermen can have a voice to represent their community's perspective in administrative decision making, but no longer will an alderman have a unilateral veto over permits or zoning, which has led to so many cases of aldermanic corruption.

Based on our recommendations, the city began webcasting and cable-casting council and committee meetings. Conflicting outside employment of aldermen has been ended, and the city's inspector general has been given authority to investigate aldermen and their staffs. The city's ethics ordinance has been amended to eliminate previous loopholes.

Since her inauguration on May 20, 2019, Mayor Lightfoot's administration has worked steadily to implement other transition team proposals, including more robust citizen hearings in the neighborhoods over the city budget and mechanisms to continue engagement of the transition team members. The transition team recommended the creation of a community engagement action plan to promote a more inclusive government and to institute mechanisms of more citizen engagement. Mayor Lightfoot also began again public hearings in the neighborhoods on the city budget, which had been discontinued under Rahm Emanuel's administration. There have been neighborhood hearings on important issues as well as a poverty summit to tackle the problem of poverty and uneven development in Chicago that led to the creation of a $750 million economic development investment program for ten of Chicago's poorest neighborhoods.

Mayor Lightfoot reported her accomplishments in the first hundred days in office, and I reproduce some of them here:

- Creation of a multifaceted comprehensive crime-fighting strategy centered on unprecedented citywide coordination that has resulted in nearly 7,000 guns recovered . . ., a three-year low in murders, shooting incidents at their lowest count since 2015, and 20-year lows in robberies, burglaries and motor vehicle thefts.
- Directing a significant expansion of school staffing and resources . . . with investments to upgrade classrooms and facilities at over 300 schools across the city in 2020.
- Passing the most comprehensive worker scheduling law in the nation . . .
- Begun reforming an historically regressive fines and fees system in order to help people move into payment plans and compliance, instead of into bankruptcy.

- Overhauling the workers' compensation program to improve benefits to workers and reduce liability and claims costs to the city.
- Achieving passage of a series of ethics and good governance reforms to ensure the City operates more efficiently, transparently and in a way that is accountable to all residents and taxpayers.
- Doubling down on protections for immigrant and refugee families by issuing an executive order to terminate ICE access to citywide databases and city facilities . . .
- Beginning steps toward a comprehensive redevelopment strategy to tackle years of disinvestment on the City's South and West sides, including creating a coalition of over 40 business leaders to participate in a corridor reinvestment strategy.
- Launching a new and improved Qualified Allocation Plan (QAP) which for the first time makes explicit collaboration with the Continuum of Care, resulting in a coordinated application process for addressing homelessness.[25]

In comparison to old-style, nonparticipatory machine politics, Chicago has made significant strides toward a more deliberative and participatory government.

Issue Voting and Governing

Additional steps are needed in the United States to create more citizen participation. If we were able to institute automatic voter registration to register all voters, eliminate outdated institutions like the Electoral College, and vote electronically and by mail-in ballots, it would improve democracy and citizen participation in elections. However, shouldn't citizens be allowed to weigh in on public policy decisions as well as just electing representatives to govern us?

We have not only to overcome structural impediments, however. As citizens, we have to be willing to play a more active role than the passive one we do now. We could add some elements of participatory democracy, such as town-hall meetings or the participatory budgeting process. At least some of us would then better understand government policy choices and create new ways to better convey our preferences to our elected representatives.

It has been suggested that technology could enable much broader participation in government decision-making. However, there are severe problems in using television in its various forms (web streaming, videos, cable TV) or the Internet (with software like Zoom or Skype) to connect citizens with our government. Some other promising options are various forms of polling, citizen juries, and town-hall meetings to allow for more direct participation in governing. The use of citizen juries and other more participatory methods of government decision-making have been tested for decades now. While the promise of these experiments has been great and most have had positive results, scaling them up in a nation of more than 330 million people across the fifty states is difficult.

The basic idea of a more participatory democracy is simple. Gather all citizens regularly (monthly or annually for a day). Debate the issues put on the agenda by a steering committee or elected officials. Provide the necessary factual information and arguments for making the decision. Conduct a debate of alternatives. Then take a vote and let the majority decide the government or community action to be taken.

There are problems with this simple idea. First, the assembly or town hall meeting as a governing institution seems to work only in communities of only a few thousand people. Yet, the nation's major cities have several million people. Many states have tens of millions of residents. No city hall, town square, or government building can hold such crowds. For instance, the relatively large Chicago city council chambers holds an audience of only 550 people. Nor does televising or web streaming the meeting solve the problem. If participation in these town hall–type meetings is voluntary, it is usually low. Current participation, even in elections in the United States, is also low, rarely reaching much more than 60 percent of registered voters even in presidential elections. In municipal elections, turnout is often only 20 percent.

Town-hall meetings in New England often have similarly low turnouts. While having a direct town hall or a virtual meeting to decide government policy involves more citizens than leaving those decisions to elected officials, these options still do not reach the democratic ideal of majority rule. The pandemic also caused many towns to revamp their format to allow virtual attendance. It is unclear how they will proceed in the post-pandemic era. Nonetheless, town-hall meetings, both in person and virtually, create a sense of civic virtue and increase the quality of citizen participation.[26]

In addition to problems of participation and attendance, issues in our time have become more complex than a simple "yes" or "no" answer on some clear policy proposal. It is normal for a major bill in Congress to run well over a thousand pages and to have complicated details, such as how many parts per billion of particular chemicals in the air we breathe should be limited in our environmental laws and regulations. For instance, the second stimulus bill, which passed in December 2020 and provided $900 billion of relief from the economic effects of the pandemic, ran 5,500 pages. Informing citizens of the facts necessary to vote on actual laws like the stimulus bill is not a simple undertaking, especially for those who haven't had experience in governing over time, who don't have staff to brief them, and who haven't spent days listening to expert testimony in legislative hearings.

Since it is unlikely that everyone could gather in a single room or meeting place, the promise of new technology to solve some of these problems has encouraged experiments in new forms of direct democracy. Cable television and web streaming allow citizens from their home or office to view the same presentations and debate before casting their vote for policies. This assumes, however, that they have the time, Internet access, and interest to do so. Yet, with the COVID-19 pandemic, millions of Americans have become more familiar with distance learning and online meetings through software like Zoom. Such programs allow further experimentation in the use of the internet for issue discussions and decision-making.

However, democracy is not a public opinion poll. Simply polling the electorate without discussion and deliberation has limitations because polls often only test prejudice or prejudgment. Without any presentation of facts or arguments pollsters ask: do you favor the death penalty, lower taxes, recreational drug use, or going to war against a particular enemy abroad? That kind of opinion taking is not democracy. However, well-designed public opinion polls can provide government officials with meaningful information about constituent attitudes and current opinions. This is useful for officials to know in casting their votes. But they may still have to decide contrary to ill-informed public opinion on some critical issues.

In the end, our model of democracy is something like what happened at the 1787 Constitutional Convention. Different competing alternatives are presented and perhaps compromises are proposed that were not in the original options, and then an informed vote is taken.

This ideal assumes that a significant number of the public are willing to devote the time and effort to participate and cast an informed vote. There are many legitimate distractions, including entertainment, work, family, friendships, recreation, hobbies, and healthy exercise. Are enough of us willing and economically secure enough to make the sacrifices necessary to increase our role as citizens? And if we can obtain a meaningful level of participation, can we develop the institutions to allow for meaningful participation in policy making? Finally, won't the wealthy, through paid ads and advocates, still dominate the decision-making, as they now dominate campaigns and lawmaking with their greater resources?

Creating a more informed public committed to democratic governance and building the processes to allow genuine citizen input into decision-making is perhaps the greatest challenge to our democracy and an essential element in democracy's rebirth in the twenty-first century.

New England Town Meeting

When we think of deliberative democracy in the United States, the most obvious case is the venerable New England town meeting. While most of the country votes on local issues the same way it does state and national issues, using what Vermont refers to as the "Australian ballot"—that is, voting by secret ballot at a polling place—some communities in New England still vote in a general meeting by raising their hands in a floor vote.[27] In some rural towns in Vermont, for instance, residents still assemble together on the first Tuesday in March for the annual town meeting, at which they discuss and vote on the town budget and the other local items put before them by the members of the select board who were elected to serve as their town council. In some cases, school boards hold their own town meeting at other times so that those policies and budgets are developed with citizen input and control as well.

The town meeting format throughout New England has morphed and evolved over time to adjust to societal changes, local needs, and a modern, voting workforce, but town meetings are still not perfect democracies. Political scientist Frank Bryan estimates attendance to be only 20 percent of the registered voters in Vermont, and only 7 percent of the voters (but 44 percent of attendees) speak at the meetings.[28] Nonetheless, this is higher participation than for most local elections elsewhere in the country. Today, many annual town meetings throughout New England are held on a weeknight and last a few hours at most, permitting many residents to attend. Vermont law requires employers to allow voters to take off from work when their town's annual meeting is held on a weekday, but this requires more planning (and probably paperwork) than would be required, for example, for submitting an absentee ballot.[29] In addition to annual town meetings, other town meetings are routinely called, depending on state and on municipal regulations, over the course of a year on additional issues requiring by statute a floor vote. Voters who do not attend these meetings are left out of the decision-making, although some towns now livestream all town meetings so people can follow the proceedings in real time. Given all these factors, citizen participation in town hall meetings is still impressive, and the format itself continues to evolve.

Direct deliberative democracy requires that citizens "in person, in face-to-face meetings of the whole [and] make laws that govern the actions of everyone within their geographic boundaries."[30] Town meetings are run by an elected moderator following *Robert's Rules of Order* to bring issues before those who attend. Everyone who wishes to do so is generally allowed to speak (depending on residency and voter status), residents make motions on specific articles to propose alternative wording, and, after discussion and deliberation, a binding decision is taken by consensus or majority vote.

Many observers from around the world, including Alexis de Tocqueville over a century ago, have observed town meetings. Most who have seen them believe these town meetings to be a well-spring of American democracy. One twentieth-century observer, Russian dissident Aleksandr Solzhenitsyn, lived in the town of Cavendish, Vermont, for eighteen years. His farewell address at the 1994 town meeting included this: "I have observed here in Cavendish, and in the surrounding towns the sensible and sure process of grassroots democracy where the local population decides most of its problems on its own, not waiting for the decisions of higher authorities. Alas, this we still do not have in Russia, and that is our greatest shortcoming."[31]

As with Athens 2,500 years ago, town meetings are particularly important because they teach democracy by practicing democracy—by making binding governmental decisions through debate and in-person voting. The skills developed in town meetings are important foundations for participation in government at state and national levels.

Some annual town meetings were suspended during the COVID-19 pandemic and reduced to balloting at the polls, so whether the floor-vote format can be fully restored in New England is still uncertain. Moreover, the larger issues are whether town meetings can handle the complexity of twenty-first-century decision-making, and whether there is a realistic way to expand the format to the rest of the country. The example of Chicago's Forty-Fourth Ward Assembly and participatory budgeting in Chicago wards suggest that the elements of "real democracy" from the town meeting can be adapted for dense urban areas with larger populations than New England towns and villages.

Jefferson's Ward System

Beyond the New England town meetings, ideas for improving our governmental system with units of deliberation and direct democracy go back to the founding of the nation. Most Americans don't know that Thomas Jefferson advocated a more participatory, federated system of government. He proposed that the country be divided into wards of a few square miles and as few as a hundred citizens each. In these wards, citizens by discussion and vote would decide on local issues in a manner similar to New England town meetings. Higher levels of state and national government would focus on general laws and their enforcement as well as national defense and foreign affairs. Under Jefferson's proposed system, citizens would have a direct voice in directing local matters that affected them directly and instructing their representatives at higher levels of their position on key issues.

As in ancient Athens, citizens would be educated in democracy by practicing democracy. Other than New England town meetings and later experiments in neighborhood governments, the Jefferson ideal was never practiced in the United States. But it provides a framework for making changes. Obviously, wards would need to be of a greater size. For instance, Chicago wards have roughly fifty thousand people, and most suburbs range from a few hundred people to more than a hundred thousand. But neighborhoods, suburbs, and rural towns could make the building blocks for the practice of deliberative democracy that Jefferson had in mind.

To make participation work as proposed in Jefferson's ward system, it would be best to make the cost of participation low by declaring meeting days as official holidays or conducting them on the Internet using new software meeting tools. We could also make the stakes higher by allowing decisions over budgets and taxes, as New England town meetings do, and by having state representatives and U.S. House representatives attend to hear directly from their constituents.

Making Congress Deliberative

Clearly, in a nation of 330 million people, we require more than ward or town government. That is the reason that our Constitution created national political institutions. We need not only more direct democracy but a way to influence our representatives at the higher levels of government. One approach to deliberative democracy is to bring deliberation to larger government units. One place to begin is with the U.S. Congress, where each member is currently charged with representing the needs, interests, and views of 750,000 constituents. In truth, it is very hard to know the views or interests of such a large constituency, much less to represent their diverse and sometimes conflicting views in the halls of government. It is equally difficult for a congressional representative to inform citizens about the issues that are to be voted upon. Mailed newsletters and occasional emails simply don't do the job. Most serve just as reelection campaign propaganda.

With job approval rating of Congress fluctuating from 13 percent in 2017 to 31 percent in May 2021 and the job approval rating of President Trump dropping to 29 percent as he left office, there can be no doubt that there is a problem with our democracy.[32] Many citizens obviously feel that they are not well represented by those they elect.

Some people claim that we still have a democracy in which Congress has the ability to deliberate well and that its deliberations are grounded "in the interests and desires of the American citizenry."[33] Or, as the U.S. Capitol Visitor Center puts it, "Through legislative debate and compromise, the U.S. Congress makes laws that influence our daily lives. It holds hearings to inform the legislative process, conducts investigations to oversee the executive branch, and serves as the voice of the people and the states in the federal government."[34] While this concept of members of Congress representing their constituents is the ideal, it will take major reforms for us to achieve it. Based on public opinion polls, a majority of voters were dissatisfied with both the president and the Congress during the Trump era. Their dissatisfaction is likely to continue at a high level even with the election of a new president and Congress.

Some analysts argue that we can cure the problems of representative democracy by some simple structural changes. Others say that the answer is more direct, participatory democracy, like the New England town meeting or the Jefferson ward system. But we must find ways to improve our national government, remove structural barriers, and improve democracy at the local level.

Political scientists Michael Neblo, Kevin Esterling, and David Lazer suggested one way to improve our national government: "We agree that the problems of modern representative democracy are real, but argue that any attempt to double down on establishment politics is likely to deepen the incipient crisis. However, the going reform proposals—direct democracy, technocracy, and reactionary populism—are unlikely to help much either. . . . There is little room for citizens to act in their deliberative capacity *as citizens*, rather than just as consumers. Contemporary democracy asks little more of citizens than their votes and money."[35]

The autocratic and often chaotic style of President Donald Trump in the White House caused many citizens to conclude that something must be done to "save democracy." These concerns became even more acute after the insurrection of January 6, 2021. Yet, the deep-seated problems with our politics have no simple fix, such as electing different officials. There is no single piece of legislation or silver bullet that can provide the cure.

The underlying flaws existed before Trump became president. It will take decades to reinvent our democracy for the twenty-first century. Given the challenges we face, incremental changes, while certainly useful, will not be enough. We must create a democratic constituency willing to undertake the role and demands of citizenship. What our founders called the Spirit of '76 and Abraham Lincoln in his famous Gettysburg Address called a "rebirth of freedom" must be rekindled.

Since status quo politics and government won't solve our problems, it is important to consider how we might move beyond them. There have been numerous experiments with different methods such as deliberative opinion polls, citizen assemblies, citizen legislative juries, town-hall meetings, neighborhood governments, and earlier participatory experiments like televote. Nearly all these experiments have been successful on their own terms, but no one deliberative democratic method has been widely adopted to make government decisions.[36]

Neblo, Esterling, and Lazer argue that any new deliberative democratic institutions that might be adopted should meet five "mutually interactive" criteria:

- Inclusion by providing "equal access and voice to attract a wide cross-section of constituents";
- Encouraging "constituents to proceed on the basis of reliable, balanced, and relevant information" to discuss constructively;
- Promoting high-quality exchanges between elected officials and their constituents by giving reasons for their policy proposals;
- Encouraging "the trust and legitimacy" when participants are not able to reconvene; and
- Be at a scale "so that a meaningful number of constituents can participate, and the process can . . . ramify through the larger deliberative system."[37]

Added to these, any effective new deliberative democratic institutions would need to be written into law to operate over time. This is one of the lessons of Chicago's Forty-Fourth Ward Assembly and the other experiments in participatory government that have eventually been destroyed because they threatened those in power.

James Fishkin suggested that as additional criteria that any deliberative method must also support democratic principles, among them political equality, mass participation, deliberation, and non-tyranny. However, all these goals cannot all be pursued at the same time. Fishkin concludes that deliberative democracy is the best form of government because it best promotes political equality and deliberation.[38] He argues that instead of the deliberation between representatives and some selected constituents, which occurred in the experiments by Neblo, that the arguments presented in deliberations must not be one-sided, such as those presented by the members of Congress or authority figures, but should be made by any participant as they are in deliberative town halls. Let us consider more closely the experiments by Neblo and Fishkin.

In the summer of 2006, Neblo, Esterling, and Lazer hosted a series of nineteen deliberative town-hall meetings over the Internet with both Republican and Democratic members of the U.S. House on controversial pending legislation, for example, an immigration proposal. For each meeting they recruited a random sample of at least a hundred of the representative's constituents. The sessions lasted thirty-five minutes, and participants afterward discussed the session with the political scientists for another twenty-five minutes. The U.S. representatives, participants, and political scientists found the discussions to be more satisfying than the usual town-hall meetings that some members of Congress hold. Usually, town-hall meetings attract mostly partisans and often end in shouting matches. After the elections of 2008, meetings in some congressional districts, especially those represented by Republicans, became so divisive that they were abandoned altogether. By contrast, in these alternative Internet meetings, the U.S. representatives explained their positions and listened to the ideas and concerns of their constituents in a deliberative way.

Of the people who were contacted to be part of the discussion with their U.S. representative, 83 percent expressed interest in participating. Afterward, it was determined that "the representatives valued the sessions, valued the constituents' input, and found the events to be of high value to them as effective representatives. . . . The sessions generally featured rational and reasoned argumentation."[39] Constituents also valued the interaction with their representative in this format. "On the follow-up survey, a large majority of participants reported that they found the sessions to be helpful and informative (78 percent). Virtually all participants (95 percent) agreed that this kind of deliberative interaction between constituents and representative is very valuable for our democracy, and would like to participate in a similar session in the future (97 percent)."[40]

In this kind of deliberative interaction, the role of the representative is changed by meaningful contact with constituents. At the theoretical level, the political scientists who conducted these deliberative sessions proposed a new "gyroscopic" model of representation. As opposed to the "trustee" model, in which a representative acts like a lawyer for a client, or a "delegate" model, in which a representative simply acts like an ambassador from the constituency delivering their message to the government, a gyroscopic representative "can maintain her orientation vis-à-vis her constituents on new issues by referencing her own pre-aligned values, in that a gyroscope constantly reorients itself into an upright position, even when buffered by external forces . . . a representative can often behave like a trustee on a given issue but produce the effects of a delegate if she 'thinks, reasons, and feels' like her constituents."[41] Such a system obviously works only if there is frequent contact between the representative and constituents as in deliberative democracy. You can't represent a constituency you don't know or whom you manipulate through money, advertising, and one-way communication, as occurs in too many election campaigns. It works only if officials aren't beholden to lobbyists and big donors.

Thus, all the reforms discussed in earlier chapters—campaign finance reform, lobbyist restrictions, and fair legislative redistricting—are needed to make these deliberative interactions effective. This alternative method of representation also provides an argument for term limits, so there aren't representatives for life who get more and more out of touch with their constituents the longer they serve. But structural reforms alone are not enough. A larger transformation is needed for democracy in the United States to be reborn in the twenty-first century. We must create institutions of deliberative democracy.

Legislative Juries

Debra Campbell and Jack Crittenden argue for a different version of deliberative democracy than the deliberative town halls of Neblo, Esterling, and Lazer. They propose legislative juries that are useful at the state level.[42] They combine the current practices of initiatives and referendums in some states with juries with which we are familiar from direct experience in trials or from films and televised accounts of court proceedings.

There already are initiatives in twenty-six states by which citizens can propose legislation directly that is then voted on in the next election. If the initiative passes, it becomes law.[43] Initiatives have been criticized as being controlled by big money and interest groups, but in the decade between 1986 and 1996 in California, only fourteen of the fifty-four initiatives originated with narrow interest groups, and the money spent by wealthy groups was not the sole factor in an initiative's success.[44]

While there are shortcomings to the initiative process, it does allow for citizens to have a voice in government policy making. What Campbell and Crittenden suggest is adding to this existing process a deliberative element based on our experience with citizen juries. This adds to the initiative process the deliberation that occurs when a law is approved by a legislature and signed (or vetoed) by an executive.

Why is deliberation so essential to the democratic processes? To deliberate means "to weigh thoroughly" from the Latin, *deliberare*, to consider carefully. In short, it means long and careful consideration and discussion in making a decision. Deliberation allows for other points of view to be presented, for positions to be challenged, unintended consequences to be uncovered, and compromises to be adopted.

Under Campbell and Crittenden's proposal, "there will be a framing jury [of twelve voters chosen at random as trial juries are] to generate and propose possible options for the wording of the ballot issue. The second tier of public forums, or the 'naming' tier, involves participants' deliberating and choosing the best alternative from the three or four possible policy or position approaches."[45] The process starts with citizens gathering voter signatures to place an issue on the ballot, as currently occurs with the initiative and referendum process. The issue is then filtered through the deliberations of two juries as the framing and naming juries reach consensus to develop the best possible alternative to present to the voters. Finally, citizens then vote the proposed initiative up or down at the next election.

The authors lay out a strong case for improving the initiative process with deliberation. However, it has yet to be tried in any of the twenty-six states that currently allow initiatives.

James Fishkin has, since the 1980s, experimented with even larger deliberative processes called deliberative polling. The deliberative opinion poll takes a representative random sample of the people and brings the people together at a place to deliberate about an issue for a weekend.

> Carefully balanced briefing materials are sent to the participants and are also made publicly available. The participants engage in dialogue with competing experts and political leaders based on questions they develop in small group discussions with trained moderators. Parts of the deliberative events are often broadcast on television, either live or in taped and edited form and/or through social media and other mediums. After the deliberations, the sample is again asked the original questions. The resulting changes in opinion represent the conclusions the public would reach, if people had opportunity to become more informed and more engaged by the issues.[46]

The decisions made in one hundred polls in twenty-nine countries have been used to elect candidates in primaries, recommend policy decisions, and to frame ballot initiatives.[47] These deliberative polls or citizen assemblies are an alternative method of allowing citizens to influence public policy, not simply to vote in elections.

Other Alternatives

Simple direct democracy in the form of voter initiatives and referenda are not the answer to our current political aliments. They are too often subverted by the influence of money and special interests in the same way that the electoral process has often been undermined by big money and dark money. In the same way, big money can overwhelm voter choice on issues with paid ads and media manipulation. Initiatives and referenda to promote democracy do need to have a deliberative aspect. But there is a danger even in cases in which citizen juries or deliberative polls are added to the decision process.

Moreover, only a few issues can be voted on by either initiative or citizen juries. Many states limit ballot issues to three per election. Whereas government enact hundreds or thousands of laws each year. There is an additional complication. Every year the City of Chicago adopts an annual budget consisting of four hundred pages and two hundred thousand line items, and the federal budget is even bigger and more complicated. It would be difficult to submit such a complicated document to either referendum or a weekend citizen jury.

Technocratic innovations such as independent commissions "and other attempts to insulate the policy process provide political cover[,] but normal imperfections in the policy outcomes become magnified, decreasing confidence in political institutions."[48] Such commissions might be used to draw maps or nominate judges, but they can't be our sole method of governing.

The introduction of new technologies, such as the Internet and social media, despite their potential and early hopes that they would automatically bring about more democracy, have been subverted by "fake news," trivia, uncivil behavior, online attacks, disinformation, hacks of democratic institutions and elections, and information overload. Technology by itself will not bring about more democracy. It must be harnessed and directed if it is to do so.

Finally, as the Trump administration and the growth of right-wing parties in Europe have demonstrated, there is a great danger that reactionary populists may gain control. Populists claim that a strong leader can overcome the messiness of representative democracies and the normal legislative processes in order to pronounce the "will of the people" directly and more accurately. Yet, we know strong leaders and weakened democratic institutions lead to autocratic rule, usually some form of fascism or communism.

Overall, it would seem that the deliberative democracy experiments by Neblo and others that involve elected official meeting by phone or forms of teleconferencing, such as Zoom meetings, in which specific policy issues are discussed hold promise for reinvigorating our democracy. But they have not yet had widespread adoption.

What all of these deliberative alternatives (neighborhood government, participatory budgeting, town meetings, congressional deliberation, and legislative juries) have in common is the effort to make our representative democracy more deliberative. To let citizens, or at least a larger representative group of them, participate in policy making.

For our system of government to become more democratic, rather than to devolve into either an autocracy or an oligarchy, we must find a way to reform our institutions to allow more citizen participation in policy making. However, that will be challenging.

Our Divisions

If democratic deliberation is to be adopted, it will have to overcome deep divisions in our society and politics. Divisions such as race, income and wealth inequality, political party identity, and polarization are obvious challenges. The widening economic gap, in particular, makes participatory democracy in any form difficult unless the institutions of deliberative democracy are specifically designed to include the poor. To give one example, there are gated communities in which hundreds of homes are enclosed and entry to outsiders is blocked. And there are high-rise condominium buildings that provide many of the services governments usually provide. In both cases political decision-making is restricted to residents and their politics are those of exclusion, not inclusion, from surrounding jurisdictions such as towns and suburbs. Homeowners in many suburbs and condominium buildings prefer restrictive zoning laws that raise property values and keep out those of lesser economic means. Those who are poorer and not condo owners are literally locked out.

We are not only divided materially and physically by wealth and property ownership. For all our patriotism and flag waving, we have what E. J. Dionne declared a "divided political heart." The fundamental division between liberty and community that has existed since our founding. The founders tried "to build protections against the excess of self regarding behavior. . . . But they also sought to build a community that fostered the virtues self-government required."[49] So there is a tension between these competing values. We have to foster both individual liberty and community if democracy is to flourish.

As Dionne reminds us, our nation "was founded not on a grand consensus but on a series of arguments" and compromises.[50] We have had a long consensus that "embodies moderation, balance, and compromise" between the principles of liberty and community.[51] However, in our time, deep divisions exist between the ideologies of the Tea Party right and the anti–Wall Street left, between Republicans and Democrats, and between pro-Trump and anti-Trump political factions. Deep divisions also divide the many races and ethnic groups in the United States. The balance between these different political perspectives, racial groups, social conditions, and fundamental values is not easy to achieve, either in Chicago or the nation. We have in the past been able to promote both liberty and community as American values. But to continue to do so in the post-Trump era, we must forge new compromises.

We must find new methods to promote a more deliberative democracy in an era of new technology, social media, and polarization. This makes our task not only challenging but more pressing. During the early period of COVID-19 pandemic, we had a spirt of community and self-sacrifice. It was visible in the heroic efforts of health care and essential workers who endangered themselves for the good of others. But tensions soon arose as many Americans refused to wear masks or avoid large in-person gatherings. Based on these experiences, it remains to be seen if community spirit can overcome our divisions. And can such a spirit be sustained for the less glamorous work of healing our democracy? While we now have vaccines to end the pandemic, it is unclear if we have the remedies to overcome our divisions.

Constitutional Crisis and Constitutional Rot

There is widespread agreement that the American political system has become dysfunctional. It is both undemocratic "because it no longer responds to popular will" and unrepublican "because it is not fairly representative, allows too much self-entrenching behavior, is deeply corrupt, and is not directed at the achievement of the public good."[52] Representative democracies like ours require vigilance and civic virtue on the part of the public and our leaders. This civic virtue includes "devotion to the public good and the ability and the willingness to sacrifice short-term political self-interest for the greater good." It is undermined by corrupt public officials who promote their own economic and political self-interests and by a public "who become cynical, internally divided and lose faith in the idea of a common good and in the possibility of a common project of governance involving their fellow citizens."[53]

Part of our dilemma in pursuing reforms lies in determining whether we are in a constitutional crisis in which the very structure of our government and the checks and balances established in the U.S. Constitution 250 years ago is in peril. In such a case, the only solution would be to call a constitutional convention or to pass a series of fundamental reforms as constitutional amendments. If on the other hand, we are in a period of democratic decay, then it is possible to demand institutional changes by law without a constitutional convention.

According to Jack Balkin, there are four interlocking features of democratic decay or constitutional rot: polarization, loss of trust in government, increasing economic inequality, and policy disasters on the order of the Vietnam War or the 2008 financial crisis and subsequent Great Recession.[54] There is clear evidence that these failings exist today. Therefore, I believe we have constitutional rot that needs to be cut out of the body politic. But I am fearful of calling a Constitutional Convention at a time of such political polarization and division.

As bad a president as Donald Trump may have been, it is clear that these political problems exist beyond his failed presidency. They require more fundamental solutions than merely electing new and better public officials. However, it will be best to institute more direct democracy at the local level, further experiment with larger reforms at the state level, and pass those laws at the national level that correct mistakes of the Trump era and remove structural barriers to representative democracy.

Balkin identifies three political cycles that explain the current level of constitutional rot and that offer hope of overcoming it. The three cycles are the current conservative, Republican Party–dominated political regime that began with the Reagan administration; the partisan polarization that began in the culture wars of the 1968 election; and the current cycle of constitutional rot in the Trump era.[55]

We can begin by recognizing the seriousness of our problems and the need to reform if we are to create a virtuous reinforcing cycle of rebirth and renewal. The conservative cycle, cultural wars, and Trump phenomenon may have run their course, and new historical trends can now be initiated.

President Biden at his inauguration promised more unity, more truth from government, and an end to our "uncivil war." He recognized that this was a time for boldness. So, it is time to begin the process of renewal and reform.

The Move to Deliberative Democracy

Given the significant challenges we face, simple incremental changes by themselves will be insufficient. We will have to amend the Constitution to cure some of our ills. And we have to improve our political system. The first step is to recognize that our democracy must be made both more deliberative and more participatory. Experiments in more direct democracy, from New England town meetings to neighborhood governments, provide guidance for what must be done. At the same time, we must limit the influence of money in our elections and make them less polarizing. We must, as well, remove structural barriers to greater democracy.

Since each approach to more deliberative democracy has their respective strengths and disadvantages, no one reform can solve all our political and governmental problems. The best alternative is to adopt a number of reforms—ward assemblies, participatory budgeting, and community hearings at the local level; citizen juries, initiatives, and deliberative polling at the state level; and more congressional deliberation with constituents at the national level. Legislation curbing campaign finance abuse, setting term limits, and ending gerrymandering—all of which stand in the way of better democratic representation—must be adopted to make these changes possible. Achieving all these reforms will require public support and an aroused public seeking to reclaim our democracy.

Citizens speak out at a Chicago City Council meeting, February 19, 2020.
(Photo courtesy John R. Boehm Photography, www.jboehmphoto.com)

11

Spirit of Democracy

Some political analysts claim that the United States is a plutocracy, moving toward an aristocracy of inherited wealth.[1] Today, the top 1 percent of Americans take home 20 percent of the income and 75 percent of the wealth is owned by the richest 10 percent. Given this unequal wealth, it is not surprising that "one percent of one percent" (0.1 percent) of the population account for $1.3 billion in federal political campaign contributions.[2] This, in turn, leads members of Congress to consistently vote for the policy preferences of the wealthy over the desires of most Americans.[3]

Beyond income inequality and the clout the wealthy have over government, Alan Wolfe argues that, "when it comes to the quality of its performance, American democracy is not doing well at all."[4] He concludes that our democracy works badly because citizens and leaders often do not act out of a sense of justice and public spirit. He asserts that, we need to act out of "a sense of duty to others rather than comfort and convenience to ourselves."[5]

The grounds for hope begin with the story of Chicago's rebirth as an example of what might be possible in the country. As the photo opening this chapter shows, despite the pandemic, economic recession, and national political turmoil, Chicago remains a vibrant city, a visible symbol of resilience and rebirth. Its citizens speak out at city council meetings and demand reform and change.

Chicago's Rebirth

On May 20, 2019, Mayor Lori Lightfoot and a more progressive Chicago City Council, having won the 2019 city elections, were sworn into office. Since the administration of President Franklin D. Roosevelt, historians, political scientists, and journalists have paid particular attention to the first hundred days of a new government on the theory that there will be a political honeymoon when the winners can sometimes get big things done, especially if the chief executive received a mandate of a landslide election. Since Mayor Lightfoot won 74 percent of the vote in the runoff elections and carried all fifty wards, she had the political capital to move forward with her reform agenda.

In 2021, there were similar hopes for the new Biden administration even if his support in Congress was less than Lightfoot's in the Chicago City Council.

It is not always the case that big things get done in the first hundred days. For instance, because he won by a much closer margin in more racially and politically fractured Chicago in 1983, Mayor Harold Washington got no honeymoon. He faced a 29–21 opposition split in the city council that blocked many of his programs for his first three and a half years in office. Only after new court-ordered elections gave him majority control after 1986, could his full agenda be implemented.

In comparison, Mayor Lightfoot won all thirty-two of the divided roll call votes on controversial issues in her first year in office and a total of seventy-seven divided votes by the end of her second year.[6] In 2020, she governed by her executive authority alone in the first months of the COVID-19 pandemic when the council couldn't meet. The economic recession created a $2 billion budget gap to be overcome and additional police accountability cases that have made city council votes closer. But Mayor Lightfoot has managed even with the pandemic and recession to balance the budget and move her progressive reform agenda forward.

Mayor Lightfoot began her term in office propitiously with a diverse and experienced transition team. Its ten committees, hundreds of experts, and community representatives compiled by her inauguration a 110-page report with recommended policy changes and goals to be implemented.[7]

As we saw in the previous chapter, on the very day that she was sworn into office, she signed an executive order eliminating aldermanic privilege in routine administrative matters. Aldermen could have a voice on decisions like awnings, signs, and building permits for developments in their wards, but they would no longer have a veto. This was particularly important because the indictment of Fourteenth Ward alderman Edward Burke during the 2019 election charged him with holding up a driveway permit for a fast-food restaurant until a bribe was paid in the form of legal fees and campaign contributions. So, eliminating aldermanic privilege was the first installment of the mayor's ethics reform package and it was accomplished by executive order within hours of becoming mayor.

Her second major victory was in the first votes in the Chicago City Council. The most important votes aldermen take are the first ones in which they adopt rules of procedure, establish council committees, their membership, and chairmanships. The first city council votes had gone against Harold Washington 29–21; whereas Mayors Richard M. Daley and Rahm Emanuel began their terms with solid majority support, which only grew as they reduced the council to a rubber stamp. In Mayor Lightfoot's case, the rules she proposed and the committees and committee chairmanships that she negotiated carried by a voice vote of more than forty of the fifty aldermen.

On July 24, 2019, she and her council allies won another victory by a unanimous vote. They passed sweeping ethics reform ordinance amendments that gave the Chicago Inspector General authority to investigate aldermen, their staff, and the mayor's office without sworn affidavits from complainants. In addition, the inspector general was given subpoena powers he had not had previously. And the new ethics rules spelled out that aldermen could not have outside employment that conflicted with their duties to the city or to their constituents. So, on ethics reform, especially as it related to aldermen and the city council, Mayor Lightfoot and her progressive allies scored major victories within the first hundred days.

Mayor Lightfoot's next big challenge was a Chicago teacher's strike in October 2019 that lasted eleven days. It was at times acrimonious, with demands for higher wages, more school librarians and nurses, and paid teacher preparation time. Teachers won most of their demands, including a 16 percent salary increase over five years. While there were some hard feelings among the teachers and their union, the strike was not as contentious as the one that resulted in the teachers' permanent political opposition to Mayor Emanuel.[8] Although the teachers' strike was settled, tensions between the teachers' union and the Lightfoot administration would continue, however.

The biggest challenge and test for Mayor Lightfoot prior to the COVID-19 pandemic was a $838 million gap in the 2020 city budget that she had to close without raising property taxes significantly. She was able to do so, and to add $10 million each to funding services for the homeless and the mentally ill, as well as opening public libraries on Sundays once again. The city council vote approving her $11.6 billion city budget on November 26, 2019, was 39–11, demonstrating the mayor's continuing dominance in the city council.[9]

Turning to the city's social and economic issues, in the first months of 2020, after her successful first hundred days, Mayor Lightfoot held a poverty summit with seven hundred participants to create an agenda for attacking the disparities among Chicago communities. Mayor Lightfoot, having successfully implemented her anticorruption reform agenda was now able to turn to progressive social reforms. Solving racial and income inequality, increasing the city's population, creating more balanced economic development, lowering the crime rate, and improving the public schools were all long-term projects. But the city was at least beginning to tackle these problems in Lightfoot's first year in office.

But in 2020 as winter was ending, the COVID-19 pandemic hit Chicago. The city became one of the disease hotspots in the country. Mayor Lightfoot, in conjunction with Illinois governor J. B. Pritzker, coordinated the battle against the spread of COVID-19. The public supported their leadership. While President Trump's approval rating stayed in the 40 percent range, public approval of the governor and the mayor was at 70 percent.[10] For a number of months the city council was not able to meet and the mayor governed by her executive authority and was later granted permission by the city council to do so.

Other challenges continued in Chicago as murder and shooting rates soared. Neighborhood economic development as well as the loss of population, affordable housing, and jobs continued to plague the city. However, Mayor Lightfoot pushed forward. Despite the pandemic and economic recession, changes were beginning to take effect. By 2021, with a second federal stimulus package passed, a change in leadership in the national government, and vaccines against the virus being distributed, progress began to be visible. By June 2021, the city was able to fully reopen and rescind its COVID-19 pandemic restrictions.

Mayors and governors have generally been more successful than the national government in coping with the pandemic during the Trump administration and were generally given a higher job approval rating from the voters. The National League of Cities summarized in its 2020 report: "The state of our cities continues to be strong even in these troubled times. Right now, mayors are battling the twin challenges of a public health crisis precipitated by the COVID-19 pandemic and the economic fallout that the novel coronavirus has wrought on our nation's communities. Mayors have been on the frontlines serving as stalwart leaders—together with the essential workers and the fire, police, sanitation, and public health employees—guiding our cities through this storm. This journey is far from over, and our essential cities will recover and rebuild."[11]

Mayor Lightfoot's accomplishments in Chicago give hope that the same type of success might occur now nationally after a new government had been sworn into office. However, as the Lightfoot experience and the experience of the first six months of the Biden administration have shown, there will be continual challenges. And the Biden administration, with a narrow partisan majority in the House of Representatives and a bare majority in the divided Senate, does not have the support in the Congress that Lightfoot was able to keep in the Chicago City Council. Nonetheless, President Biden has thus far been able to get the funding necessary to fight the pandemic and begin economic recovery. By executive authority, he has also been able to reverse many of the Trump policies on environment, trade, and civil rights. It is a promising beginning.

A Democratic Movement for Change

Winning a single election for president or mayor is the first step in democracy's recovery and rebirth, not the end point. In the 1990s, there was a great increase in democratization worldwide, especially with the revolutions in 1989 and the collapse of the Soviet Union in 1991.[12] Then in the twenty-first century the pattern reversed, with populism and authoritarianism surging around the world. As Freedom House observes, there have been fifteen consecutive years of decline in global freedom since 2006 and nearly 75 percent "of the world's population lived in a country that faced deterioration last year."[13] Here in the United States, President Trump and his allies ruled for four years.

Now with the election of President Joe Biden and Mayor Lori Lightfoot, it is possible to reverse many of the policies of former administrations. But a genuine democratic resurgence in the face of the challenges in the twenty-first century and the adoption of the reforms advocated in this book will require a broader strategy. It starts with a broader social and political movement for change.

As Page and Gilens argue, a movement to increase government's responsiveness to average citizens and decrease political power to the wealthy and corporations, "can only be attained through a broad energetic and persistent social movement; a coalition of millions of people joined together to bring about democratic reforms over the long term."[14] It will have to be a movement such as the one that elected Mayor Lightfoot and a more progressive city council in Chicago. The times require that we, the people, elect better officials and create the demand for democratic reforms.

This historical time may allow, that just as progressive movements developed after the Gilded Age, we may now be able to create a movement for reform. In *The Upswing*, Robert Putnam and Shaylyn Garret argue that we have moved from an "I" society to a "we" society back to "I." However, after the "I" period of the Gilded Age "came more than six decades of imperfect but steady upward progress toward *greater* economic equality, *more* cooperation in the public square, a *stronger* social fabric, and a *growing* culture of solidarity."[15] Then in the 1960s this upswing "abruptly reversed direction" and we had a downturn and "re-created the socioeconomic chasm of the last Gilded Age."[16] The authors conclude that in the twenty-first century we again have the opportunity to re-create the progress achieved by the social and political movements that ended the Gilded Age.

According to Putnam and Garret, to achieve the monumental changes we need requires "starting in our own communities and recognizing the latent power of collective action not just to protest but to build the foundations of a reimagined America."[17] In short, we must reimagine a more just and democratic society. Then re-create the "spirit of democracy" that animated the American Revolution, Civil War, and civil rights movement. We must make the sacrifices and do the hard work, starting in our communities, to give democracy once again its rebirth.

In a similar vein, Vascha Mounk writes that even the election of Donald Trump and the turn to the right doesn't doom our effort at renewal. He argues that it wasn't "until strongmen gained a second or third victory at the polls that they completed their countries' descent toward outright dictatorship." When Donald Trump and other populists come up for reelection and they are defeated, as he was in the 2020 election, "liberal democracy—at least for the short run—is likely to recover." But in a democracy, the only protection against the slide to oligarchy and autocracy is to persuade people to vote against populists.

To have citizens vote against populists with their siren songs of enemies within and abroad demands that we right the economic and social wrongs that cause the politics of resentment. As Mounk puts it, "joining a political movement that has a real hope of success at the polls remains one of the best ways to stand up for democracy."[18]

Page and Gilens outline three conditions for success of such social and political movements for change: "widespread agreement that we have serious problems"; these problems are understood as "failures of government"; and "enough people . . . care enough about these problems to devote a lot of time and energy to bring about change."[19]

President Barack Obama recounts in his memoir, *A Promised Land*, what such a movement feels like and what hard work it is. This is especially obvious in his retelling of the retail politics and citizen mobilization in the critical Iowa caucuses that made his win of the broader 2008 election possible. As he writes about the spirit of campaigning in 2007 in Iowa just before the caucus votes were taken, "Right there, in that high school in the middle of the country on a cold winter night, I had witnessed the community I had so long sought, the America I imagined, made manifest."[20] It is the campaign spirit and people turning out to caucus, discuss with neighbors, and vote, that is the spirit we need now and the community we need to create.

There have been the Black Lives Matter protests, Women's Marches, and various anti-Trump protests, but building a broader movement for reinventing democracy in America in our time is still a work in progress.

Solutions

Democracy's rebirth requires political action like what is occurring in Chicago and occurred on that cold winter night in Iowa in 2007. We must act to make structural reforms that promote democracy. Since a new national government came to power in 2021, much of the first six months of the Biden administration was taken up with ending the pandemic, preparing for economic recovery, and rolling back the negative actions of the Trump administration on climate change, foreign policy, immigration, and racial justice. That work continues.

It is important to remember that we have faced national crises before. We have weathered previous rebellions, wars, and depressions. We have survived inept leaders. By unifying and mobilizing Americans, the crises and challenges of the last few years make radical changes more possible now.

We are at a turning point to determine if we can create a viable deliberative democracy in the midst of the twenty-first century. Even if we have the courage and the wisdom to meet these challenges and a movement to back reforms, we still need an explicit agenda for change.

Each chapter in this book outlines the interrelated problems that need to be solved and solutions at both the national and local level. Among the specific recommendations are the following:

- Create a fairer tax system so that the wealthy and corporations pay significantly higher taxes.
- Better regulate transnational corporations.
- Institute a shorter work week, better education, and job training programs for citizens and workers, along with programs to rebuild the middle class along with the leisure time to engage in civic activities.
- Enact fairer immigration rules and citizenship for the twelve million immigrants already in the United States without legal status. As part

- of the new rules, immediately enact DACA protections for those who came to the United States as young children.
- Robustly enforce civil rights laws and reinstitute the Voting Rights Act of 1965 or pass the broader HR 1 For the People Act to prevent voter suppression laws and make voting easier.
- Publicly finance political campaigns and restrict private campaign contributions.
- In the longer term, repeal *Citizens United* by a constitutional amendment to clarify that corporations are not citizens, that campaign contributions can be regulated, and that corruption can be broadly defined and prohibited.
- Implement automatic voter registration in all states and the District of Columbia.
- Institute ranked-choice voting to end uncompetitive districts and single-party dominance.
- Ensure greater transparency in government so citizens can better hold officials accountable. This will require not only posting the information on the Internet but making it available in easy-to-use forms, public meetings to explain the data, and freedom of information procedures that allow citizens to demand relevant information from their government in a timely manner.
- Require civic education and civic engagement courses in schools and enact the Civics Secures Democracy Act to make civic engagement a priority in K–12 education.
- Establish nonpartisan redistricting commissions to end partisan gerrymandering after 2021.
- Prohibit outside employment of public officials that conflicts with their public duties.
- Strengthen the role of inspectors general in all units of government.
- Destroy machine politics by eliminating patronage, favoritism, and crooked contacts.
- Create more participatory neighborhood government in our cities and towns.
- Create deliberative democratic institutions at the state and national levels.
- Work to eliminate the culture of corruption and institutional corruption.
- Reform the Electoral College so that the results reflect the national popular vote for president and vice president.
- Enact term limits for all elected offices.
- Create longer early voting periods, easier vote-by-mail systems, and, when safeguards are in place, institute electronic voting.

- Institute merit selection and term limits for judges.
- Amend the Constitution to rebalance the Senate to make it more democratic. Limit the filibuster, the hold on appointments, and use of the Hastert rule.
- Limit political polarization and resentment by solving underlying social and economic injustice and by providing more voice and citizen control of their governments.
- Increase the individual civic virtue and willingness to sacrifice necessary to mobilize citizens to enact the other reforms.

None of us can work on all these reforms, nor can they be achieved at the same time. But we can each work on a few of them. These reforms will not be achieved as quickly as many of us would wish. Some reforms are more difficult and will take longer to accomplish. They will not be a simple fix instituted by a single election or by the passage of a single law. But they can be accomplished if we join movements to demand their adoption. For their adoption depends on a reform movement that is broader than a single issue or a single demographic. Elites currently in power will not enact them unless there is a strong public demand.

None of these reforms can be achieved without building civic virtue in individuals and broader social and political movements. They will happen only when the public demands change. We will have to elect officials pledged to carry them out. But many of these reforms will first have to be adopted locally to build the popular support to enact them nationally. So, we can begin where we live.

Civic Virtue

Our nation's founders knew the history of the fall of the Roman Republic and the corruption in British politics at the time of our revolution. This caused them to believe that civic virtue and the willingness to sacrifice, as they and their compatriots had in the revolution of 1776, was essential to preserving a democratic nation. When Benjamin Franklin was asked at the conclusion of the Constitutional Convention if we were to have a republic or a monarchy, he is reputed to have answered, "A republic, if you can keep it." To keep a representative democracy requires constant reinvention and renewal. Democracy demands a democratic people.

Today, we are faced with the need of massive reforms. Fundamental changes are required to create a deliberative democracy adequate to the challenges and opportunities of the twenty-first century. The reforms listed above and described in earlier chapters depend on civic virtue and our willingness to resist personal *and* institutional corruption. We must be willing to sacrifice personal ease and gain for the sake of our community and nation.

To call forth such selflessness, we must purify our institutions, politics, and ourselves. We must hold free, fair, and frequent elections whose outcomes are not warped by the misuse of technology, dominated by economic elites, or tainted by interference by enemies abroad. Our partisanship must not become so extreme as to foster hate, resentment, polarization, and gridlock. We must uphold the guardrails and norms of democracy, such as tolerance and forbearance, as well as its laws.

Our economic system must be made fairer. Currently, the top economic earners do not pay their fair share of taxes, the middle class on whom democracy rests is shrinking, and the poor are too oppressed in their effort to eke out a living and cope with day-to-day problems to participate meaningfully.

Added to this, transnational corporations are insufficiently regulated. Wealthy global corporations corrupt our politics for their own benefit. A society composed only of the very wealthy and the poor, powerful corporations and the powerless, cannot sustain democracy.

Although we are a nation of immigrants, we have built walls to keep out future workers, entrepreneurs, inventors, and citizens. Many immigrants have special contributions to make to our culture and society. This is why we have a message of welcome on the Statue of Liberty in the New York Harbor. The United States takes refugees from other lands and transforms them into productive citizens. We have since our beginning. And while we cannot have completely open borders, our current anti-immigrant policies must change. We have to offer a reasonable path to citizenship to undocumented immigrants and especially the "dreamers" who came here as young children.

In many cases, we know what reforms are needed and the best ways to achieve them. But gaining the resources, support, and political will to enact those best practices is the problem. Because any fundamental transformation will take many years to achieve, we must begin by instilling the ideal of civic virtue by training a new generation of citizens capable of democratic citizenship.

Teaching Civic Engagement

The Association of American Colleges and Universities in its document, *What Liberal Education Looks Like*, makes explicit the link between education and democracy: "Democracy is not self-sustaining; rather, it depends on the sustained engagement of a free people who are united in their commitment to the fundamental principles it is intended to preserve and advance—justice, liberty, human dignity, equality of persons. The task of an education allied to democracy is not simply to help students gain knowledge and skills, but in so doing also to form the habits of heart and mind that liberate them and that equip them for, and dispose them to, civic involvement and the creation of a more just and inclusive society."[21]

As the ancient Athenians knew, a liberal education is essential, but democracy is best learned by practicing democracy. Citizenship requires civic knowledge, motivation, and experience. Allowing more citizen participation in a more deliberative democracy lets us and the next generation learn by practice how to become democratic citizens.

A necessary step in creating a better citizenry is teaching civic engagement in our schools from early grades straight through college. If we are to have a democracy, we must educate for democracy.

On Constitution Day, September 17, 2020, U.S. Representatives Rosa DeLauro (CT-03) and Tom Cole (OK-04), chair and ranking member of the Labor, Health and Human Services, Education, and Related Agencies Appropriations Subcommittee, introduced the Educating for Democracy Act, which has since been reintroduced as the Civics Secures Democracy Act, to make civic education a priority and to provide major funding for the effort and careful testing of its impact.[22] It has strong bipartisan support in Congress and support of more than a hundred educational organizations pressing for its adoption. Passing it is an important first step in prioritizing civic education in schools once again.

The current movement to promote civic engagement has followed earlier democratic education renewals. Perhaps the most famous centered on John Dewey and progressive educators at the beginning of the twentieth century. Now we have a renewed effort to teach democracy once more in the United States and globally.[23]

The beginning of the current civic education effort was marked by the publication of *A Crucible Moment* by the National Task Force on Civic Engagement in 2012 during the Obama administration.[24] Over the last decade, an ever-greater effort to teach civic engagement reached a high point in the 2020 elections. This election had more participation by high school and college students than in previous decades, which had been marked by much lower student voting. Turnout among young people ages eighteen to twenty-nine reached 55 percent according to the Center for Information and Research on Civic Learning and Engagement—up at least 8 percent from the youth turnout of 2016.[25] The youth vote, and especially the vote by minority youths, was pivotal in many key states in electing Biden and Harris.

At the same time as youth participation increased, the pedagogy for teaching civic engagement also improved. In two books that I coedited for the American Political Science Association, *Teaching Civic Engagement* and *Teaching Civic Engagement across the Disciplines*, nearly seventy authors developed methods for teaching civic engagement in a range of political science courses.[26] More importantly, we encouraged civic engagement across college campuses in different disciplines and fields of study. The third book in the series published September 2021, *Teaching Civic Engagement Globally*, shares lessons learned from civic engagement efforts around the world. The challenge is to expand these programs of educating for democracy universally.

As these methods were adapted to civic engagement in the COVID-19 pandemic, the basic goals remained the same. They included the following:

1. Incorporating civic engagement as a university goal in the mission statement and in priorities of the university president or chancellor. Getting a firm commitment from university leadership is a necessary first step to organizing campus-wide civic engagement efforts.
2. Creating a core group of at least a dozen faculty, administrators, and students to coordinate civic engagement efforts on campus. It should meet at least once a month to plan the campus civic engagement programs and to pool resources.
3. Setting explicit goals including the number of students to be registered to vote, percentage of students who vote, and community civic engagement activities to be done per semester.
4. Developing a common campus engagement calendar of events.
5. Getting commitments to coordinate and pay for these events:
   a. Voter registration as new students obtain their student IDs or as students register for classes.
   b. Constitution Day programs held on September 17 each year.
   c. National Voter Registration Day. It is federally mandated that universities inform students of registration deadlines and encourage voter registration.
   d. TurboVote or similar software that provide students with voter registration and voting reminders by e-mail throughout the year as well as links to electronic voter registration and vote-by-mail applications.
   e. Sign-up for information on registration and voting participation through the National Study of Learning, Voting, and Engagement to gauge the level of participation.[27]
   f. Primary-election debates and election-night watch discussions.
   g. Alternative spring break programs to allow intensive student community engagement.

h. Internship and service learning opportunities in all departments.
i. Opportunities like Model UN, Mock Trial, Congressional Debate, Model State Legislature, and National Student Issues Convention.
j. Lobbying at state capitols and Congress for more funding for students and universities.

6. Creating early voting and regular polling places on campus to make student voting easier.
7. Instituting automatic voter registration where allowed under state law.
8. Reminding students to vote by mail and to utilize early voting opportunities.
9. Promoting social media efforts like "I Vote" or "Student March to the Polls," in which students post their voting activities on twitter, Instagram, Facebook, and other social media to build student enthusiasm.
10. Arranging political speakers and candidate debates on campus.
11. Creating distinct learning opportunities and a ladder of civic engagement experiences through multiple courses.

There have been many other civic engagement efforts at individual college campuses and parallel efforts to teach civic engagement at the high school and middle school levels. Some states, including Illinois, passed laws mandating civic engagement courses as a graduation requirement. Many schools have adopted service-learning requirements to expose students to problems in their own communities and to allow them to advocate what might be done to alleviate problems like hunger, homelessness, and poverty.

As a part of the renewed civic engagement effort in 2020, national university organizations adopted a goal of a 20 percent increase in student voter registration and a 5 percent increase in student voting over the 2016 presidential election levels. In the end, despite the pandemic, students registered in record numbers and the total student vote was about 55 percent, surpassing the goals.[28]

The United States still falls far short of nearly universal voter registration and nearly 90 percent turnout in many mature democracies. For instance, Belgium has an 87 percent voting rate and Sweden 82 percent.[29] We still have a long way to go in our electoral participation to match what is regularly achieved in other democracies. But civic engagement education is making a difference.

Beyond voting, it is important to create institutions and to instill skills of deliberative discussion and decision-making among the public. And that will require a reorganization of our education system to make civic engagement a central part of school and college education.

Democracies Do Die

It is insufficient only to adopt institutional structural reforms and teach democracy. Democracies can die. The takeover of Germany by Nazis in the twentieth century, along with the current threats to democracy, and the rise of populism in the United States and Europe, provide a clear warning that democracy's rebirth will require greater efforts.

Surprisingly, democracies often die at the hands of elected leaders: "presidents or prime ministers who subvert the very process that brought them to power."[30] Adolph Hitler, Vladimir Putin, and Hugo Chávez are examples of the type of elected autocrats who undermine democracy. To prevent the ascension of autocrats, formal checks and balances written into laws and constitutions are insufficient. They must be reinforced by unwritten democratic norms, two of which in the United States have been mutual tolerance and institutional forbearance. These guardrails of democracy keep societies from veering off the road and becoming autocracies or totalitarian nations. Both guardrails were weakened in the Trump era.

As Robert Rowland describes it,

> By undercutting rhetorical norms that have shaped American politics for decades, Trump created fear and hatred and sowed division. In a political system in which partisans view their political opponents not as misguided but as dangerous or evil, winning at all costs will become the norm. This could lead to the gradual loss of basic democratic institutions or in a crisis threatened the democratic system itself.
>
> Trump's nationalist populist message also threatens American democracy by undercutting the very idea of truth itself. . . .
>
> When the distinction between truth and lies disappears, there is no basis for the rational discourse on which the organization of a free society, governed by laws depends. . . . "Lies and untruths are the enemy of honest democratic deliberation."[31]

Trump also undermined the free press and increased the levels of polarization and alienation. Finally, he ignored tolerance and forbearance in attempting to aggrandize his power. So, the effects of the Trump era were not just in laws, regulations, and appointments, but in undermining democratic norms and the guardrails on which democracy ultimately depends.

Why are tolerance and forbearance so important? "Mutual toleration is politicians' collective willingness to agree to disagree." It recognizes that opponents may have legitimate motives for the positions they hold. It allows for civic discourse and compromise. Forbearance is "the action of restraining from exercising a legal right."[32] Forbearance restrains the government from crushing opponents in ways that would invite rebellion and violence. This means that, although it is legal to refuse, for instance, to hold hearings on Supreme Court nominations or to stack the federal courts with partisan ideologues, it is not prudent to do so because it undermines impartial justice and soon imperils democracy.

As Levitsky and Ziblatt put it, norms like tolerance and forbearance are the

> soft guardrails of democracy, preventing day-to-day competition from devolving into a no-holds-barred conflict.
> Norms are more than personal dispositions. . . . They are shared codes of conduct.[33]

When parties become too extreme, polarized, and aligned along economic, racial, or religious dimensions, then democracy itself is threatened. Formal laws and constitutions can be falsely interpreted and subverted if norms don't uphold ideals such as fair elections and fair play by common rules.

When democratic norms no longer hold, an autocratic populist leader is elected who rejects democratic rules of the game and the legitimacy of the opposition, creating a situation that then encourages violence, curtails civic liberties, takes over the judicial and law enforcement agencies, and permanently changes the balance of power. Slowly, step by baby step, democracy is undermined and eventually dies.

Many observers believe that President Donald Trump was just such an autocratic leader and fear that democracy in America might die as a result. Today we rebuild in the hope that democracy—more specifically, a more equal, multiracial, better deliberative democracy—may be reborn after the pandemic, economic recession, and Trump political era end. America has survived democratic breakdowns as great as the Civil War in the past and recovered. It is time, once again, to foster democracy's rebirth.

Political Action

The reaction against Trump's erratic and regressive administration provides a unique opportunity for making substantial reforms. The 2020 election of new leaders across the country creates the opportunity to make major strides forward. Just as the "new normal" in which we will live after the COVID-19 pandemic and economic recession provides a basis for change. Because our old lives have been upended, we are prepared to do things differently. In this time of change, we may be open to radical political transformations unthinkable only a few years ago.

While the pandemic in the United States has not entirely ended, immunization of a significant majority of the population has made the crisis less acute. We are moving into a new normal as schools and universities, restaurants, bars, ballparks, and theaters are reopening.

At the same time, the economy is recovering as the stock market remains at an all time high and jobless rates drop. The insurrection of January 6, 2021, however, remains a powerful warning of our democracy's fragility.

The wave of books analyzing our challenges as a democracy continue to pour forth.[34] Their conclusions about the severity of our problems are remarkably consistent. Many agree with George Packer, who writes that "American under Trump became less free, less equal, more divided, more alone, deeper in debt, swampier, dirtier, meaner, sicker, and deader."[35] We will be dealing with the legacy of the Trump administration for many years, and our problems were shown in high relief by his election and presidency. But, as William Howell and Terry Moe put it, "Trump himself is not the main reason America faces such troubled times. He is a symptom of powerful socioeconomic forces unleashed by modernity."[36]

In 2021, a new administration took office in Washington, D.C. New members of Congress and state legislators were sworn in. Reform mayors like Chicago's Lori Lightfoot led many U.S. cities. Many of the new officials had run on reform platforms with specific pledges to bring hope and change.

There have been positive steps taken since President Biden took office, including massive federal spending on pandemic relief, economic recovery, and infrastructure. The elections of 2022 and 2024 will determine whether the political pendulum will swing back toward the Trump. But even if those elections are won by progressive candidates, the dangers outlined in this book, will remain if major reforms are not undertaken.

Again, Chicago provides an example of what can be achieved. Mayor Lightfoot successfully completed her first two years in office despite a school strike, continued racial and income inequality, a once-in-a-century pandemic, and turnover among her top staff members. In her time in office, she has not permanently lost a single city council vote on issues she has championed. The old rubber-stamp city council is a thing of the past. So the mayor, constantly pushed by progressive groups and the progressive bloc in the city council, is now able to move forward more aggressively on her original agenda of reform. There is hope in the air as the city comes out of the COVID-19 lockdown, masks are removed, and most Chicagoans return to jobs and pre-pandemic activity.

Given the changes taking place in society, the economy, and government, this is the time to build a stronger political movement to eliminate structural barriers and to establish a more deliberative democracy. Despite partisan divides that remain in the country, there is consensus that much needs to be done to heal the rifts in our society.

Political scientists like Howell and Moe believe that "institutional reform is the key challenge of our times, and national success at meeting it will determine our future as a democratic nation . . . populism will be defused only when the public's genuine needs are met by a government capable of effective action."[37]

Others, like my University of Illinois at Chicago colleague Zizi Papademos, argue that we live in an imperfect democracy. In interviewing hundreds of people around the globe, she found that "none [of the people interviewed] find democracy ideal. . . . Little is right, and a lot must change." She and those interviewed propose eliminating this disconnect between the people and their government. She advocates a ten-point plan to improve democracy by a more participatory government at the micro level, reinventing journalism, and using technology more effectively to create new civic avenues for participation.[38]

In truth, we need both institutional reforms and a revitalization of the democracy itself with greater and more informed citizen participation. And to get either, we must have a movement of change comparable to the abolitionist movement before the Civil War or the civil rights movement of the 1960s.

Democracy's rebirth will take decades. It will require a sustained effort. As we move in this direction, we will need to conserve and protect our political heritage as we make changes. We will have to reflect on our actions and make course corrections. But it is essential that we act. It is time to begin.

We face a great challenge, which is also a great opportunity, to preside at democracy's rebirth.

Acknowledgments

No book is possible without the help of many. I would not have written this one without the support of my partner Margaret and my family, Kate, Jeffrey, Lilian, and Polly. Too many friends to name here have bolstered my efforts and spirits. I hope you know of my gratitude.

I have been part of reform movements and campaigns for more than sixty years. My fellow reformers have taught me what I know about politics and democracy. I have tried to pass on some of that knowledge in this book.

My students, fellow faculty, and coauthors have furthered my understanding with the wisdom they have imparted. I am most thankful to the University of Illinois at Chicago, which has allowed me to teach there for more than five decades. I am especially grateful for my undergraduate and graduate student classes in 2019 and 2020 who worked through these chapters with me.

My friend and frequent coauthor, Tom Gradel, obtained all the photographs that illustrate this book.

At the University of Illinois Press, I am thankful as well for the guidance of Editor-in-Chief Daniel Nasset, who pushed me to develop the Chicago focus. I am also grateful to the senior production editor, Tad Ringo, and my wonderful copy editor, Deborah Oliver, who caught so many of my errors. I am responsible for all that remain.

Notes

Chapter 1. Challenges to Democracy

1. See, for example, Steven Levitsky and Daniel Ziblatt, *How Democracies Die* (New York: Crown Books, 2018), 227; Danielle Allen, "Charlottesville Is Not the Continuation of an Old Fight. It Is Something New," *Washington Post*, August 13, 2017; and Christopher Hayes, *Twilight of the Elites: America after Meritocracy* (New York: Random House, 2012), 59–63. A fuller description of racial and economic inequality appears in chapter 3 of this book.

2. Gregory Scruggs, "'Everything We've Heard about Global Urbanization Turns Out to Be Wrong: Researchers," *Reuters*, July 12, 2018.

3. Aristotle defines "civic virtue" as "citizens taking part in ruling and being ruled." The Romans among others thought civic virtue was one of the principal and essential elements needed to build a successful polity. See https://www.britannica.com/topic/civic-virtue.

4. For a discussion of how we might better teach democracy in schools and universities, see Alison Rios Millett McCartney, Elizabeth A. Bennion, and Dick Simpson, eds., *Teaching Civic Engagement* (Washington, DC: American Political Science Association, 2013) and the other books in this series published by the association.

Chapter 2. The Rise and Fall of Democracy

1. "This week [April 2018], The Heritage Foundation added 26 new entries to its election fraud database [www.heritage.org/voterfraud], bringing the searchable ledger to a total of 1,132 proven instances of election fraud. That includes 983 cases that ended in a criminal conviction, 48 that led to civil penalties, 79 where defendants were enrolled in a diversion program, and 22 cases of official or judicial findings of fraud." Jason Snead, "Add These Voter Fraud Cases to the Growing List," Com-

mentary: Election Integrity, Heritage Foundation, April 19, 2018, www.heritage.org/election-integrity/commentary/add-these-voter-fraud-cases-the-growing-list.

2. Mike Royko, *Boss: Richard J. Daley of Chicago* (New York: Dutton, 1971), 77.

3. The quotation from Rechtenwald is from Dick Simpson (producer) and William Machine (director), "The Chicago City Council," Chicago: University of Illinois at Chicago, 1982. Available on YouTube and my Chicago Politics website (https://pols.uic.edu/chicago-politics/).

4. Many newspaper and magazine headlines called Richard J. Daley "the last boss." The phrase is even quoted in the definitive Encyclopedia of Chicago History in the entry written by historian Roger Biles (http://www.encyclopedia.chicagohistory.org/pages/774.html).

5. "Extract from Thomas Jefferson to Adamanntios Coray," October 31, 1823, Jefferson Quotes and Family Letters, Thomas Jefferson Foundation, https://tjrs.monticello.org/letter/424.

6. Joyce Appleby and Terence Ball, eds., *Thomas Jefferson, Political Writings* (New York: Cambridge University Press, 1999), 231–319. See also Thomas Jefferson, *The Writings of Thomas Jefferson*, Memorial ed., edited by Andrew A. Lipscomb and Albert Ellery Bergh, 20 vols. (Washington, DC: Issued under the auspices of the Thomas Jefferson Memorial Association of the United States, 1903–4).

7. "Tyranny" is defined in *The Federalist Papers* by James Madison, Alexander Hamilton, and John Jay. Any edition of the book is fine, but the Library of Congress version is online at https://guides.loc.gov/federalist-papers/full-text. One of the best discussions of the key philosophy of the Constitution and the Federalist Papers is Robert A. Dahl, *Preface to Democratic Theory* (Chicago: University of Chicago Press, 2006).

8. See especially Ian Shapiro, *The State of Democratic Theory* (Princeton, NJ: Princeton University Press, 2003).

9. Hanna Pitkin, *The Concept of Representation* (Berkeley: University of California Press, 1967).

10. Rachel Hinton and Mitch Dudek, "City Council Poised to Have Most Latinos, Fewest Whites Ever," *Chicago Sun-Times*, April 2, 2019, https://chicago.suntimes.com.

11. David Llorens, "The Only Real 'Negro Voice' in the Chicago City Council," *Negro Digest* 16, no. 2 (December 1966): 44–48.

12. See Quote Investigator, https://quoteinvestigator.com/2014/01/12/history-rhymes/.

13. Abraham Lincoln's House Divided Speech (June 16, 1858) is at www.abrahamlincolnonline.org/lincoln/speeches/house.htm.

14. The concept of the permanent underclass was first developed in William Julius Wilson, *The Truly Disadvantaged: The Inner City, the Underclass, and Public Policy* (Chicago: University of Chicago Press, 1987).

Chapter 3. Income and Racial Inequality

1. Biographical information is from "About Lori Lightfoot," Lightfoot for Chicago, May 2019, http://lightfootforchicago.com/about-lori/, accessed April 12, 2019. Mayor

Byrne, who also had not held elected office prior to her election as mayor, had been Mayor Daley's commissioner of Consumer Sales, Weights, and Measures and cochair of the Cook County Democratic Party.

2. Benjamin I. Page, Jason Seawright, and Matthew J. Lacombe, *Billionaires and Stealth Politics* (Chicago: University of Chicago Press, 2019). This is the best and most current source on billionaires and their effect on our political life.

3. Stephen Caliendo, *Inequality in America: Race, Poverty, and Fulfilling Democracy's Promise*, 2d ed. (New York: Westview, 2018), 47.

4. Christopher Ingram, "The Richest 1 Percent Now Owns More of the Country's Wealth Than at Any Time in the Last Fifty Years," *Washington Post*, December 6, 2017, www.washingtonpost.com.

5. Larry Bartels, *Unequal Democracy: The Political Economy of the New Gilded Age* (Princeton, NJ: Princeton University Press, 2008), 35.

6. See for instance, Benjamin I. Page, and Martin Gilens, *Democracy in America? What Has Gone Wrong and What Can We Do about It?* (Chicago: University of Chicago Press, 2017), 187–89.

7. Aamer Madhani, "Nasty Illinois Governor's Race Could Be the Most Expensive in U.S. History," *USA Today*, November 2, 2018, www.usatoday.com.

8. The best source for the cost of campaigns is Open Secrets (www.opensecrets .org/elections-overview/most-expensive-races?cycle=2020&display=allcands).

9. For an explanation of why local campaigns cost so much, see Dick Simpson and Betty O'Shaughnessy, *Winning Elections in the 21st Century* (Lawrence: University Press of Kansas, 2016).

10. Victoria Masterson, "Fewer Women CEO's Have Been Appointed since the Start of the COVID-19 Crisis—Here's Why," World Economic Forum, December 3, 2020, www.weforum.org/agenda/2020/12/fewer-women-ceos-covid-gender-gap/.

11. Katherine Schaeffer, "Racial, Ethnic Diversity Increases Yet Again with the 117th Congress," Pew Research Center, January 28, 2021, www.pewresearch.org/fact -tank/2021/01/28/racial-ethnic-diversity-increases-yet-again-with-the-117th -congress/, and "Women in the U.S. Congress 2020," Center for American Women and Politics, https://cawp.rutgers.edu/women-us-congress-2020.

12. William Frey, "The U.S. Will Become 'Minority White' in 2045, Census Projects," blog post, https://Brookings.edu. See also William Frey, *Diversity Explosion: How New Racial Demographics Are Remaking America* (Washington, DC: Brookings Institution, 2015).

13. Pierre De Vise, *Chicago's Widening Color Gap* (Chicago: Report No. 2, Inter-University Social Research Committee, 1967).

14. There is an enormous literature on Chicago's segregation. One of the newspaper summaries of the change in the segregation index is Lolly Bowean, "Segregation Declines in Chicago, But City Still Ranks High, Census Data Show," *Chicago Tribune*, January 4, 2016.

15. "Quick Facts: Chicago City, Illinois" (2018), U.S. Census Bureau, https://www .census.gov/quickfacts/chicagocityillinois.

16. De Vise, *Chicago's Widening Color Gap*.

17. Carl Sandburg, "Chicago," in *Chicago Poems* (New York: Henry Holt, 1916). This poem has been widely anthologized.

18. Suzanne Hanney, "Chicago's Community Trust's 'On the Table' Returns . . . (with an) Emphasis on Eliminating the Wage Gap," Chicago StreetWise, May 1, 2019, 12. Original data from Chicago Community Trust.

19. Nirmal Milaikal and Nader Issa, "Chicago's Job Gap," *Chicago Sun-Times*, May 4, 2019, 6.

20. "Latest Data," Chicago Department of Public Health, www.chicago.gov/city/en/sites/covid-19/home/latest-data.html, accessed May 29, 2021.

21. Sage Kim, "Racial Inequality in the Distribution of COVID-19 Cases and Deaths in Chicago," University of Illinois at Chicago School of Public Health, April 16, 2020, https://publichealth.uic.edu/news-stories/racial-inequality-distribution-covid-19-cases-deaths-chicago/.

22. Fran Spielman, "Racism Is Public Health Crisis in Chicago, Lightfoot Declares," *Chicago Sun-Times*, June 18, 2021, 10.

23. Lisa Wade, "Chicago's Disappearing Middle Class," *Sociological Images* (blog), April 3, 2014, https://thesocietypages.org/socimages/2014/04/03/chicagos-disappearing-middle-class/.

24. Abraham Lincoln's House Divided Speech (June 16, 1858) is at www.abrahamlincolnonline.org/lincoln/speeches/house.htm.

25. Janie Boschma, Fredreka Schouten, and Priya Krishnakumar, "Lawmakers in Forty-Seven States Have Introduced Bills that Would Make It Harder to Vote," CNN, April 2021, www.cnn.com.

26. Stephen Wayne, *Is This Any Way to Run a Democratic Election?* (New York: Routledge, 2018), 45. Source of data is "Global Database on Elections and Democracy," International Institute for Democracy and Electoral Assistance, www.idea.int/data-tools/data/voter-turnout.

27. See, for instance, the classic voting study, University of Michigan Survey Research Center [Angus Campbell, Philip E. Converse, Warren E. Miller, and Donald E. Stokes,] *The American Voter* (1960; reprint Chicago: University of Chicago Press, 1976).

28. This view of Thomas Jefferson's beliefs is provided by Jim Ross-Nazzal, "The Agrarian Republic and the Symbolic End of the Revolution," PressBooks, https://ourstory.pressbooks.com/chapter/the-agrarian-republic-and-the-symbolic-end-of-the-revolution/.

29. Katherine Cramer, *The Politics of Resentment: Rural Consciousness in Wisconsin and the Rise of Scott Walker* (Chicago: University of Chicago Press, 2016). See also Jestin Gest, *The New Minority: White Working Class Politics in an Age of Immigration and Inequality* (New York: Oxford University Press, 2016).

30. Kari Lydersen, *Mayor 1%: Rahm Emanuel and the Rise of Chicago's 99%* (Chicago: Haymarket Books, 2013).

31. Kelly Bauer, "Here's How Every Chicago Ward Voted in the 2020 Presiden-

tial Election," Block Club Chicago, November 4, 2020, https://blockclubchicago.org/2020/11/04/just-1-chicago-ward-voted-for-president-trump-over-joe-biden/.

32. Yoni Appelbaum, "How America Ends: A Tectonic Demographic Shift Is Under Way. Can the Country Hold Together?," *Atlantic*, December 2019, 47.

33. Ibid., 51.

34. Caliendo, *Inequality in America*, 13–21.

35. Ibid., 9.

36. Dave Gilson and Carolyn Perot, "It's the Inequality, Stupid," *Mother Jones*, March/April 2011, www.motherjones.com/politics/2011/02/income-inequality-in-america-chart-graph. Peter G. Peterson Foundation, "Who Pays Taxes?," April 15, 2016, www.pgpf.org/budget-basics/who-pays-taxes, quoted in Caliendo, *Inequality in America*, 49.

37. Heather Cherone, "Push to Boost Investment on South, West Sides Starting to Pay Off: Lightfoot," WTTW, October 26, 2020, https://news.wttw.com/2020/10/26/push-boost-investment-south-west-sides-starting-pay-lightfoot. See also "15 New Projects Proposed for INVEST South/West Opportunity Sites," Planning and Development, Chicago Department of Public Health, April 16, 2021, www.chicago.gov/city/en/depts/dcd/provdrs/invest_sw/news/2021/april/15-new-projects-proposed-for-invest-south-west-opportunity-sites.html.

38. Cherone, "Push to Boost Investment."

Chapter 4. Money in Politics

1. The most extensive coverage of mayoral fund-raising was in stories by Tanner Ali and Alexandra Arriga, for example, "Chicago Mayoral Money-Tracker: Preckwinkle Beats Lightfoot in Final Money Chase," *Chicago Sun Times*, March 29, 2019, https://chicago.suntimes.com/news/chicago-mayor-election-2019-mayoral-money-tracker-candidates-campaign-fundraising-contributions-spending/. John Byrne and Gregory Pratt covered the final fund-raising in "Money and Manpower Could Decide Chicago's Tight Mayor's Race," *Chicago Tribune*, February 16, 2019.

2. There are many news stories on Alderman Burke's corruption case. See, for example, Claire Bushy, "Ed Burke Charged in Attempted Extortion Case," *Crain's Chicago Business*, January 3, 2019, www.chicagobusiness.com.

3. "City Council Elections in Chicago, Illinois (2019)," BallotPedia, https://ballotpedia.org/City_council_elections_in_Chicago_Illinois_(2019), accessed May 30, 2021.

4. "Everett Dirkson Quotes," BrainyQuote, www.brainyquote.com/quotes/everett_dirksen_201172.

5. For information on these contributions, see "Outside Spending by Disclosure, Excluding Party Committees," OpenSecrets, Center for Responsive Politics, www.opensecrets.org/outsidespending/disclosure.php.

6. Thomas J. Gradel and Dick Simpson, *Corrupt Illinois: Patronage, Cronyism, and Criminality* (Urbana: University of Illinois Press, 2015). Dick Simpson, Thomas J. Gradel, Michael Dirksen, and Marco Rosaire Rossi, "Chicago Is Still the Corruption

Capital," Chicago, University of Illinois at Chicago Department of Political Science, Anti-Corruption Report no. 11, February 17, 2020.

7. The original tally of the different type of elected officials convicted of corruption is from my book *Corrupt Illinois*. Additional officials had been convicted by the time of our latest publication, "Chicago Is Still the Corruption Capital." Trials in federal court of state and city officials are still going forward as of 2021 and 2022.

8. Benjamin I. Page and Martin Gilens, *Democracy in America? What Has Gone Wrong and What We Can Do about It* (Chicago: University of Chicago Press, 2017, 2020), 113–14. The 2020 edition includes a new afterword on the challenges of the Trump administration.

9. Stephen Wayne, *Is This Any Way to Run a Democratic Election?* 6th ed. (New York: Routledge, 2018), 99. See also Karl Evers-Hillstrom, Raymond Arke, and Luke Robinson, "A Look at the Impact of Citizens United on Its 9th Anniversary," OpenSecrets, Center for Responsive Politics, January 21, 2019, www.opensecrets.org, accessed January 3, 2020.

10. "Total Outside Spending by Election Cycle, Excluding Party Committees," OpenSecrets, www.opensecrets.org.

11. Wayne, 103.

12. "Total Spending," OpenSecrets, www.opensecrets.org/elections-overview/cost-of -election?cycle=2020&display=T&infl=N.

13. Ibid.

14. Sun-Times Staff, "Pritzker Price Tag: Victory in Gov Race Costly, No Matter How You Slice It," *Chicago Sun-Times*, November 7, 2018, https://chicago.suntimes.com/ 2018/11/7/18385028/pritzker-price-tag-victory-in-gov-race-costly-no-matter-how -you-slice-it.

15. William Tweed quoted in Lawrence Lessig, *America, Compromised* (Chicago: University of Chicago Press, 2018), 7.

16. "Most Expensive Races," OpenSecrets, www.opensecrets.org/elections-overview/ most-expensive-races?cycle=2020&display=allcands.

17. Robert Maguire, "$1.4 Billion and Counting in Spending by Super PACs, Dark Money Groups," OpenSecrets, Center for Responsive Politics, November 9, 2016, www.opensecrets.org, accessed January 3, 2020.

18. Bernie Sanders, "2019," New Year's e-mail to supporters from Bernie Sanders, January 1, 2019, info@berniesanders.com.

19. Associated Press and *New York Times* election results at "U.S. House Election Results 2018," *New York Times*, November 6, 2018, www.nytimes.com, accessed January 2, 2019.

20. "U.S. House Election Results 2018," *New York Times*, November 6, 2018. See also "Blue Wave of Money Propels 2018 Election to Record-Breaking $5.2 Billion in Spending," OpenSecrets, October 29, 2018, www.opensecrets.org.

21. Page and Gilens, *Democracy in America?*, 111–13.

22. Nicholas Carnes, *White-Collar Government: The Hidden Role of Class in Economic Policy Making* (Chicago: University of Chicago Press, 2013); Russ Choma,

"Millionaires' Club: For First Time, Most Lawmakers Are Worth $1 Million-Plus," OpenSecrets, January 9, 2014, www.opensecrets.org; and Page and Gilens, *Democracy in America?*, 112.

23. Nicholas Carnes, *The Cash Ceiling: Why Only the Rich Run for Office and What We Can Do about It* (Princeton, NJ: Princeton University Press, 2018), 5.

24. Page and Gilens, *Democracy in America*, 132.

25. See Benjamin I. Page, Larry M. Bartels, and Jason Seawright, "Democracy and the Policy Preferences of Wealthy Americans," *Perspectives on Politics* 11, no. 1 (March 2013): 51–73, for a description of the data and how they were obtained. The data they collected would then be further reported in Page and Gilens, *Democracy in America*.

26. Page and Gilens, *Democracy in America*, 118.

27. Carnes, *Cash Ceiling*, 9. Carnes cites nine social science studies to support his claims.

28. Dick Simpson, Constance A. Mixon, and Melissa Mouritsen, eds., *Twenty-First Century Chicago*, 3rd ed. (San Diego: Cognella Academic Publishing, 2019), parts 1 (5–14) and 3 (67–150).

29. Gradel and Simpson, *Corrupt Illinois*; Dick Simpson and Thomas J. Gradel, "The Cost of Corruption in Chicago," in *Chicago Is Not Broke!*, ed. Tom Tresser (Chicago: Civic Lab, 2016), 20–23.

30. Clarence Stone, *Regime Politics: Governing Atlanta, 1948–1988* (Lawrence: University Press of Kansas, 1989). See also Harvey Molotch, "The City as a Growth Machine," Oregon State University, Occasional Papers Series, 1980, and Paul Petersen, *City Limits* (Chicago: University of Chicago Press, 1981). For how the growth machine operates in a global city today, see Simpson, Mixon, and Mouritsen, *Twenty-First Century Chicago*, 64–67.

31. Larry Diamond, *The Spirit of Democracy: The Struggle to Build Free Societies throughout the World* (New York: Times Books, Henry Holt and Company, 2008), 345–46. The original study by the Kettering Foundation is "Public Thinking about Democracy's Challenge: Reclaiming the Public's Role," November 13, 2006, https://www.kettering.org/content/democracy%E2%80%99s-challenge-reclaiming-public%E2%80%99s-role.

32. Len O'Connor, *Clout—Mayor Daley and His City* (Chicago: H. Regnery, 1975), 9.

33. "Public Financing of Campaigns: Overview," National Conference of State Legislators, February 8, 2019, www.ncsl.org/research/elections-and-campaigns/public-financing-of-campaigns-overview.aspx.

34. Ibid.

35. See ibid. for an overview of the public funding systems that campaigns use.

36. Page and Gilens, *Democracy in America*, 132

37. Kay Lehman Schlozman, Sidney Verba, and Henry E. Grady, *The Unheavenly Chorus: Unequal Political Voice and the Broken Promise of American Democracy* (Princeton, NJ: Princeton University Press, 2012). These facts were first drawn to my attention in an unpublished UIC graduate paper by Daniel Williams in 2019.

38. Susan Schmidt and James V. Grimaldi, "The Fast Rise and Steep Fall of Jack Abramoff," *Washington Post*, December 29, 2005, www.washingtonpost.com.

39. Carnes, *Cash Ceiling*, 18–20.

Chapter 5. Nonparticipation

1. Annie Goldsmith, "The 2020 Election Had the Highest Voter Turnout in Modern History," *Town and Country*, November 7, 2020, https://www.townandcountrymag.com/society/politics/a34574744/2020-election-voter-turnout-high/. See also Kevin Schaul, Kate Rabinowitz, and Ted Mellnik, "2020 Turnout Is the Highest in Over a Century," *Washington Post*, November 5, 2020, www.washingtonpost.com.

2. Mike Maciag, "Voter Turnout Plummeting in Local Elections," *Governing*, August 28, 2014, www.governing.com/archive/gov-voter-turnout-municipal-elections.html.

3. John Dewey, *Democracy and Education* (New York: McMillan, 1916). Dewey considers how a progressive education could prepare students to be democratic citizens. For a modern take on educating for democracy, see Anne Colby, Elizabeth Beaumont, Thomas Ehrlich, and John Corngold, *Educating for Democracy: Preparing Undergraduates for Responsible Political Engagement* (San Francisco: Josey-Bass, 2007).

4. The original classic study of the effect of party identity on voting was Angus Campbell, Phillip E. Converse, Warren E. Miller, and Donald E. Stokes, *The American Voter* (New York: John Wiley and Sons, 1960).

5. See for instance, Michael X. Delli Carpini and Scott Ketter, *What Americans Know about Politics and Why It Matters* (New Haven, CT: Yale University Press, 1996).

6. See for example, Christopher H. Achen and Larry M. Bartels, *Democracy for Realists: Why Elections Do Not Produce Responsive Government* (Princeton, NJ: Princeton University Press, 2016), 89–145.

7. "States with Initiative or Referendum," Ballotpedia, https://ballotpedia.org/States_with_initiative_or_referendum.

8. The various voting statistics come from Kyle Bentle, "Voter Turnout in February 24 Election, 32.7%," *Chicago Tribune*, February 25, 2015, and Leonore Vivanco, "Voter Turnout Slightly Higher in Chicago's Runoff Election," *Chicago Tribune*, April 8, 2015, www.chicagotribune.com.

9. See Harold F. Gosnell, *Machine Politics: The Chicago Model* (Chicago: University of Chicago Press, 1937). Mike Royko, *Boss: Richard J. Daley of Chicago* (New York: Penguin, 1971).

10. Keith Koeneman, *First Son, Biography of Richard M. Daley* (Chicago: University of Chicago Press, 2013).

11. Dick Simpson, Constance A. Mixon, and Melissa Mouritsen, eds., *Twenty-First Century Chicago*, 3rd ed. (San Diego: Cognella Academic Publishing, 2020), 64–66.

12. See, for example, Edward C. Banfield, *Political Influence* (Glencoe, IL: Free Press, 1961).

13. Tahman Bradley, "Inside Internal Polls for Chicago Race for Mayor," WGN-TV, June 11, 2018, https://wgntv.com/news/politics/inside-internal-polls-in-the-race-for-chicago-mayor/.

14. "FBI Raids Alderman Ed Burke's Office in Chicago, Cover Windows with Brown Paper," CBS News, November 29, 2018, www.cbsnews.com.

15. Chicago Tribune Staff, "Read the Criminal Complaint Filed against Ald. Ed Burke," *Chicago Tribune*, January 3, 2019, www.chicagotribune.com.

16. For more on Chicago corruption see, Dick Simpson and Thomas J. Gradel, *Corrupt Illinois: Patronage, Cronyism, and Criminality* (Urbana: University of Illinois Press, 2015).

17. "Cleaning Up City Government," Lori Lightfoot for Chicago, https://lightfootforchicago.com/wp-content/uploads/2018/08/LL-Position-paper-template_L2.pdf, accessed June 1, 2021.

18. Edward McClelland, "Chicago's Mayoral Candidates, Ranked by Chances of Victory," *Chicago*, last updated February 24, 2019, www.chicagomag.com/city-life/October-2018/Who-Will-Win-Chicago-Mayor-Race-2019/.

19. Robert Dahl, *On Democracy* (New Haven, CT: Yale University Press, 1998), 38.

20. Ibid., 85.

21. Ibid., 90.

22. Ibid., 2.

23. "Newspaper Fact Sheet," Pew Research Center, July 9, 2019, www.journalism.org/fact-sheet/newspapers/.

24. Victor Pickard, "The Misinformation Society," in *Antidemocracy in America: Truth, Power, and the Republic at Risk*, ed. Eric Klinenberg, Caitlin Zaloom, and Sharon Marcus (New York: Columbia University Press, 2019), 40–41.

25. "Newspaper Fact Sheet."

26. Shobhit Seth, "The World's Top Media Companies," Investopedia, last updated October 7, 2020, https://www.investopedia.com/stock-analysis/021815/worlds-top-ten-media-companies-dis-cmcsa-fox.aspx. Many of the problems of media were drawn to my attention by Ken Mitchell's unpublished UIC graduate student paper, "Journalism Reform and Democracy," December 2019.

27. Stephen Wayne, *Is This Any Way to Run a Democratic Election?* 3rd ed. (New York: Routledge, 2018), 112.

28. Mark Jurkowitz, Amy Mitchell, Elisa Shearer, and Mason Walker, "U.S. Media Polarization and the 2020 Election: A Nation Divided," Pew Research Center, January 24, 2020, www.journalism.org/2020/01/24/u-s-media-polarization-and-the-2020-election-a-nation-divided/.

29. Ibid.; S. Robert Lichter, "Take This Campaign—Please," *Media Monitor*, September/October 1996, 2; S. Robert Lichter, "Campaign 2000 Final," *Media Monitor*, November/December 2000, 2.

30. Jurkowitz et al., "U.S. Media Polarization."

31. Pickard, "Misinformation Society," 42–43.

32. Ibid., 32 and 45. There are various ways of calculating voter turnout depending

on whether voting age population, eligible voter population, or registered voters is used as the denominator. Thus, various authors report slightly different percentage voting in elections. However, all of the statistics for U.S. elections are below what would be expected in a strong representative democracy.

33. Drew Desilver, "In Past Elections, U.S. Trailed Most Developed Countries in Voter Turnout," Pew Research Center, November 3, 2020, www.pewresearch.org/fact -tank/2020/11/03/in-past-elections-u-s-trailed-most-developed-countries-in-voter -turnout/.

34. See Joshua A. Douglas, *Vote for US: How to Take Back Our Elections and Change the Future of Voting* (Amherst, NY: Prometheus Books, 2019), 15–28.

35. Ibid., 25. For the original studies, see Alan S. Gerber, Donald P. Green, and Ron Schachar, "Voting May be Habit Forming: Evidence from a Randomized Field Experiment," *American Journal of Political Science* 47 (2003): 540.

36. Douglas, *Vote for US*, 33.

37. Ibid., 205.

38. "What Is Political Participation?," *American Government and Politics for the Internet Age*, 2011, accessed at https://open.lib.umn.edu/americangovernment/ chapter/8–1-what-is-political-participation/.

39. Phil Parvin, "Democracy without Participation: A New Politics for a Disengaged Era," *Res Publica* 24, no. 1 (February 2018): 32–52.

40. Ibid.

41. Dahl, *On Democracy*, 178.

42. Benjamin I. Page and Martin Gilens, *Democracy in America? What Has Gone Wrong and What Can We Do about It?* (Chicago: University of Chicago Press, 2017), 202.

43. William Riker and Peter Ordeshook, "A Theory of the Calculus of Voting," *American Political Science Review* 62, no. 1 (March 1968): 25–42.

44. Bernard L. Fraga, *The Turnout Gap: Race Ethnicity, and Political Inequality in a Diversifying America* (New York: Cambridge University Press, 2018), 3.

45. Ibid., 109.

46. Ibid., 42.

47. Achen and Bartels, *Democracy for Realists*, 299.

48. Ibid., 12.

49. Ibid., 4.

50. Pickard, "Misinformation Society," 43.

Chapter 6. Polarization and the Politics of Resentment

1. AOC Curator, "A Most Magnificent Ruin: The Burning of the Capitol during the War of 1812," *Architect of the Capitol* (blog), August 22, 2012, www.aoc.gov/explore -capitol-campus/blog/most-magnificent-ruin-burning-capitol-during-war-1812.

2. "Election 2020 Results and Live Updates," ABC News, https://abcnews.go.com/ Elections/2020-us-presidential-election-results-live-map/, accessed December 4, 2020.

3. Aaron Freeman invented the term "Council Wars." See Rick Kogan, "There's a Lot More to Aaron Freeman than 'Council Wars,'" *Chicago Tribune*, July 12, 1985, www.chicagotribune.com.

4. Dick Simpson, *Rogues, Rebels, and Rubber Stamps: The Politics of the Chicago City Council from 1863 to the Present* (Boulder, CO: Westview, 2001), 15–45.

5. For more information on the 2019 election, see WBEZ Staff and Associated Press, "2019 Chicago Municipal Election Results," WBEZ Chicago, February 26, 2019, www .wbez.org/stories/2019-chicago-municipal-election-results/ed40602f-1773-4570 -8c70-84e97e242cd8.

6. For a more detailed analysis of the Chicago City Council during Mayor Lightfoot's first year in office, see Dick Simpson, Marco Rosaire Rossi, and Thomas J. Gradel, "From Rubber Stamp to Political Divisions, June 12, 2019–April 24, 2020," Chicago City Council Report no. 11, Department of Political Science, University of Illinois at Chicago, April 28, 2020, https://pols.uic.edu/chicago-politics/city-council -voting-records/.

7. Fran Spielman, "Lightfoot Poll Shows Strong Support for Her and the Police Reforms She Champions," *Chicago Sun-Times*, July 2, 2020, https://chicago.suntimes .com/city-hall/2020/7/2/21311448/lightfoot-poll-approval-rating-chicago-police -reform-contract.

8. Pew Research Center, "Most Americans Say Trump Was Too Slow in Initial Response to Coronavirus Threat," April 16, 2020, www.pewresearch.org/politics/ 2020/04/16/most-americans-say-trump-was-too-slow-in-initial-response-to -coronavirus-threat/.

9. Herbert M. Kritzer, "Polarized Justice? Changing Patterns of Decision-Making in the Federal Courts," University of Minnesota Law School Working Papers, *SSRN Electronic Journal*, 2018, www.ssrn.com/abstract=3157153, accessed December 29, 2019. This was drawn to my attention by Marc Lopez in his UIC student paper, "A Tale of Two Countries: Polarization in America," December 2019.

10. Among many other studies, see Edward G. Carmines, Michael J. Ensley, and Michael W. Wagner, "Who Fits the Left-Right Divide? Partisan Polarization in the American Electorate," *American Behavioral Scientist* 56, no. 12 (2012): 1631–53.

11. Pew Research Center, "In a Politically Polarized Era, Sharp Divides in Both Partisan Coalitions," December 17, 2019, www.people-press.org/2019/12/17/in-a -politically-polarized-era-sharp-divides-in-both-partisan-coalitions/. See also Morris Fiorina and Samuel Abrams, "Political Polarization in the American Public," *Annual Review of Political Science* 11, no. 1 (2008): 563–88, and Nolan McCarthy, "Polarization, Congressional Dysfunction, and Constitutional Change," *Indiana Law Review* 50, no. 1 (2016): 223–45, among many other articles and books.

12. Pew Research Center, "In a Politically Polarized Era."

13. John Gramlich, "20 Striking Findings from 2020," Pew Research Center, December 11, 2020, www.pewresearch.org/fact-tank/2020/12/11/20-striking-findings -from-2020/.

14. A summary of the literature on polarization in Congress is provided in Michael Barber and Nolan McCarthy, "Causes and Consequences of Polarization," in *Political*

Negotiation: A Handbook, ed. Jane Mansbridge and Cathy Jo Martin (Washington, DC: Brookings Institution, 2015). See also key studies of congressional polarization such as Kenneth T. Poole and Howard Rosenthal, "The Polarization of American Politics," *Journal of Politics* 43, no. 4 (November 1984): 1061–79, and Christopher Hare and Kenneth T. Poole, "The Polarization of Contemporary American Politics," *Polity* 46, no. 3 (July 2014): 411–29.

15. John Campbell, *American Discontent: The Rise of Donald Trump and the Decline of the Golden Age* (New York: Oxford University Press, 2018), 9.

16. See "January 2021 Insurrection: A Curated Collection of Links," Marshall Project (www.themarshallproject.org/records/10207-trump-riot-insurrection-january-2021) for the most extensive news analysis of the insurrection and the aftermath.

17. "January 2021 Insurrection."

18. John Campbell, "Critical Dialogue: Response to Bryan Gervais and Irwin Morris' Review of *American Discontent: The Rise of Donald Trump and the Decline of the Golden Age*," *Perspectives on Politics* 17, no. 1 (March 2019): 214.

19. Amy Mitchell, Jeffrey Gottfried, Jocelyn Kiley, and Katrina Eva Matsa, "Political Polarization and Media Habits," Pew Research Center, October 21, 2014, November 15, 2019, www.journalism.org/2014/10/21/political-polarization-media-habits/. See also Yochai Benkler, Robert Faris, and Hal Roberts, *Network Propaganda: Manipulation, Disinformation, and Radicalization in American Politics* (New York: Oxford University Press, 2018).

20. John Campbell, "Review of Gervais and Morris' *Reactionary Republicanism: How the Tea Party in the House Paved the Way for Trump's Victory*," *Perspectives on Politics* 17, no. 1 (2019): 215.

21. Bryan Gervais and Irwin Morris, "Review of *American Discontent: The Rise of Donald Trump and Decline of the Golden Age*," *Perspectives on Politics* 17, no. 1 (2019): 212.

22. Katherine Cramer, *The Politics of Resentment: Rural Consciousness in Wisconsin and the Rise of Scott Walker* (Chicago: University of Chicago Press, 2016), 2.

23. Ibid., 5–6.

24. Ibid., 7.

25. Ibid., 25.

26. Ibid., 40.

27. Jeffrey Goldberg, "The Places Where the Recession Never Ended: A Conversation with Tara Westover on the Urban/Rural Divide," *Atlantic*, December 2019, 53.

28. Ibid., 211.

29. Stephen Levitsky and Daniel Ziblatt, "The Crisis of American Democracy," *American Educator*, Fall 2020, 9.

30. Ibid.

31. Andrew Hall, *Who Wants to Run? How the Devaluing of Political Office Drives Polarization* (Chicago: University of Chicago Press, 2019), 3.

32. Ibid., 10–11.

33. Ibid., 14–15.

34. Ibid., 15.

35. Ibid., 57.

36. Richard Wike, Laura Silver, and Alexandra Castillo, "Many Across the Globe Are Dissatisfied with How Democracy Is Working," Pew Research Center, April 29, 2019, www.pewresearch.org/global/2019/04/29/many-across-the-globe-are-dissatisfied -with-how-democracy-is-working/.

37. E. J. Dionne Jr., *Our Divided Political Heart: The Battle for the American Idea in an Age of Discontent* (New York: Bloomsbury, 2012), 74–75.

38. Robert D. McFadden, "Ross Perot, Brash Texas Billionaire Who Ran for President, Dead at 89," *New York Times*, July 9, 2019, www.nytimes.com.

39. For an account of the division in the 1990s, see Steve Kornacki, *The Red and the Blue: The 1990s and the Birth of Political Tribalism* (New York: Harper Collins, 2018).

40. All Cook County elected executive officials are Democrats, as are fifteen of the seventeen Cook County Commissioners. The two Republicans were elected from suburban districts.

41. Kelly Bauer, "Here's How Every Chicago Ward Voted in the 2020 Presidential Election," Block Club Chicago, November 4, 2020, https://blockclubchicago .org/2020/11/04/just-1-chicago-ward-voted-for-president-trump-over-joe-biden/.

42. Illinois will lose a U.S. representative in 2022; see, for example, Lynn Sweet, "Illinois to Lose One Seat in Congress due to Population Shifts in 2020 Census," *Chicago Sun-Times*, April 26, 2021, https://chicago.suntimes.com/2021/4/26/22403917/ illinois-congress-seats-house-representatives-reapportionment-census-population.

43. These accounts follow my descriptions in *Rogues, Rebels, and Rubber Stamps*, which also contains additional sources for these accounts.

44. The original NBC-5 editorial opposing racial and ethnic political maneuvering was broadcast on December 28–29, 1976. Copies of the written text are in the Dick Simpson Papers, Special Collections of the Richard J. Daley Library at the University of Illinois at Chicago.

45. These distinctions were first written about by William Grimshaw, "Is Chicago Ready for Reform?," in *The Making of the Mayor, Chicago, 1983*, ed. Melvin G. Holli and Paul M. Green (Grand Rapids, MI: Eerdmans, 1984), 141–63.

46. Paul Kleppner, *Chicago Divided: The Making of a Black Mayor* (DeKalb: Northern Illinois University Press, 1985), 177.

47. Melvin Holli, "Daley to Daley," in *Restoration 1989: Chicago Elects a New Daley*, ed. Paul Green and Melvin Holli (Chicago: Lyceum, 1991), 202.

48. R. Bruce Dold and Ann Marie Lipinski, "The Making of the Mayor," *Chicago Tribune*, December 6, 1987, www.chicagotribune.com.

49. Mark Edmundson, "Walt Whitman's Guide to a Thriving Democracy," *Atlantic*, May 2019, 110.

50. WBEZ Staff and Associated Press, "2019 Chicago Municipal Election Results: The Runoff," WBEZ Chicago, April 2, 2019, www.wbez.org/stories/chicago-mayoral -election-runoff-results/e1a08ba2-d784-4e78-9499-10819e75e436, accessed April 14, 2020.

51. Simpson, Rossi, and Gradel, "From Rubber Stamp to Political Divisions."

Chapter 7. Corruption

1. Larry Diamond, *Ill Winds: Saving Democracy from Russian Rage, Chinese Ambition, and American Complacency* (New York: Penguin, 2019), 184.

2. Nearly every article or book on corruption develops a similar definition of corruption but it is, in fact, a complicated and contested term. For a fuller discussion, see Jonathan Rose, "The Contested Definition of Corruption," in *Global Corruption and Ethics Management*, ed. Carole L. Jurkiewicz, 3–10 (Lanham, MD: Rowman and Littlefield, 2020), and Bo Rothstein and Aiysha Varraich, *Making Sense of Corruption* (New York: Cambridge University Press, 2017).

3. Andrew C. McCarthy, "The 'Anti-Establishment' Candidate Boasts About His History of Bribing Politicians," *National Review*, January 25, 2016. www.nationalreview.com.

4. Robert I. Rotberg, *Anticorruption* (Cambridge, MA: MIT Press), 2020, 191.

5. For a description of the emoluments clause (Article 1, section 9, clause 8) and the reasons that it is included in the Constitution, see Zephyr Teachout, *Corruption in America: From Benjamin Franklin's Snuff Box to Citizens United* (Cambridge, MA: Harvard University Press, 2014).

6. See, for instance, the *Guardian*, Politico, and Business Insider, including Peter Stone, "Inside Trump's DC Hotel, Where Allies and Lobbyists Flock to Peddle Their Interests," *Guardian*, July 18, 2019, www.theguardian.com, and Alexandra Ma, "At Least One Foreign Government Allegedly Tried to Suck Up to Trump by Booking Rooms in His Hotel But Never Staying in Them," *Business Insider*, October 3, 2019, www.businessinsider.com.

7. Nicholas Confessore, Karen Yourish, Steve Eder, Ben Protess, Maggie Haberman, Grace Ashford, Michael LaForgia, Kenneth P. Vogel, Michael Rothfeld, and Larry Buchanan, "The President's Taxes; The Swamp That Trump Built," *New York Times*, October 10, 2020, www.nytimes.com.

8. See, for instance, Kevin Wack, "8 Banks Entangled in Trump-Related Probes," American Banker, August 19, 2018, www.americanbanker.com/list/8-banks-entangled-in-trump-related-probes.

9. The G7 meeting was originally scheduled for June 2020 but was postponed because of the COVID-19 pandemic and ultimately canceled. One of the many news stories on the siting of that meeting is Julian Borger's "G7 Summit: Last Rites of Old Order as Trump's Theatre Looms Next Year," *Guardian*, August 26, 2019, www.theguardian.com, accessed August 27, 2019.

10. Meghan Keneally, "5 Controversial Dictators and Leaders Donald Trump Has Praised," ABC News, July 6, 2016, https://abcnews.go.com, accessed November 15, 2019.

11. See Washington Post Staff, "The Mueller Report, Annotated," *Washington Post*, last updated December 2, 2019, www.washingtonpost.com.

12. Reuters lists those convicted at "Factbox: Here Are Eight Trump Associates Arrested or Convicted of Crimes," Reuters, August 20, 2020, www.reuters.com/article/us-usa-trump-bannon-associates-factbox-idUSKBN25G1YU.

13. Kevin Johnson, "How Many Trump Advisers Have Been Criminally Charged? Manafort, Stone and Steve Bannon Makes 7," *USA Today*, August 20, 2020, last updated August 21, 2020. Reuters counts the total as eight ("Factbox").

14. Michael Balsamo, "A Look at 29 People Trump Pardoned or Gave Commutations," AP News, December 24, 2020, https://apnews.com/article/election-2020-donald-trump-robert-mueller-paul-manafort-elections-2793e154c7eec45dc81fdeaf9b432b6f, accessed January 12, 2021.

15. Tessa Berenson, "Donald Trump Calls on Russia to Hack Hillary Clinton's Emails," *Time*, July 27, 2016, time.com.

16. Chuck Todd, Mark Murray, and Carrie Dann, "How Trump took advantage of Russian interference: Amplifying Wikileaks," *NBC News*, February 19, 2018, www.nbcnews.com.

17. Peter Baker, "Senate Acquits Trump, Ending Historic Trial," *New York Times*, February 6, 2020, www.nytimes.com, accessed April 2, 2020.

18. David Bennett, "Donald Trump Has Hit the Corruption Trifecta," *Daily Beast*, November 9, 2019, www.thedailybeast.com, accessed December 20, 2019.

19. David Graham, "The Unchecked Corruption of Trump's Cabinet," *Atlantic*, May 2019, www.theatlantic.com.

20. Juliet Eiperin, Josh Dawsey, and Darryl Feris, "Interior Secretary Zinke Resigns Amid Investigation," *Washington Post*, December 15, 2018.

21. Brakkton Booker, "House Oversight Panel Asks HUD for Documents Amid Accusations of Lavish Spending," NPR, February 28, 2018, www.npr.org, accessed November 15, 2019.

22. Stephen Collinson, "Trump's False Crusade Rolls on Despite Devastating Supreme Court Rebuke," CNN Politics, December 9, 2020, www.cnn.com, accessed December 10, 2020, and Dominico Montanaro, "Trump Continues to Push Election Falsehoods. Here Is Why That Matters," National Public Radio, May 20, 2021, www.npr.org/2021/05/20/998352776/out-of-the-spotlight-trump-continues-to-command-the-republican-message.

23. Erick Tucker and Frank Bajak, "Repudiating Trump, Officials Say Election 'Most Secure,'" AP News, November 13, 2020, https://apnews.com/article/top-officials-elections-most-secure-66f9361084ccbc461e3bbf42861057a5, accessed December 10, 2020.

24. Brett Samuels, "Barr Says DOJ Hasn't Uncovered Widespread Voter Fraud in the 2020 Election," *Hill*, December 1, 2020, www.msn.com/en-us/news/politics/barr-says-doj-hasnt-uncovered-widespread-voter-fraud-in-2020-election/ar-BB1bxkry.

25. "U.S. House Votes to Impeach Trump," *Crains Chicago Business*, January 13, 2020, www.chicagobusiness.com, accessed January 13, 2020.

26. Transparency International, Corruption Perception Index, 2018 (www.transparency.org/cpi2018), and Corruption Perception Index, 2020, (www.transparency.org/en/cpi/2020/index/usa), accessed December 20, 2019, and June 7, 2021.

27. *Report to Congress on the Activities and Operations of the Public Integrity Section of the U.S. Department of Justice for 2019*, Public Integrity Section, Criminal Division, U.S. Department of Justice, 22, www.justice.gov/criminal-pin/file/1346061/download.

28. News21 Staff, "Election Fraud in America," News21, August 12, 2012, https://votingrights.news21.com/interactive/election-fraud-database/.

29. Dick Simpson, Thomas J. Gradel, and Marco Rosaire Rossi, "Corruption Spikes in Illinois," Chicago, University of Illinois at Chicago Department of Political Science, Anti-Corruption Report no. 13, February 22, 2021.

30. In addition to Report no. 13, see Dick Simpson, Thomas J. Gradel, Marco Rosaire Rossi, and Katherine Taylor, "Continuing Corruption in Illinois," Chicago, University of Illinois at Chicago Department of Political Science, Anti-Corruption Report no. 10, May 15, 2018, 2; Dick Simpson, Thomas J. Gradel, Michael Dirksen, and Marco Rosaire Rossi, "Chicago Is Still the Corruption Capital," Chicago, University of Illinois at Chicago Department of Political Science, Anti-Corruption Report no. 11, February 17, 2020, 2–3.

31. Thomas J. Gradel and Dick Simpson, *Corrupt Illinois: Patronage, Cronyism, and Criminality* (Urbana: University of Illinois Press, 2015). These figures are updated in Anti-Corruption Report no. 13.

32. Pam G. Dempsey, "Illinois Gets D+ Grade in 2015 State Integrity Investigation: History of Scandal Holds Back Progress on Transparency," Center for Public Integrity, last updated November 12, 2015, https://publicintegrity.org/state-politics/state-integrity-investigation/illinois-gets-d-grade-in-2015-state-integrity-investigation/.

33. Jeffrey M. Jones, "Illinois Residents Least Confident in Their State Government," Gallup, February 17, 2016, https://news.gallup.com/poll/189281/illinois-residents-least-confident-state-government.aspx; Lydia Saad, "Half in Illinois and Connecticut Want to Move Elsewhere," Gallup, April 30, 2014, http://news.gallup.com/poll/168770/half-illinois-conneticul-move-elsewhere.aspx, accessed September 2, 2019.

34. Monica Davies, "Jury Finds Blagojevich Guilty of Corruption, *New York Times*, June 27, 2010.

35. For an account of the impeachment trial, see Bernard H. Sieracki, *A Just Cause: The Impeachment and Removal of Governor Rod Blagojevich* (Carbondale: Southern Illinois University Press, 2016).

36. Jeff Cohen and John Case, *Golden: How Rod Blagojevich Talked Himself Out of the Governor's Office and into Prison* (Chicago: Chicago Review Press, 2012), 26.

37. Kevin Liptak and Kaitland Collins, "Trump Commutes Blagojevich Sentence and Grants Clemency to 10 Others," CNN, February 19, 2020, www.cnn.com/2020/02/18/politics/donald-trump-rod-blagojevich-commutation-sentence/index.html, accessed April 2, 2020. See also Brie Stimpson, "Rod Blagojevich, Freed by Trump Commutation, Returns to Illinois," *Fox News*, February 19, 2020, www.foxnews.com/politics/ex-gov-blagojevich-released-from-prison-after-trump-pardon.

38. Daniel Egler, "Vote Fraud Started When Chicago Did," *Chicago Tribune*, September 8, 1948, 1–2. Many of these examples are taken from my earlier book, Gradel and Simpson, *Corrupt Illinois*.

39. "Sangamon County Grand Jury, the Great Canal Script Fraud Minutes of Proceeding," 1859, Internet Archive, http://archive.org/stream/greatcanalscripfoosang#page/ns/mode/2up, accessed November 15, 2013.

40. Jim Nowlan, "Corruption in Illinois: An Enduring Tradition," paper presented at Ethics and Reform Symposium on Illinois Government, Paul Simon Public Policy Institute, Southern Illinois University, Carbondale, September 27–28, 2012, 3.

41. Ron Grossman, "Bigger than a Shoe Box," *Chicago Tribune*, February 24, 2013, 19.

42. Gradel and Simpson, *Corrupt Illinois*, esp. 45.

43. Ibid., 46–47.

44. Ibid., 14; see also later writings on corruption by the authors in the UIC Corruption Reports nos. 1–13 at https://pols.uic.edu/chicago-politics/.

45. Flint Taylor, *The Torture Machine: Racism and Police Violence in Chicago* (Chicago: Haymarket, 2019).

46. Teachout, *Corruption in America*, 18.

47. Ibid., 47.

48. Ibid.

49. Ibid., 50.

50. Thomas Frisbie, "Rule Models: Authors Cite the Need for Ethical Government," *Literary License*, December 2020/January 2021, 2. From a talk to the Society of Midland Authors by Jill Long Thompson, author of *The Character of American Democracy: Preserving Our Past, Protecting Our Future* (Bloomington: Indiana University Press, 2020).

51. Lawrence Lessig, *America, Compromised* (Chicago: University of Chicago Press, 2018), xi.

52. Ibid., 12.

53. See the chapters on different forms of corruption in Gradel and Simpson, *Corrupt Illinois*.

54. James Madison, *The Federalist Papers #52*, https://founders.archives.gov/documents/Hamilton/01-04-02-0200.This was drawn to my attention by Nicholas Anderson in his UIC student paper, "The Institutional Corruption of Congress," December 2019.

55. Lessig, *America, Compromised*.

56. Ibid., 199.

57. Thompson, *Character of American Democracy*, 3.

58. Mary Frances Berry, *Five Dollars and a Pork Chop Sandwich: Vote Buying and the Corruption of Democracy* (Boston: Beacon, [2016]), 148.

Chapter 8. Structural Problems

1. Mary Frances Berry, *Five Dollars and a Pork Chop Sandwich: Vote Buying and the Corruption of Democracy* (Boston: Beacon, [2016]). The author provides examples of vote buying in more than a half-dozen states. The payoff of a pork chop sandwich occurred in Louisiana.

2. See, for instance, "Summary of Voter Suppression Efforts," National Organization for Women, https://now.org/summary-of-voter-suppression-efforts/, accessed June 8, 2021.

3. Tom Ginsburg and Aziz Z. Huq, *How to Save a Constitutional Democracy* (Chicago: University of Chicago Press, 2018), 72–73.

4. For one list of democracies failing or under attack, see Sara Repucci and Amy Slipowitz, "Democracy Under Siege," Freedom House, http://freedomhouse.org/report/freedom-world/2021/democracy-under-siege, accessed June 8, 2021.

5. "Losing the Popular Vote and Winning," in "Why Does the U.S. Have an Electoral College?," How Stuff Works, https://people.howstuffworks.com/question4721.htm.

6. Caroline Tolbert and Kellen Gracey, "Changing How America Votes for President," in *Changing How America Votes*, ed. Todd Donovan (Lanham, MD: Roman and Littlefield, 2018), 72.

7. "2020 Electoral College Results," National Archives, www.archives.gov/electoral-college/2020, accessed January 16, 2021.

8. Tolbert and Gracey, "Changing How America Votes for President," 73.

9. Reid Wilson, "Republicans Want to Reform the Electoral College to Help Themselves," *Atlantic*, December 17, 2012; Thomas H. Neale, "The Electoral College: How it Works in Contemporary Presidential Elections," *Congressional Research Service*, report 7-5700, May 14, 2017, https://fas.org/sgp/crs/misc/RL32611.pdf, accessed January 2, 2020.

10. Ruth Bader Ginsburg quoted in Tina Sfondales, "The Notorious RBG," *Chicago Sun-Times*, September 10, 2019, 16.

11. For a definitive analysis of why the Electoral College continues to exist, see Alexander Kayssar, *Why Do We Still Have the Electoral College?* (Cambridge, MA: Harvard University Press, 2020).

12. "National Popular Vote Interstate Compact," BallotPedia, https://ballotpedia.org/National_Popular_Vote_Interstate_Compact, accessed June 8, 2021.

13. Ibid.

14. Trent England, "The Danger of the Attacks on the Electoral College," *Imprimis* 49, no. 6 (June 2019): 7.

15. Brian Murphy and Will Doran, "New Congressional Maps in North Carolina Will Stand for 2020, Court Rules," *Raleigh (NC) News and Observer*, December 2, 2019, www.newsobserver.com/news/politics-government/election/article237958719.html, accessed December 20, 2019.

16. Wendy K. Tam Cho and Simon Rubinstein-Salzedo, "Understanding Significance Tests from a Non-Mixing Markov Chain for Partisan Gerrymandering Claims," *Statistics and Public Policy* 6, no. 1 (2019), https://doi.org/10.1080/2330443X.2019.1574687. These statistical studies and court cases were originally brought to my attention by Nicholas Anderson in his UIC student paper, "The Institutional Corruption of Congress," December 2019.

17. Rucho et al. v. Common Cause et al., 18–422, 588 U.S. (2019), https://www.supremecourt.gov/opinions/18pdf/18-422_9oll.pdf.

18. George Pillsbury, "Nonpartisan Redistricting: Citizen Commissions Drawing Districts," Nonprofit VOTE, March 29, 2017, www.nonprofitvote.org/nonpartisan-redistricting-citizens-not-incumbents-charge/.

19. Vladimir Kogan and Eric McGhee, "Redistricting and Representation," in Donovan, *Changing How America Votes*, 93.

20. Gary Jacobson, "Competition and U.S. Congressional Elections," in *Marketplace of Democracy*, ed. Michael McDonald and John Samples, 27–52 (Washington, DC: Brookings Institution, 2006); also cited in Benjamin I. Page and Martin Gilens, *Democracy in America? What Has Gone Wrong and What Can We Do About It?* (Chicago: University of Chicago Press, 2017), 161.

21. Pillsbury, "Nonpartisan Redistricting."

22. Wendell Hutson, "Is Englewood Represented by Too Many Aldermen?," *Weekly Citizen*, January 22, 2020, https://citizennewspapergroup.com/news/2020/jan/22/englewood-represented-too-many-aldermen/, accessed December 15, 2020.

23. Tammy Xu, "A Chinatown Civics Lesson," *South Side Weekly*, February 19, 2019, https://southsideweekly.com/chinatown-civics-lesson-building-power-representation-25th-ward/, accessed December 15, 2020.

24. The fifteen states with term limits and the six states that have repealed are listed by the National Council of State Legislatures (www.ncsl.org/research/about-state-legislatures/chart-of-term-limits-states.aspx).

25. "Fighting Voter Suppression," ACLU, www.aclu.org/issues/voting-rights/fighting-voter-suppression, accessed December 15, 2020.

26. "Automatic Voter Registration, a Summary," Brennan Center for Justice, July 19, 2019, www.brennancenter.org/analysis/automatic-voter-registration, accessed December 15, 2020.

27. "Felon Voting Rights," National Conference of State Legislatures, http://www.ncsl.org/research/elections-and-campaigns/felon-voting-rights.aspx, accessed May 13, 2021.

28. Lawrence Mower and Langston Taylor, "Florida Ruled that Felons Must Pay to Vote. Now, It Doesn't Know How Many Can," *Tampa Bay Times*, October 11, 2020. https://www.tampabay.com/news/florida-politics/elections/2020/10/07/florida-ruled-felons-must-pay-to-vote-now-it-doesnt-know-how-many-can/. Accessed on December 17, 2020.

29. Ron Hayduk, "One Step Forward, Two Steps Back: The Curious Case of Immigrant Voting Rights," in Donovan, *Changing How America Votes*, 67.

30. Pippa Norris, *Why Elections Fail.* (New York: Cambridge University Press, 2015), fig. 2.2, 54. The book explains in detail the ranking and the underlying theory and methodology.

31. James M. Lindsey, "The 2020 Election by the Numbers," Council on Foreign Relations, www.cfr.org/blog/2020-election-numbers.

32. Robert S. Mueller III, *Report on the Investigation into Russian Interference in the 2016 Presidential Election*, U.S. Department of Justice, www.justice.gov/storage/report.pdf.

33. See for instance, Michael Golden, *Unlock Congress: Reform the Rules, Restore the System* (Pacific Grove, CA: Why Not Books, 2015), 223–32.

34. Golden, *Unlock Congress*, 220–23; Larry Diamond, *Ill Winds: Saving Democ-*

racy from Russian Rage, Chinese Ambition, and American Complacency (New York: Penguin, 2019), ch. 13.

35. Jessica Piper and Michael Shepherd, "Maine's GOP Says It Has Signatures to Force 3rd Rank Choice Referendum in 4 Years," *Bangor Daily News*, June 15, 2020, https://bangordailynews.com/2020/06/15/politics/maine-gop-says-it-has-signatures -to-force-3rd-ranked-choice-voting-referendum-in-4-years/. See also BallotPedia, https://ballotpedia.org/Maine_Ranked-Choice_Voting_for_Presidential_Elections_ Referendum_(2020) for updates.

36. Page and Gilens, *Democracy in America*, 229.

37. Golden, *Unlock Congress*, 154–55.

38. Page and Gilens, *Democracy in America*, 213.

39. Ibid.

40. Rebecca Rifkin, "Public Faith in Congress Falls Again, Hits New Low," *Gallup*, June 19, 2014 https://news.gallup.com/poll/171710/public-faith-congress-falls-again -hits-historic-low.aspx.

41. Golden, *Unlock Congress*, 163.

42. "FEC Adopts Interim Verification Procedure for Filings Containing Possibly False or Fictitious Information (2016)," Federal Elections Commission, August 19, 2016, www.fec.gov/updates/fec-adopts-interim-verification-procedure-for-filings -containing-possibly-false-or-fictitious-information-2/.

43. This material on sham candidates was originally researched and written as testimony for my expert witness report in a lawsuit challenging the sham candidates put up in Michael Madigan's election in 2016 by my research assistant Marco Rosaire Rossi.

44. Other news stories about sham candidates around the country include Abby Spegman, "Mailer in Thurston County Commission Race Called Misleading—by the Person It Claims to Support," *Olympia (WA) Olympian*, October 20, 2018, www .theolympian.com; Marc Lacey, "Republican Runs Street People on Green Ticket," *New York Times*, September 6, 2010, www.nytimes.com; Jonathan J. Cooper, "AZ Green Party 'Sham' Candidates to Stay on Ballot," *Seattle Times*, September 14, 2010, www.seattletimes.com; "Write-in Loophole Creates Election Trickery Once Again," editorial, *South Florida Sun-Sentinel*, July 2, 2018, www.sun-sentinel.com; "The Spectacle of Sham Write-In Candidates Must End," editorial, *Jacksonville Florida Times-Union*, June 3, 2016, www.jacksonville.com.

45. "Evidence of Fraud in a Florida Election. Where's the Outrage?," editorial, *South Florida Sun-Sentinel*, November 25, 2020, www.sun-sentinel.com, accessed December 18, 2020.

46. Jason Gonzales v. Michael Madigan, 16C7915, 403 F. Supp. 3d 670 (N.D. Ill. 2019), https://casetext.com/case/gonzales-v-madigan-4.

47. For details on the sham candidates in the Gonzales/Madigan election, see my Expert Witness Report in ibid.

48. Jason Meisner, "Election Fraud Allegations from 2016 Heard in Appellate Court as Federal Probe Swirls around Democratic Boss Michael Madigan," *Chicago Tribune*, November 10, 2020, www.chicagotribune.com, accessed December 18, 2020.

49. "Merit Selection: The Best Way to Choose the Best Judges," American Judicial Society, www.judicialselection.us/uploads/documents/ms_descrip_1185462202120.pdf.

50. Jed Handelsman Shugerman, *The People's Courts: Pursuing Judicial Independence in America* (Cambridge, MA: Harvard University Press, 2012).

51. This was drawn to my attention Samuel Scruby in his UIC student paper, "Judicial Selection and Democracy," November 18, 2019.

52. "Supreme Court," Gallup News, https://news.gallup.com/poll/4732/supreme-court.aspx, accessed January 2, 2020.

53. For more information on possible judicial reforms, see Sanford Levinson and Jack M. Balkin, *Democracy and Dysfunction* (Chicago: University of Chicago Press, 2019), and Thomas Phillips, "The Merits of Merit Selection," *Harvard Journal of Law and Public Policy*, Winter 2009, 75.

54. Rachel Kleinfeld, Richard Youngs, and Jonah Belser, "Renewing U.S. Political Representation: Lessons from Europe and U.S. History," Carnegie Endowment for International Peace, March 12, 2018, http://carnegieendowment.org/2018/03/12/renewing-u.s.-political-rerpesentation-lessons from europe-and-u.s.-history-pub-75758, accessed November 15, 2019. See also "Fusion Voting," BallotPedia, https://ballotpedia.org/Fusion_voting.

55. Ganesh Sitaraman, *The Crisis of the Middle-Class Constitution: Why Economic Inequality Threatens Our Republic* (New York: Alfred A. Knopf, 2017), 299.

Chapter 9. Cascading Crises

1. See the Department of Justice report and media stories at the time on the Michael Brown shooting. *Memorandum: Department of Justice Report Regarding the Criminal Investigation into the Shooting Death of Michael Brown by Ferguson, Missouri Police Officer Darren Wilson*, U.S. Department of Justice, March 4, 2015, www.justice.gov/sites/default/files/opa/press-releases/attachments/2015/03/04/doj_report_on_shooting_of_michael_brown_1.pdf.

2. "Black Lives Matter: A Timeline of the Movement," *Cosmopolitan*, www.cosmopolitan.com/uk/reports/a32728194/black-lives-matter-timeline-movement/.

3. "1 Million per Shot—How Laquan McDonald Settlement Unfolded after That Initial Demand," *Chicago Sun-Times*, June 24, 2016, https://chicago.suntimes.com/2016/6/24/18465327/1-million-per-shot-how-laquan-mcdonald-settlement-unfolded-after-that-initial-demand.

4. Mark Guarino, Tim Elfrink, and Teo Armus, "Looters Smash Windows Along Chicago's Magnificent Mile after Police-Involved Shooting," *Washington Post*, August 10, 2020, www.washingtonpost.com.

5. David Sirota, "Polls Showed Many Americans Opposed to Civil Rights Protests in the 1960s. But That Changed," *Jacobin*, June 12, 2020, www.jacobinmag.com/2020/06/polls-george-floyd-protests-civil-rights-movement. Kim Parker, Juliana Horowitz, and Monica Anderson, "Amid Protests, Majorities across Racial and Ethnic Groups Express Support for the Black Lives Matter Movement," Pew Research Center, June

12, 2020, www.pewsocialtrends.org/2020/06/12/amid-protests-majorities-across
-racial-and-ethnic-groups-express-support-for-the-black-lives-matter-movement/.

6. "Black Lives Matter."

7. Tribune News Service, "Dylann Roof Sentenced to Death for Killing 9 Church Members in South Carolina," *Chicago Tribune*, January 10, 2017, www.chicagotribune .com/nation-world/ct-dylann-roof-sentencing-20170110-story.html, accessed December 19, 2020.

8. "Two Years Ago, They Marched in Charlottesville. Where Are They Now?," ADL blog, August 8, 2019, www.adl.org/blog/two-years-ago-they-marched-in-charlottesville -where-are-they-now, accessed December 19, 2020.

9. Brakkton Booker and Mark Katkow, "Illinois Teen Arrested after Fatal Shootings of 2 Kenosha, Wis., Protestors," WBEZ Chicago, August 26, 2020, www.npr.org, accessed December 21, 2020.

10. "Chicago Race Riot of 1919," Encyclopedia Britannica, www.britannica.com/ event/Chicago-Race-Riot-of-1919. The definitive study by the appointed commission after the riots was published as *The Negro in Chicago—A Study of Race Relations and a Race Riot* (Chicago: University of Chicago Press, 1922).

11. "Race Riots," Encyclopedia of Chicago, www.encyclopedia.chicagohistory.org/ pages/1032.html.

12. Ibid.

13. Dick Simpson, Constance A. Mixon, and Melisa Mouritsen, eds., *Twenty-First Century Chicago*, 3d ed. (San Diego: Cognella Academic Publishing, 2020), 6.

14. Pierre De Vise, *Chicago's Widening Color Gap* (Chicago: Report No. 2, Inter-University Social Research Committee, 1967).

15. William Julius Wilson, *The Truly Disadvantaged: The Inner City, the Underclass, and Public Policy* (Chicago: University of Chicago Press, 1987).

16. Flint Taylor, *The Torture Machine: Racism and Police Violence in Chicago* (Chicago: Haymarket Books, 2019).

17. Peter C. Baker, "In Chicago, Reparations Aren't Just an Idea. They're the Law," Guardian, March 8, 2019.

18. Taylor, *Torture Machine*, 57.

19. Ibid., 508.

20. Sam Charles, "Violence Rebounds with a Vengeance," *Chicago Sun-Times*, January 1, 2020, 8. See also "Tracking Chicago Homicide Victims," *Chicago Tribune*, www .chicagotribune.com/news/breaking/ct-chicago-homicides-data-tracker-htmlstory .html, accessed December 19, 2020.

21. See, for example, Ta-Nehisi Coates, "The Case for Reparations," *Atlantic*, June 2014, www.theatlantic.com, accessed January 19, 2021.

22. Sklyar Mitchell and Suzanne Malaveux, "Evanston, Illinois Approves the Country's First Reparation Program for Black Residents," *CNN*, March 24, 2021, www.cnn.com/2021/03/22/us/reparations-evanston-hr-40-legislation-whats-next/ index.html.

23. Cedric Johnson, *After Black Lives Matter* (Minneapolis: University of Minnesota Press, forthcoming), 10.

24. Ibid., 349.

25. "Graphic: Coronavirus Deaths in the U.S., per Day," *NBC News*, www.nbcnews.com/health/health-news/coronavirus-deaths-united-states-each-day-2020-n1177936, accessed June 10, 2021.

26. Global Map, Coronavirus Resource Center, John Hopkins University, https://coronavirus.jhu.edu/map.html, accessed June 20, 2021.

27. Mitchell Armentrout, "Illinois Records 12th Straight Day with More than 100 Virus Deaths," *Chicago Sun-Times*, December 20, 2020, 22.

28. Tim Nickens, "Six Closer Looks into the Pandemic's Impact on Minorities and the Poor," Poynter, September 17, 2020, www.poynter.org.

29. John Whitesides, "Trump's Handling of Coronavirus Pandemic Hits Record Low Approval: Reuters/Ipsos Poll," Reuters, October 8, 2020, www.reuters.com.

30. Derek Thompson, "How Disaster Shaped the Modern City," *Atlantic*, October 2020, 70.

31. George Packer, "Making America Again," *Atlantic*, October 2020, 50.

32. The data are from "Chart Book: Tracking the Post Great-Recession Economy," Center on Budget and Policy Priorities, October 2020, www.cbpp.org/research/economy/chart-book-tracking-the-post-great-recession-economy.

33. "Chart Book."

34. Sarah Jones, "Essential Workers Are Still Dying from Coronavirus," *New York Magazine*, June 26, 2020, https://nymag.com/intelligencer/2020/06/essential-workers-are-still-dying-from-coronavirus.html.

35. "COVID-19 Vaccine Distribution: The Process," U.S. Department of Health and Human Services, www.hhs.gov/coronavirus/covid-19-vaccines/distribution/index.html.

36. "See How Vaccinations Are Going in Your County and State," *New York Times*, www.nytimes.com/interactive/2020/us/covid-19-vaccine-doses.html.

37. "2020 Election to Cost $14 Billion, Blowing Away Spending Records," Open Secrets, October 28, 2020, www.opensecrets.org/news/2020/10/cost-of-2020-election-14billion-update.

38. Steve Chapman, "Can the Republic Survive Trump's Attack on the Election?," *Chicago Tribune*, December 13, 2020, www.creators.com/read/steve-chapman/12/20/can-the-republic-survive-trumps-attack-on-the-election, accessed June 11, 2021.

39. Evelyn Kenya, "Capitol Attack, the Five People Who Died," *Guardian*, January 8, 2021, www.theguardian.com/us-news/2021/jan/08/capitol-attack-police-officer-five-deaths, accessed June 11, 2021.

40. Madison Hall, Skye Gould, Rebecca Harrington, Azmi Haroun, and Taylor Ardrey, "521 People Have Been Charged in the Capitol Insurrection So Far," *Insider*, June 11, 2021, www.insider.com/all-the-us-capitol-pro-trump-riot-arrests-charges-names-2021, accessed June 12, 2021.

41. "Rahm Emanuel Quotes," BrainyQuote, www.brainyquote.com/quotes/rahm_emanuel_409199.

Chapter 10. Deliberative Democracy

1. "Results from the Bright Line Watch U.S. Democracy Survey," Bright Line Watch, https://brightlinewatch.org/results-from-the-bright-line-watch-u-s-democracy-survey.

2. "American Democracy at the Start of the Biden Administration," Bright Line Watch, http://brightlinewatch.org/american-democracy-at-the-start-of-the-biden-presidency/.

3. "Results."

4. "Democracy in the COVID-19 Era: Bright Line Watch August 2020 Expert Survey," Bright Line Watch, http://brightlinewatch.org/bright-line-watch-august-2020-expert-survey/.

5. Ibid.

6. "Bright Line Watch Survey Report: Wave 3," Bright Line Watch, http://brightline watch.org/blw-survey-wave3/.

7. "Democracy in the COVID-19 Era" and "American Democracy."

8. "A Democratic Stress Test—The 2020 Election and Its Aftermath: Bright Line Watch November 2020 Surveys," Bright Line Watch, http://brightlinewatch.org/american-democracy-on-the-eve-of-the-2020-election/a-democratic-stress-test-the-2020-election-and-its-aftermathbright-line-watch-november-2020-survey/, accessed December 24, 2020.

9. Benjamin Barber, *Strong Democracy: Participatory Politics for a New Age* (Berkeley: University of California Press, 2004). I was reminded of Barber's terminology by Marco Rosaire Rossi's UIC graduate student paper, published as "Chicago's Little Known Experiment in Radical Democracy," *ROAR*, January 17, 2020.

10. Ron Formisano, *American Oligarchy* (Urbana: University of Illinois Press, 2017), and Eric Klinenberg, Caitlin Zaloom, and Sharon Marcus, eds., *Antidemocracy in America: Truth, Power, and the Republic at Risk* (New York: Columbia University Press, 2019).

11. Jeffery Jones, "Illinois Residents Least Confident in Their State Government," Gallup, February 17, 2016, https://news.gallup.com/poll/189281/illinois-residents-least-confident-state-government.aspx, accessed April 22, 2020.

12. Rick Pearson, "Census Figures Show Illinois 1 of 3 States to See Population Drop in Last Decade, Costing It One Congressional Seat and Some Clout in Washington," *Chicago Tribune*, April 26, 2021, and "Census: 7th Year of Illinois Population and the Worst Yet," editorial, *Chicago Tribune*, December 22, 2020.

13. "Democratic Stress Test."

14. James Bohman and William Rehg, eds., *Deliberative Democracy: Essays on Reason and Politics* (Cambridge, MA: MIT Press, 2006).

15. See "Districts," Città di Firenze, http://en.comune.fi.it/administration/municipality/districts.htm, accessed December 29, 2019.

16. "The 44th Ward Assembly Charter and By-Laws," in *Neighborhood Government in Chicago's 44th Ward*, ed. Dick Simpson, Judy Stevens, and Rick Kohnen (Cham-

paign, IL: Stipes, 1977), 227. Quote also cited in Dick Simpson and George Beam, *Strategies for Change: How to Make the American Political Dream Work* (Chicago: Swallow Press, 1976), 204.

17. *44th Ward Assembly Brochure* (Chicago: 44th Ward Service Office, 1971), in Dick Simpson Papers, Special Collections, Richard J. Daley Library, University of Illinois at Chicago.

18. The same point is made by Debra J. Campbell and Jack Crittenden in *Direct Deliberative Democracy: How Citizens Can Rule* (Montreal: Black Rose Books, 2019), 138, in their discussion of deliberative democracy and civic engagement in schools.

19. Simpson, Stevens, and Kohnen, *Neighborhood Government*, 54.

20. The most complete academic study of the ward assembly is the dissertation by Greta Salem, *The 44th Ward Assembly* (Chicago: Center for Urban Policy, Loyola University Urban Insight Series, 1980). She quotes Sherry Arstein, "A Ladder in Participation," in Robert Yin, ed., *The City in the Seventies* (Itasca, IL: Peacock, 1972), as stressing "that decentralized institutions without sufficient power to carry out their tasks are bound to fail." For additional information on the ward assembly and Forty-Fourth Ward neighborhood governments, see Rossi, "Chicago's Little Known Experiment," and Simpson, Stevens, and Kohnen, *Neighborhood Government*.

21. "Public Budgeting in Chicago," PB Chicago, www.pbchicago.org/pb-in-chicago.html.

22. This account of participatory budget in Brazil is taken from Campbell and Crittenden, *Direct Deliberative Democracy*, chapter 6.

23. "49th Ward—Participatory Budgeting in Chicago," www.pbchicago.org/previous-cycles5.html, accessed June 13, 2021.

24. City of Chicago 2019 Transition Team Report, City of Chicago Office of the Mayor, www.chicago.gov/city/en/depts/mayor/supp_info/transition-report.html, accessed June 13, 2021.

25. "Mayor Lightfoot Joins Transition Team and Community to Review First Hundred Days, Look Ahead to Key Priorities for City," Office of the Mayor, August 28, 2019, www.chicago.gov/city/en/depts/mayor/press_room/press_releases/2019/august/Review100Days.html, accessed December 24, 2020.

26. See, for instance, Frank Bryan and John McClaughry, *The Vermont Papers: Recreating Democracy on a Human Scale* (White River Junction, VT: Chelsea Green, 1998).

27. On the Australian ballot, see "Town Meeting and Local Elections," Elections Division, Office of the Vermont Secretary of State, https://sos.vermont.gov/elections/election-info-resources/town-meeting-local-elections/, accessed June 25, 2021, and "Secret Ballot," Wikipedia, https://en.wikipedia.org/wiki/Secret_ballot, accessed June 25, 2021.

28. Frank M. Bryan, *Real Democracy: The New England Town Meeting and How It Works* (Chicago: University of Chicago Press, 2004), 280. Bryan and his students recorded 1,435 Vermont town meetings from 1970 to 1998, from which these statistics are derived.

29. *A Citizen's Guide to Vermont Town Meeting*, Elections Division, Office of the Vermont Secretary of State, 2008, 5, https://sos.vermont.gov/media/uomghd2h/citizen-guide-text-2.pdf, accessed June 25, 2021.

30. Bryan, *Real Democracy*, 4.

31. Town of Cavendish, "Minutes of the Cavendish Town Meeting—1994," *Town Report*, year ending December 1994, reprinted in Bryan, *Real Democracy*, xvi.

32. Gallup, "Congress and the Public," https://news.gallup.com/poll/1600/congress-public.aspx; Scott Keeter, "How We Know the Drop in Trump's Approval Rating in January Reflected a Real Shift in Public Opinion," FactTank, Pew Research Center, January 20, 2021, www.pewresearch.org/fact-tank/2021/01/20/how-we-know-the-drop-in-trumps-approval-rating-in-january-reflected-a-real-shift-in-public-opinion/.

33. Joseph Bessette, *The Mild Voice of Reason: Deliberative Democracy and American National Government* (Chicago: University of Chicago Press, 1997), 5.

34. "About Congress," U.S. Capitol Visitor's Center, www.visitthecapitol.gov/about-congress, accessed June 13, 2021.

35. Michael A. Neblo, Kevin M. Esterling, and David M. J. Lazer, *Politics with the People: Building a Directly Representative Democracy* (New York: Cambridge University Press, 2018), 3.

36. There are various accounts of the individual experiments in deliberative democracy, but for an overview see John Gastil and Peter Levine, eds., *The Deliberative Democracy Handbook: Strategies for Effective Civic Engagement in the Twenty-First Century* (San Francisco: Josey-Bass, 2005). For additional experiments in citizen panels and congress, see Steve Kull's organization, Voice of the People (www.vop.org).

37. Neblo, Esterling, and Lazar, *Politics with the People*, 29–31.

38. Jame Fishkin, *Democracy When the People Are Thinking: Revitalizing Our Politics through Public Deliberation* (New York: Oxford University Press, 2018). See also the series of reviews and responses between Fishkin, Neblo, Esterling, and Lazer in "Critical Dialogue," *Perspectives on Politics* 17, no. 2 (June 2019): 527–31. For Fishkin's core democratic principles, see "Critical Dialogue," 529.

39. Neblo, Esterling, and Lazer, *Politics with the People*, 99.

40. Ibid., 103.

41. Ibid., 100. See also Jane Mansbridge, "Clarifying the Concept of Representation," *American Political Science Review* 104, no. 3 (August 2011): 621–30.

42. Campbell and Crittenden, *Direct Deliberative Democracy*, chapter 5.

43. "Initiative States Compared by Number of Initiatives on Their Ballot," Ballotpedia, https://ballotpedia.org/Initiative_states_compared_by_number_of_initiatives_on_their_ballot.

44. See Todd Donovan, Shaun Bowler, David McCuan, and Ken Fernandez, "Contending Players and Strategies," in *Citizen as Legislators: Direct Democracy in the United States*, ed. Shaun Bowler, Todd Donovan, and Caroline J. Tolbert (Columbus: Ohio State University Press, 1998), 84, and Elizabeth Gerber, *The Populist Paradox: In-*

terest Group Influence and the Promise of Direct Legislation (Princeton, NJ: Princeton University Press), 8, as summarized in Campbell and Crittenden, *Direct Deliberative Democracy*, 61–64.

45. See Campbell and Crittenden, *Direct Deliberative Democracy*, chapter 5, for a fuller description of the legislature jury proposal. The quote is from 92–93.

46. "What Is Deliberative Polling®?," Stanford Center for Deliberative Democracy, https://cdd.stanford.edu/what-is-deliberative-polling/, accessed January 22, 2021.

47. Ibid.

48. Campbell and Crittenden, *Direct Deliberative Democracy*, 10.

49. E. J. Dionne Jr., *Our Divided Political Heart: The Battle for the American Idea in an Age of Discontent* (New York: Bloomsbury, 2012), 75.

50. Ibid., 130.

51. Ibid., 252.

52. Sanford Levinson and Jack M. Balkin, *Democracy and Dysfunction* (Chicago: University of Chicago Press, 2019), 2.

53. Ibid., 67.

54. Ibid., 106.

55. Ibid., 191–93.

Chapter 11. Spirit of Democracy

1. In addition to books cited earlier, see Ron Formisano, *American Oligarchy: The Permanent Political Class* (Urbana: University of Illinois Press, 2017).

2. Formisano, *American Oligarchy*, 2–8, quote on 8.

3. See, for instance, Larry Bartels, *Unequal Democracy: The Politics of the New Gilded Age* (Princeton, NJ: Princeton University Press, 2008), and Benjamin I. Page and Martin Gilens, *Democracy in America? What Has Gone Wrong and What We Can Do about It*, updated ed. (Chicago: University of Chicago Press, 2020).

4. Alan Wolfe, *Does American Democracy Still Work?* (New Haven, CT: Yale University Press, 2006), 14.

5. Ibid., 138.

6. Dick Simpson, Marco Rosaire Rossi, and Thomas J. Gradel, "From Rubber Stamp to Political Divisions, June 12, 2019–April 24, 2020," Chicago City Council Report no. 11, Department of Political Science, University of Illinois at Chicago, April 28, 2020, https://pols.uic.edu/chicago-politics/city-council-voting-records/, and Dick Simpson, Marco Rosaire Rossi, and Thomas J. Gradel, "Emanuel and Lightfoot City Councils: Chicago City Council," Report no. 12, Department of Political Science University of Illinois at Chicago, May 2021, https://pols.uic.edu/wp-content/uploads/sites/273/2021/05/City-Council-Report-%5eN12-Corrected-5-17-21-Final.edits_.pdf.

7. City of Chicago 2019 Transition Team Report, City of Chicago Office of the Mayor, www.chicago.gov/city/en/depts/mayor/supp_info/transition-report.html, accessed June 14, 2021.

8. For one account of the school strike, see Mitch Smith and Monica Davey, "Chi-

cago Teachers' Strike, Longest in Decades, Ends," *New York Times*, October 31, 2019, www.nytimes.com.

9. Fran Spielman, "City Council Approves Lightfoot's $11.6 Billion Budget—with 11 'no' Votes," *Chicago Sun-Times*, November 26, 2019, https://chicago.suntimes.com/city-hall/2019/11/26/20983774/chicago-city-council-lightfoot-budget-vote, accessed January 2, 2020.

10. Rich Miller, "Note to GOP: Suburban Voters Give Gov High Marks on Handling of Pandemic," *Chicago Sun-Times*, May 3, 2020, 36.

11. Anita Yadavalli, Rose Kim, and Christiana K. McFarland, "State of the Cities," National League of Cities, 2020, www.nlc.org/wp-content/uploads/2020/10/NLC_StateOfTheCities2020–1–1.pdf, 1.

12. For the short version of these events, see "Collapse of the Soviet Union," Britannica, www.britannica.com/event/the-collapse-of-the-Soviet-Union.

13. Sara Repucci and Amy Slipowitz, "Democracy Under Siege," Freedom House, http://freedomhouse.org/report/freedom-world/2021/democracy-under-siege.

14. Page and Gilens, *Democracy in America*, 239.

15. Robert Putnam with Shaylyn Garrett, *The Upswing: How America Came Together a Century Ago and How We Can Do It Again* (New York: Simon and Schuster, 2020), 10.

16. Ibid., 11.

17. Ibid, 331.

18. Yascha Mounk, *The People vs. Democracy: Why Our Freedom Is in Danger and How to Save It* (Cambridge, MA: Harvard University Press, 2018), 188–89.

19. Page and Gilens, *Democracy in America*, 264.

20. Barack Obama, *A Promised Land* (New York: Random House, 2020), 107.

21. Association of American Colleges and Universities, *What Liberal Education Looks Like: What It Is, Who It's for, and Where It Happens*, (Washington D.C.: AACU, 2020).

22. "DeLauro, Cole Introduce the Educating for Democracy Act, Historic Investments in Civic Education," press release, Rosa DeLauro, September 17, 2020, https://delauro.house.gov/media-center/press-releases/delauro-cole-introduce-educating-democracy-act-historic-investments.

23. See Elizabeth C. Matto, Alison Rios Millett McCartney, Elizabeth A. Bennion, Alasdair Blair, Taiyi Sun, and Dawn Whitehead, eds., *Teaching Civic Engagement Globally* (Washington, DC: American Political Science Association, 2021).

24. National Task Force on Civic Learning and Democratic Engagement, *A Crucible Moment: College Learning and Democracy's Future* (Washington, DC: Association of American Colleges and Universities, 2012), www.aacu.org/sites/default/files/files/crucible/Crucible_508F.pdf.

25. "Youth Vote Up Significantly in 2020; Young People of Color Pivotal," Tufts Now, November 19, 2020, https://now.tufts.edu/news-releases/youth-vote-significantly-2020-young-people-color-pivotal.

26. Alison Rios Millett McCartney, Elizabeth A. Bennion and Dick Simpson, eds., *Teaching Civic Engagement: From Student to Active Citizen* (Washington, DC: American Political Science Association, 2013), and Elizabeth C. Matto, Alison Rios Millett McCartney, Elizabeth A. Bennion, and Dick Simpson, eds., *Teaching Civic Engagement across the Disciplines* (Washington, DC: American Political Science Association, 2017).

27. Information on NSLVE can be found at https://idhe.tufts.edu/nslve.

28. "Youth Vote Up Significantly in 2020."

29. Drew DeSilver, "U.S. Voter Turnout Trails Most Developed Countries," Pew Research Center, May 21, 2018, www.pewresearch.org.

30. Steven Levitsky and Daniel Ziblatt, *How Democracies Die* (New York: Crown, 2018), 3.

31. Robert C. Rowland, *The Rhetoric of Donald Trump: Nationalist Populism and American Democracy* (Lawrence: University Press of Kansas, 2021), 163–69. In turn, Rowland quotes E. J. Dionne Jr., Norman J. Ornstein, and Thomas E. Mann, *One Nation after Trump: A Guide for the Perplexed, the Disillusioned, the Desperate, and the Not Yet Deported* (New York: St. Martin's, 2017), 286.

32. Levitsky and Ziblatt, *How Democracies Die*, 102, 104.

33. Ibid., 100.

34. See for instance, Robert Reich, *The System: Who Rigged It and How We Fix It* (New York: Knopf, 2020); William G. Howell and Terry M. Moe, *Presidents, Populism, and the Crisis of Democracy* (Chicago: University of Chicago Press, 2020); and Morris Pearl and Erica Payne, *Tax the Rich: How Lies, Loopholes, and Lobbyists, Make the Rich Even Richer* (New York: New Press, 2021); along with earlier books, such as Christopher Hayes, *Twilight of the Elites: America After Meritocracy* (New York: Random House, 2012), and Gar Alperovitz, *What Then Must We Do? Straight Talk about the Next American Revolution* (White River Junction, VT: Chelsea Green, 2013).

35. George Packer, "The Legacy of Donald Trump," *Atlantic*, January/February 2021, 10.

36. Howell and Moe, *Presidents, Populism*, 1.

37. Ibid., 8 and 13.

38. Zizi Papademos, *After Democracy: Imaging Our Political Future* (New Haven, CT: Yale University Press, 2021), 86, 111–17.

Index

Note: *Italicized* page numbers indicate material in photo captions.

Abramoff, Jack, 59
absentee/mail-in ballots, 120, 123, 126, 137, 139, 140, 175, 178, 200
active representation, 13–15
Adams, John Quincy, 127
African Americans: Black Power movement, 154, 156; as Chicago mayors (*see* Lightfoot, Lori; Washington, Harold); civil rights movement and, 32, 36, 80, 135–36, 200; descriptive underrepresentation in politics, 14, 27; in federal office (*see* Harris, Kamala; Obama, Barack); Silent Six on the Chicago City Council, 14; slavery as basis of permanent underclass, 16, 23, 32, 152. *See also* income/wealth inequality; racial inequality; racism and racial tensions
age for voting, 76, 77, 119, 120, 136, 138, 203, 205
American Civil Liberties Union (ACLU), 135
American Community Survey, 31
American Legislative Exchange Council (ALEC), 51
American Political Science Association, 204
American Revolution, 83–84, 198, 201
American Samoa, voting rights and, 128
anticorruption commissions, 119
apartheid, 23

Appelbaum, Yoni, 36
Arizona: Electoral College votes, 127–28; Internet voting, 139; voter-suppression laws, 32
Asian Americans: descriptive underrepresentation in politics, 14, 27; income/wealth inequality in Chicago and, 30. *See also* racial inequality; racism and racial tensions
Association of American Colleges and Universities, 202–3
Australia, anticorruption commissions, 119
autocracy, 33, 49, 187, 198, 206, 207
automatic voter registration (AVR), 32, 80, 120, 126, 136–37, 200

Balkin, Jack, 189
Bannon, Steve, 106
Barber, Benjamin, 167
Barrios, Joe, 70
Bartels, Larry, 25, 52
Bennett, David, 107
Berry, Mary Frances, 118
Better Government Association, 173
Biden, Joe: in the elections of 2020 (*see* elections of 2020); opportunity for new beginning and, 15, 35, 72, 101, 136, 151, 189, 194, 196–99, 207–9
Bilandic, Michael, 21, 96–98, 100
Bischoff, Kendra, 31
Black Lives Matter (BLM) movement, *xii,* 34, 71, 94, *150,* 151, 152–56, 199

Blacks. *See* African Americans

Blagojevich, Rod, 110–11, 113, 115, 120, 121

Bohman, James, 168

Brennan Center for Justice, 136

bribery and extortion: Rod Blagojevich and, 110–11, 113, 115, 120, 121; in campaign finance, 45–46, 112; in the definition of corruption, 46–47, 112–13, 114, 120; election fraud and, 125–26; institutional corruption and, 116; state corruption and, 111–12; Donald Trump and, 105–6

Bright Line Watch, 165–67

Brown, Michael, 151, 152

Bryan, Frank, 178

Buckley v. Valeo (1976), 46

Buffett, Warren, 38

Burge, Jon, 113, 154–55

Burke, Ed: corruption scandal, 44, 69, 70, *104*, 105, 194; election fraud and, 123, 125; lack of term limits and, 135, 145; mayoral succession in Chicago (1977) and, 96–97

Bush, George W., 127

Bush, Jeb, 70

Byrne, Jane, 21, 84, 98

cable television, 44, 67, 74, 174–75, 177

Caliendo, Stephen, 37

campaign finance: anticorruption laws, 45–46; bribery and, 45–46, 112; Chicago mayoral elections of 2019, 44, 69–71; *Citizens United* (2010) and, 25, 46–47, 56, 114, 119–20, 200; contribution limits, 45, 46–47, 57; corruption and, 45–46, 112, 116; cost of elections, 25–26, 43–45, 47–50, 70, 73, 92, 110, 116, 128, 142; dark-money contributions, 25, 45, 47–50, 56, 73, 186; global corporations and, 66; government influence and, 44, 50–53, 116, 118; illicit use of funds, 46; individual contributions to candidates, 77; in machine politics, 65, 67, 68; political action committees (PACs) and, 25, 44, 47–49; public funding in, 45–47, 56–59, 120, 200; public-private partnership regimes and, 40, 53, 64; regulating, 45–47, 56–57, 59; reporting requirements, 45, 46, 47–48, 56–57, 59; Watergate scandal and, 45, 111, 121

Campbell, Debra, 184–85

Campbell, John, 88

capitalist economic system, 23–24, 37–39, 77–78

Carnes, Nicholas, 52, 59

Carson, Ben, 107

Center for Public Integrity, 109

Center for Responsive Politics, Open Secrets website, 47–48

Cermak, Anton, 8

challenges to democracy, 1–4; Chicago as case study in, 1–2, 45–46, 69, 109 (*see also* Chicago); COVID-19 pandemic (*see* COVID-19 pandemic); dangers of ignoring, 4, 7, 198; economic recession (*see* economic recessions); gender inequality (*see* gender inequality); income inequality (*see* income/wealth inequality); nonparticipation of voters (*see* nonparticipation of voters); participatory and deliberative democracy as solution to (*see* participatory/deliberative democracy); polarization and politics of resentment (*see* political polarization; resentment); political corruption (*see* corruption; machine politics); racial inequality (*see* racial inequality); racism and racial tension (*see* racism and racial tensions); structural barriers to democracy (*see* structural barriers to democracy); times of crisis and, 33–35, 151, 162–63; Donald Trump as symbol and example of, 1, 4, 14, 17, 33–35, 88, 162, 165–67, 180–82, 208

Chapman, Steve, 160

Chicago: Blagojevich corruption scandal, 110–11, 113, 115, 120, 121; as case study in the challenges to democracy, 1–2, 45–46, 69, 109; cost of elections in, 43–45, 70; Council Wars under Harold Washington, 84–85, 86, 97, 101–2, 144–45, 194, 195; COVID-19 pandemic in, 31, 40, 86, 102, 157, 167, 173–74, 194–96; election fraud in, 9–10, 11, 111, 123, 124–26; as global city, 33–34, 52, 66, 67, 68, 95; history of racial tension in, 98, 153–55; income/wealth inequality in, 21–23, 27–32, 52; machine politics in (*see* machine politics); mayoral succession of 1977 and, 95–97; mayoral succession of 1987 and, 99–100; nonparticipation of voters in, 63–67, 76–78; political polarization in, 84–86, 97, 101–2; racial inequality in, 21–23, 27–32, 95; rebirth under Lori Lightfoot, 174–75, 193–97, 208; reformers and progressive leaders in, 10–11, 15–17, 18, 84–86 (*see also* Lightfoot, Lori; Washington, Harold); residential segregation in, 27–30, 34,

77–78, 166–67 (*see also* machine politics); lessons from the past, 15–18; participatory democracy and (*see* participatory/deliberative democracy); potential death of, 206–7; renewal of the "spirit of democracy" and, 4, 55–56, 59, 101, 181–82, 193–209; representative democracy and (*see* representative democracy); transformative change and, 4, 199–201

Democratic Party: bias in news sources, 74; as diverse and expanding, 91; dominance in Chicago (1933-present), 8–10, 63–67, 84, 94–101, 124, 195 (*see also* machine politics); in the elections of 2018, 49–50; in the elections of 2020, 35; gerrymandering in Chicago, *122*, 130, *131*, *132*, 144–45; leftward swing of, 87, 88, 94

descriptive representation, 14, 21–23, 27

Despres, Leon, 14

De Vise, Pierre, 28–29

Dewey, John, 62, 203

Diamond, Larry, 105

Dionne, E. J., 93–94, 187–88

direct democracy. *See* participatory/deliberative democracy

Dirksen, Everett, 44

District of Columbia: automatic voter registration and, 136, 200; voting rights of felons and, 137

Donovan, Tom, 96

Douglas, Joshua, 77

Downs, Anthony, 78

Dunne, "Gentleman" George, 125

early voting polling places, 17, 32, 120, 126, 137, 200

economic inequality. *See* income/wealth inequality

economic recessions, 88, 158–60; of 2001, 25; COVID-19 pandemic and, 1, 24, 25, 31, 32, 86, 151, 158–60, 194–96; elections of 2020 and, 15; Great Recession (2008), 24–25, 32, 33, 34–35, 90, 158, 189

Edmundson, Mark, 101

education: changes in the nature of work and, 38–39; during the COVID-19 pandemic, 74; inequality of, 33, 34; for participation in democracy, 4, 55, 62, 118–19, 200–205

Eisenhower, Dwight D., 37

election dates, 145–46

election fraud: in Chicago, 9–10, 11, 111, 123,

124–26; cyberattacks in, 11, 54, 75, 80, 106, 139; Heritage Foundation database on, 9; in machine politics, 9–10, 11, 16; as structural barrier to democracy, 124–26; Trump administration claims of (2020), 9, 17, 75, 83, 88, 107–8, 160–62, 165–66; voting machines vs. paper ballots, 125–26

elections of 1960, 9

elections of 1968, 124, 189

elections of 1983, 11. *See also* Washington, Harold

elections of 2000, 9, 128–29, 139, 140

elections of 2015, 63

elections of 2016: corruption charges, 106; cost of elections, 47–48; cyberattacks and, 11, 139; gerrymandering in North Carolina, 130–33; polarization and politics of resentment and, 7, 34, 88, 127; popular vs. Electoral College votes, 127, 128–29; Republican primary candidates, 70, 75; sham candidates, 146, 147; size of campaign contributions, 47; Trump elected president, 11, 33, 34, 70, 83, 88, 89, 127; voter turnout by ethnic/racial group, 79; voter turnout in Chicago, 76

elections of 2018: cost of elections, 48, 49; Illinois gubernatorial race, 23, 25, 48; as referendum on the Trump administration, 49–50; voter participation, 176; voter turnout, 63, 76

elections of 2019: candidates in Chicago mayoral race, 44, 68–72, 75; progressive reform administration in Chicago and, 11 (*see also* Lightfoot, Lori); voter turnout, 63

elections of 2020, 160–62; Biden election and opportunity for new beginning, 15, 35, 72, 101, 136, 151, 189, 194, 196–99, 207–9; Capitol insurrection (January 6, 2021) following, 55, 75, 83, 88, 91, 94, 108, 152–53, 161–62, 165–66; cost of elections, 48, 50, 160; cyberattacks and, 11, 139; defeat of Trump, 15; Democratic primary candidates, 70, 75; gerrymandering in North Carolina, 130–33; polarization and politics of resentment and, 7, 35, 88, 100–101; popular vs. Electoral College votes, 107–8, 127; progressive presidential candidates and, 38, 49, 87; as a referendum on the Trump administration, 15, 35, 86; sham candidates, 146; Trump election fraud claims, 9, 17, 75, 83, 88, 107–8,

and, 76–78; election dates and, 145–46; elitist vs. populist approaches to, 80; improving citizen participation, 120; income inequality and, 77; public opinion of public officials and, 53–56, 57–59, 66; reform proposals, 80–81; retrospective voting and, 62, 81; voter initiatives and referenda, 63, 133–34, 137, 147, 184–86, 190; voting rates in the U.S., 32–33, 76, 205

Nonpartisan Vote, 133

North Carolina, gerrymandering in, 130–33

Northern Mariana Islands, voting rights and, 128

Obama, Barack, 87, 110, 128, 143, 198–99, 203

Oberman, Martin, 97

Ocasio-Cortez, Alexandria, 87

Occupy Wall Street movement, 93–94, 156

O'Connor, Pat, 44

Ohio, Electoral College votes, 127–28

oligarchy, 16, 17, 23, 33, 45, 167, 187, 198

one-party dominance: in Chicago, 63–67; ending, 80; in machine politics, 8, 9, 11, 16, 63–67. *See also* gerrymandering

open primaries, 149

Open Secrets website, 47–48

Orr, David, 173

Orwell, George, 54

Packer, George, 208

"packing," in gerrymandering, 130

Page, Benjamin, 24, 50, 52, 78, 141, 143, 197, 198

Papademos, Zizi, 209

participatory/deliberative democracy, 165–90; in ancient Greece and the Roman Republic, 62, 72, 134, 180, 203; citizen juries or assemblies and, 63, 176, 184–85, 186, 190; Constitutional Convention (1787) as model for, 13, 114, 177, 201; deliberative polling in, 185; education for civic engagement, 4, 55, 62, 118–19, 200–205; inspectors general in, 56–57, 119, 174, 195, 200; issue voting and governing in, 175–78; Jefferson and, 12–13, 179–80; lack of, at the federal level, 62, 188–89; legislative juries and, 184–85; "mutually interactive" criteria for, 182; nature of, 13; need for public belief in government and, 165–68; New England town meetings and, 12, 62, 175, 176, 178–79, 180, 183, 184; other alter-

natives and, 186–87; in overcoming polarization, 187–88; participatory budgeting experiment (2009), 171–72, 179; and public support in movement for change, 2, 3–4; reforms of Lori Lightfoot in Chicago, 174–75, 193–97, 208; renewal of the "spirit of democracy" and, 4, 55–56, 59, 101, 181–82, 193–209; risks of, 186; steps in moving toward, 189–90, 200; teleconferencing/Zoom meetings and, 175–76, 177, 180, 186–87; U.S. Congress and, 180–84; voter initiatives and referenda in, 63, 133–34, 137, 147, 184–86, 190. *See also* voting rights; ward-based democracy

Parvin, Phil, 77

patriarchy, 23

patronage jobs, 8, 9, 16, 64–66, 67, 95, 96, 111, 112–13, 120

Pelosi, Nancy, 87

Pennsylvania, Electoral College votes, 127–28

Perception of Election Integrity index, 138

Permanent Apportionment Act (1929), 141

Perot, Ross, 93

Pew Research Center, 59, 86, 87, 88–89, 93

Pickard, Victor, 75, 80–81

political action committees (PACs), 25, 44, 47–49

political corruption. *See* corruption

political machines. *See* machine politics

political participation. *See* nonparticipation of voters; participatory/deliberative democracy; voter registration; voting rights

political polarization, 83–102; asymmetry of political parties and, 91; Black Lives Matter and, 94, 152–53; Capitol insurrection (January 6, 2021) and, 55, 75, 83, 88, 91, 94, 108, 152–53, 161–62, 165–66; in Chicago, 84–86, 97, 101–2; current level of polarization, 83–84; dangers of, 87; democratic deliberation in overcoming, 187–88; dissatisfaction with democracy, 93–94; "divided political heart" (Dionne) and, 93–94, 187–88; extreme candidates and, 87, 93–94; ideological polarization, 81, 87–88; mass media/social media role in, 54–55, 88–89; national-level, 86–89; origins of U.S. tribalism, 86, 93; overcoming, 101–2, 187–88 (*see also* participatory/ deliberative democracy); polarization of elected officials, 87–88, 91–93; in the political parties, 86–87; reform proposals,

mented immigrants, 13, 77, 137–38; for U.S. commonwealth territories, 128; voter turnout in the U.S. and, 32–33, 61, 76, 78–80; voting age and, 76, 77, 119, 120, 136, 138, 203, 205

voting systems, 127–28, 140, 149, 200

Vrdolyak, "Fast Eddie," 96–97, 98, 111

Walker, Scott, 89–90

ward-based democracy: in Chicago, 65–66, *122*, 124–26, 130, 131, *132*, 144–45, 168–78; Forty-Fourth Ward, Chicago experiment (1972–81), 168–72, 181; increasing citizen participation through, 120; Independent Precinct Organization (IPO) experiment, 124–26, 171; Thomas Jefferson and, 12–13, 179–80; Lightfoot transition team and, 173–75, 194; participatory budgeting experiment (2009), 171–72, 179; size of Chicago wards, 180; ward gerrymandering and, *122*, 130, 131, *132*, 144–45

War of 1812, 83, 161

Washington, Harold: Council Wars and, 84–85, 86, 97, 101–2, 144–45, 194, 195; death in office (1987), 95, 99; on the "death" of the Chicago machine politics, 11, 18; mayoral succession of 1987 and, 95, 99–100; as progressive reform mayor of Chicago, 16, 18, 21, 28, 35, 84–85, 95, 97–99, 144–45

Watergate scandal, 45, 111, 121

Wayne, Stephen, 47

wealth gap. *See* income/wealth inequality

Westover, Tara, 91

Whites: counterprotests of the Black Lives Matter (BLM) movement, 152–53; Electoral College votes and White supremacy, 128; as majority of the electorate, 79; as non-majority of Chicago electorate, 98; voter turnout gap with racial/ethnic minorities, 79; White male dominance in government, 15–16, 21–23, 28, 32–33. *See also* income/wealth inequality; racial inequality

Wilson, Andrew and Jackie, 154–55

winner-take-all voting, 127–28, 140

Wolfe, Alan, 193

women. *See* gender inequality

Women's March (January, 2017), 34, 199

work: changes in the nature of, 38–39, 199; impact of COVID-19 pandemic on, 24, 74, 159–60

working class: disconnect of governing class from, 26, 50–51, 59, 90; economic recessions and, 88 (*see also* economic recessions)

World War II, 4, 24, 37, 38, 157

young adults: DACA (Deferred Action for Childhood Arrivals) and, 36; income/wealth inequality and, 31; voting age and participation, 76, 77, 119, 120, 136, 138, 203, 205

Ziblatt, Daniel, 207

Zinke, Ryan, 107

DICK SIMPSON is a professor, former head of the Department of Political Science at the University of Illinois at Chicago, and a former Chicago alderman and congressional candidate. His books include *Corrupt Illinois: Patronage, Cronyism, and Criminality*; *Winning Elections in the 21st Century*; and *The Politics of Compassion and Transformation*.

The University of Illinois Press
is a founding member of the
Association of University Presses.

———————————————

Composed in 10.5/13 Adobe Minion Pro
with Avenir display
by Jim Proefrock
at the University of Illinois Press
Manufactured by Sheridan Books, Inc.

University of Illinois Press
1325 South Oak Street
Champaign, IL 61820-6903
www.press.uillinois.edu